RAISING CHILDREN IN THE MIDST OF GLOBAL CRISIS

Raising Children in the Midst of Global Crisis

A COMPASSIONATE GUIDEBOOK FOR NEW PARADIGM PARENTING

Jo delAmor

Radiant Balance

Copyright © 2023 by Jo delAmor

Published by Radiant Balance.

All rights reserved. No part of this book may be reproduced, stored in a retrieval system, or transmitted in any form or by any means without written permission by the publisher, except in the case of brief quotations embodied in critical articles and reviews.

Inquiries regarding requests to translate or reprint all or part of *Raising Children in the Midst of Global Crisis* should be submitted through the contact form on www.RadiantBalance.com

First Printing, 2023

Paperback ISBN: 979-8-98967-190-8
eBook ISBN: 979-8-98967-191-5

Library of Congress Control Number: 2024900320

Subjects:
FAM034000 - FAMILY & RELATIONSHIPS / Parenting / General
SOC037000 - SOCIAL SCIENCE / Future Studies
PHI048000 - PHILOSOPHY / Environmental

This book is dedicated to the wellbeing and mutual thriving of every being in the great interconnected web of existence across the span of all time.

It is dedicated to Asher, Ryker, Mia and all the young ones I've loved who didn't make it through.

And to Blue, for teaching me how to be your mama.

EARLY PRAISE

"There seems to be no better a time to reconceptualize parenting than now, here at the precipice of a broken civilization. Why? It's because parenting is ecological. Parenting is more-than-human care. Parenting is a strange grace that inhabits the suffocating architecture of the familiar. Jo feels that and she writes her yearning for new paradigms of parenting into our bones with this book. This book is a prayer, not a prescription. A sitting-with, a yearning-alongside. A glimpse of the possible. And it begins - as Jo imagines it does - right in the swirling mass of space that exists between us and the children the world has gifted itself through us."

– **Bayo Akomolafe, Ph.D.,** Author of *These Wilds Beyond our Fences: Letters to My Daughter on Humanity's Search for Home;* Inaugural Global Senior Fellow, Othering and Belonging Institute; Inaugural Global Scholar, Aspen Institute

"Jo delAmor offers an inspiring and practical vision of parenting as a form of activism, as a powerful way to seed a new Thriving Life paradigm into our world in deep crisis and travail. New Paradigm Parenting means learning alongside our children, healing the collective wounds passed down to us, while cultivating courage, creativity, and resilience in ourselves and our children. Jo offers simple and age-appropriate practices for both parents and children to support this ongoing process."

– **Molly Brown, M.A., M.Div,** Co-author, with Joanna Macy, of *Coming Back to Life;* Editor of the WTR Network *DeepTimes* Journal; Co-director of Spiral Journey Facilitator Development Program

"Frozen in place, overwhelmed, blindsided, confused - how do we parent in this era of planetary and human upheaval? Jo delAmor helps us truly visualize the journey we are on – one that requires letting go, the unlocking of our feelings and our emotions. By opening ourselves up, we can respond with creativity and with the courage required. Jo helps guide us to find our unique path where we can claim agency, hone our abilities, and build hope. As we find our path, we can help our children find theirs - ones that are personal, intuitive, and informed. This is an important book for our times."

– **Harriet Shugarman,** Author of How to Talk to Your Kids About Climate Change: Turning Angst Into Action; Executive Director of ClimateMama; Professor of Climate Change and Society and World Sustainability; Inaugural co-chair, Our Kids Climate.

"Collectively, we are going through it. If you are a parent, grandparent, relative, guardian or even envisioning bringing children into this time, what is the first question in your heart? For most it is unequivocally – What will happen with our children? However we answer this, we seek honest resolve to hold our children in the midst of great uncertainty with more love and less fear. Without denial, in Raising Children in the Midst of Global Crisis, Jo delAmor gives us courage to take heart as she teaches skills and inspires us to live beyond mere grappling so we can ground and build our present futures with more trust, presence, gratitude and resilience."

- **ALisa Starkweather,** Co-founder of Women in Power initiations and the Red Tent Movement

Contents

Introduction	xi

PART ONE: Greeting This Precious and Precarious Moment — 1

1	RAISING CHILDREN ON THE EDGE OF A CRUMBLING WORLD	2
2	SEEKING LIFE	10
3	GLOBAL CRISIS	22
4	SEEDING A NEW PARADIGM	40
	The Great Remembering	55

PART TWO: Moving Through the Spiral — 59

5	GROUNDING IN GRATITUDE	60
6	EMBRACING EMOTION	81
7	NURTURING NEW PARADIGM QUALITIES	113
	A Mother's Day Message	136

PART THREE: New Paradigm Parenting — 137

8	OUR ROLE AS NEW PARADIGM PARENTS	139

9	CREATING CONDITIONS FOR KIDS TO THRIVE	159
10	IT TAKES A VILLAGE	183
11	PARTNERING WITH OUR KIDS	200
12	GUIDING GROWTH	241
13	THRIVING LIFE EDUCATION	279
Musical Interlude: Maiden The Flower		304
14	PHASES AND STAGES	305
15	FORGET THE PERFECT OFFERING	335

About the Author	345
Acknowledgments	347
Endnotes	351

Introduction

"Do not be dismayed by the brokenness of the world.
All things break. And all things can be mended.
Not with time, as they say, but with intention.
So, go. Love intentionally, extravagantly, unconditionally.
The broken world waits in darkness for the light that is you."
– L.R. Knost [0.1]

Raising healthy, joyful kids in this time of social, economic and environmental collapse can feel like an impossible mission. Many of the parents I work with express panic and fear about the state of the world and the future their children will inherit. They doubt themselves and worry about their children.

But they were made for these times. Just like you, and just like your children.

Caring for children at this tumultuous time on Earth is a sacred task calling us to show up fully with *all* our love, *all* our fear, *all* our courage and *all* our creativity. Instead of adding to our overwhelm, this *all-in* engagement can free up our vital energy and bring us into alignment with the radical, healing transformation that is already occurring in our world. Along the way, we get to discover just how well-equipped we truly are to meet this moment, together with our children.

New Paradigm Parenting

With all that vital energy freed up, we can embrace parenting as an adventurous opportunity to transform the way we see the world and our relationship with it, to heal the wounds we've been carrying and to care for our precious world in meaningful ways, for the sake of our children and the Earth.

New Paradigm Parenting is a powerful form of activism that begins in our own hearts and households as we disentangle ourselves from the Power Over Paradigm and learn new ways of living into the Thriving Life Paradigm. Through this journey, we begin to see things from different perspectives, interrupt generations-long unhealthy patterns and learn to partner with our children (and all Life) for mutual wellbeing. Many of us haven't been raised with the level of presence and respect that this way of living requires, so it takes conscious, concerted effort to cultivate this awareness in our relationships with our children. But it's well worth the effort because it makes life so much better!

If you really apply these New Paradigm Parenting practices to the care of your children, it will make your entire parenting experience exceptionally easier and way more enjoyable. You can basically say goodbye to whining, temper tantrums, defiance and most of the really scary parts of the teenage years, because you'll be working together with your children to support their development, instead of engaging in a decades-long power struggle. And, even better, you'll be raising and educating children who can contribute to the possibility of a livable future.

A Little About Me

I'm a mom and stepmom to two young adults, both of whom graduated high school in 2020, right in the midst of Covid lockdowns and school closures. Over the past twenty plus years, I've also worked with and cared for hundreds of other people's children of all ages in a wide variety of situations, including public schools, long-term co-parenting community, wilderness camps, preschools and in-home nannying.

Motivated by my deep love for children and my dedication to personal and cultural transformation as catalysts for planetary healing, I've paid close attention to what this new generation needs at this pivotal time on planet Earth. I've charted what works and what doesn't, and what is being called forth from us as parents. Since 2013, I've been facilitating the Work That Reconnects with a focus on dismantling oppression, transforming our cultural paradigm and supporting parents through these unprecedented and challenging times.

I'm a third generation United States citizen, born on the traditional lands of the Wampanoag people beside the wild Atlantic Ocean on the shores of what is now called Massachusetts. I'm the great grandchild of immigrants from the lands of Sienna, Avellino, Foggia and Sicily in Italy and from County Tipperary, County Cork and Waterford in Ireland.

Just like you, I'm a living link between those who have come before me and those who will come after me. I offer this work on behalf of my ancestors, my children and the ones yet to be in the long lineage of Life that we all share.

Praise for my Beloved Teachers and Elders

Over the course of my life, I've been blessed with many exceptional teachers and elders. The content of this book is deeply informed by the lessons and perspectives I've learned from them as well as the lessons I've learned through my direct experience of caring for young ones.

Throughout the book, I quote and reference several teachers, philosophers, authors, childcare experts, and others who have influenced the way I understand the world and our role as parents. I've woven these threads of knowledge into the fabric of this book and have provided extensive information in the endnotes for you, in case you want to follow any of these threads for further exploration.

The root teachers I reference throughout this book, who have significantly influenced my orientation in life are Joanna Macy, [0.2] Martín Prechtel [0.3] and Woman Stands Shining (Pat McCabe).[0.4] Each of these three individuals lives with eyes wide open and hearts committed to profound healing. I am deeply grateful for their work in this world and for the opportunities I have had to learn from them.

A Deep Bow to the Great Mystery and All that I Do Not Know

I am boldly taking on *some very big things* in this book: global crisis and parenting! There are no complete answers to these topics. I can truly only speak from my personal perspective, education and experience. Each one of us has our own vantage point that is, by definition, limited. I acknowledge that I am speaking from the singular vantage point of a white, middle-class woman from the United States. I've done my best with what I know in this moment to address these bigger concepts of global issues and raising children in a way that honors and respects all human beings living on Earth at this time. But like any of us, I see through my own eyes based on my own experiences.

I deeply appreciate the lived experience of parents and families from cultural contexts and social locations that are different from my own. I know that race, class, ability, nationality and many other factors significantly impact our experience of raising children within oppressive social structures. I'm continually inspired by and learning from BIPOC parents and teachers who are particularly motivated to dismantle systems of oppression and live beyond the confines of the Power Over Paradigm (POP) because of the ways that it explicitly harms them and their families. Through their courage and resilience, they demonstrate what's possible when we stretch beyond the POP and cultivate authentic freedom, dignity and empowerment. As you engage in this work, I invite you to bring the wisdom and intuition provided by your own unique experiences, cultural roots, social location and identity into your exploration.

This book is *not* a "how to" book or a book of doctrine. This is a book of concepts that I believe will help you contemplate how you want to parent in these times. It's full of personal insights, observations and reflections gathered through my experience of caring for children in this precious and perilous time on Earth. Please do not impose the ideas in this book on children with any kind of rigidity. Every child is unique, and every child/adult relationship brings its own particularities that cannot be calculated or submitted to a prescribed method.

My hope is that this book helps you pay attention more closely to your *own* personal experience with the children in your life; to raise your own consciousness and ignite your own intuition as you raise your children; and that it will offer clear and compassionate guidance that awakens your presence and inspiration in the care you give to the children you love now, at this pivotal time in our collective story. Please take what you gather here and breathe life into it by being present, paying close attention and being brave and loving with yourself and the children in your life.

Caring for children is nothing if not humbling. The Great Mystery is at hand in every moment and Letting Go is the constant order of the day. In these times of global crisis, we can easily become overwhelmed by despair and feel like we can't go on. And yet, here we are. And here are the children we love. All of us are being held within some mysterious Grace that allows us to keep on living and growing and learning, at least for now. So, let's move forward with gratitude in our hearts for all the little miracles that carry us along and for this awesome opportunity we have to love and care for our children – right here, right now.

My prayer for you as a parent is that you will find a lifetime friend, companion and comrade in your child. That you will grow closer and closer to them as they move out of childhood and into their teenage years and adult life. That your deep respect for them will allow you to continue to get to know them as they grow, change and blossom. And that your children will want to share this tumultuous and exhilarating adventure of human life on planet Earth with you and will become your accomplices in caring for this living world and all our relations.

My prayer for your children is that they will have the fertile ground of unconditional love, authentic respect and belonging deeply laid within their beings – so they can get on with the good work of caring for this glorious planet and can bring forth a future of wellbeing for all, beyond our wildest dreams.

My prayers are for connection. Deep, lifetimes-long connection. A reweaving of the fabric of life, kinship and wellness.

Some Notes About Language

When using the words "we" and "us" it's always important to be clear about who that "we" really is. The "we" in this book refers to parents who are engaged in, complicit to, dependent on and/or imposed upon by the Industrial Growth Society in relation to our income, housing, food, civic services, education, entertainment, etc. There is *a lot* of diversity within that "we." The use of the word "we" isn't meant to imply that we all see things the same way or have the same experiences. It is not meant to overshadow the important differences that exist within our cultural lineages and positionality with the Industrial Growth Society. It is meant to indicate that "we" are all affected by the Industrial Growth Society and the Power Over Paradigm on some level and therefore have a shared interest in and need to understand it and respond to it consciously.

Throughout the book I've used the pronouns they, them and theirs instead of he/she or him/her when referring to our children in order to include the full gender spectrum. My child is gender fluid and uses the pronouns he, they and she interchangeably. Although one pronoun doesn't describe the fullness of their gender expression, they do identify as my daughter and feel that we have a mother/daughter relationship. For that reason, and with their full consent, I refer to them using the pronoun "she" throughout the book. All sections of the book that are directly about my child have been read and approved by her.

I've attempted to use the most inclusive and universal language that I can throughout this book. When I refer to "parents" I mean adults of any gender who are actively caring for children as a major aspect of their lives. This includes biological parents, adoptive parents, foster parents, stepparents and any other adults who prioritize the care of the children in their lives, whether they are "their own" children or not.

Likewise, the word "family" is meant to include all shapes, sizes and forms of adult/child configurations of care; whether you live with your children full time, part time or not at all; whether there is only one adult and one child or many adults and many children; whether community members and co-parents and "other people's children" are part of the story; whether your family consists of a constantly shifting combination of all the above, your family is included and this book is for you.

PART ONE: Greeting This Precious and Precarious Moment

1

RAISING CHILDREN ON THE EDGE OF A CRUMBLING WORLD

*"Let this darkness be a bell tower and you the bell.
As you ring, what batters you becomes your strength."*

– Rainer Maria Rilke [1.1]

Parenting on the Edge

If you're feeling overwhelmed and stressed out by parenting in these precarious times, you are not alone. It's scary to be raising kids right now. Many of us feel that we don't know how to do it. That we don't have the resources or knowledge to support our children's mental and emotional health in a world that seems so crazy, so out of balance and so desperately futureless.

In recent years, I've heard many parents ask questions like… *"Am I crazy for having kids right now? Was that a totally insane choice? Was it selfish of me to bring a child into the world the way it is now? Have I just added* to the Earth's burden? Have I set my children up for a life of suffering? How are they going to manage as the climate chaos accelerates? What will their lives be like? When they find out how bad things really are, will they hate me for having them or blame me for not doing enough to fix all the problems?"

Some people wrestle with these questions and feelings before becoming parents. Some find that questions like these come rushing in once the gravity of their parental responsibilities sets in. For others, the questions creep up slowly as they become more and more aware of the complex global crises we're facing and how they affect our children.

Many parents worry that they won't be able to adequately support their kids financially, physically, and emotionally amid social, economic and political upheavals and the increasing pressures of industrialized, techno-driven society. They're afraid they won't be able to give their children the skills and awareness they'll need to deal with all the challenges that they'll encounter in their lives. They worry that their children will give in to hopelessness as they learn about the world they're inheriting. Or, conversely, that they'll get wrapped up in cynicism and denial as a way to insulate themselves from the harshness of reality.

As a parent in these troubled times, you may find yourself walking the daily tight rope between trying your best to create a positive childhood experience for the precious little ones you love so much and being overwhelmed by the stressors of our world in crisis on personal and collective levels.

At times feelings of guilt and shame for being tacitly complicit with the environmental harm and social injustice of industrial society may weigh you down. You may feel like you have to take big urgent actions to stop it all and then get frustrated or stuck in feeling that any action you take could never be big enough. You may judge yourself and others for not "doing enough" and fret over the decisions you're making and what kind of impact they'll have (or not) on the unfolding crises. And sometimes you may push it all away and just try to focus on the positive. You might try to pour your heart and energy into the little lives you're caring for and the little world of your own household and your own family where you feel like you can make a difference. But even then, from time to time, a profound anxiety may creep into your consciousness.

You may struggle with how to talk to your children about the state of the world and prepare them for the challenges ahead. How could you possibly make them aware of what they are facing without completely overwhelming them? How do you find the right words and the right moments, in age-appropriate ways? You don't want to tell them too much too soon, but you're afraid it's already too little, too late.

If you have a partner or co-parent(s) you might find it difficult to talk with them about all these feelings. You might actually find it hard to talk with *anyone* about all of this. It's not exactly a great party conversation and your friends and family might avoid "going there" with you. If these feelings weigh heavy on your heart, it is easy to wind up feeling isolated, like you have to figure this all out on your own. And you might be afraid that if you ever let yourself *really* feel and express the pain and fear that it will wreck you and you'll get stuck in despair.

As the days, weeks and years of their childhoods go by, you might find yourself skipping these difficult conversations and going along with the status quo more than you want, just to meet your children's daily needs with the resources you can access. The current of mainstream culture is so strong that it can easily sweep you and your kids along with it. Although going with the flow often seems easier than paddling against it, you may find that the mainstream comes with all the consequences of the dysfunctional and crumbling society from which it flows. As your kids grow older, you may encounter behavioral problems, mental health concerns, addiction and other symptoms of our societal illness of disconnection.

Facing Our Biggest Fears

As parents, one of the most terrifying things we can imagine is to lose our children in some way and to wonder if there is anything we could have done differently to prevent it. Suicide, addiction, despair, apathy and alienation have become far too prevalent among our young people. We are raising our children within multiple epidemics. Too many children give up and sink into addiction and apathy or choose to end their lives because they have no compelling connection to a livable, inspiring future. This type of devastating loss has likely happened in your own neighborhood or community. It could happen in your family. It could happen in mine.

The problems our kids face are enormous. They might be too big for us to overcome. There is no guarantee that anything we do will protect them and keep them from harm. But we have to do everything we can to support them in this outrageously challenging time.

An important place for us to begin is to understand that many of these outcomes are not the result of personal pathologies. They are symptoms of overwhelming systemic disconnection and responses to the breakdown of healthy, functional social structures. This generation of young people is inheriting a hundreds-of-years-old debt of devastating loss of culture, wholesale displacement, intergenerational trauma and environmental plundering. The check is due. And they *know* it.

The most powerful thing we can do to help our children want to stay alive and be engaged in their lives is to *join them* in facing this unprecedented time on Earth with honesty, courage and a lot of love. We can work together to unlearn the ways of disconnection and relearn the ways of connection. We can cultivate wellness in our households and communities as we learn to care for each other and Earth. The world our children are currently facing is full of confusion, pain and fear. Unless we create something different together, they will only experience more of the same.

Partnering with Your Children for a Bright Future

Although many of our worries are well-founded, they are not the whole story. Right alongside all that pain, confusion and disconnection is the possibility for joy and wellness. This is part of the magic of parenting. We are at the crossroads of potential, holding space for emergence. Even with all the destruction that industrialized humans have wreaked on the planet, each new baby born reminds us of the possibility of beauty, brilliance and wellness that exists within the relationship between human beings and the Earth. I'm sure you've felt it. In your baby's giggles, the preciousness of the soft curl of your toddler's fingers around yours as you walk together, the curious open-hearted questions and authentic wonder that rise from them, the sweetness and compassion you see them offer a friend on the playground or a bug on the sidewalk.

You and your children are essential to the wellbeing of the world. You are here on planet Earth right now for important reasons and you are equipped with all the abilities required to fulfill them. This is a unique time on Earth, and a pivotal time in the human experience. There's a lot about the way industrialized human beings have conducted ourselves that needs to radically change. And the time for that change is now. This is an all-hands-on-deck time. Everyone who is alive on the planet right now is here to participate in this dynamic transition. The world needs us – and our children – now, more than ever before. It needs us working together on behalf of Life at every level.

Where does that change begin? With ourselves? Yes!

It begins in each of our hearts. In our thoughts, words and actions. And in our *parenting*. We are raising brand-new humans. We are orienting this next generation to their experience on Earth. We're showing them what it means to be human. In that process we have the opportunity to deeply consider what we *actually* want to teach them. The values and ways of thinking we expose them to in their childhoods will have a profound impact on how they live as adults. It will affect the kind of dreams they can dream. The kind of solutions they may conjure. The type of responsibility they will take. The level of connection and compassion they can feel. And, in all these ways, it will have a dramatic effect on our collective future.

This is why we're here. To love and care for our children, ourselves and this wild, beautiful, generous Earth with everything we have. To feed Life, dismantle the empires of oppression and co-create the possibility of a future worth living for. We were born for precisely this planet-time and so were our children. It can be hard and scary, no doubt. It can feel like a lonely road sometimes, but we *are* in it together.

We need to remember to turn toward each other, stay focused on healing, learning, loving and caring. We need to learn how to partner with our children at each stage of their growth in empowering ways that respect them as our most important allies and accomplices. Our work is to learn how to skillfully navigate this precious and perilous time on Earth and activate the opportunities for healing that are available to us while teaching and learning alongside our kids so they can do the same! Every little bit is important. Every moment and every connection count.

It's not going to be easy and it's not going to be perfect, but you can help your kids find their footing in this wild world while becoming stronger, healthier people as you learn, together, how to care for our world. When you're partnering with your children and engaged in the care of our world, the overwhelm eases and transforms into passionate, empowered action.

> Your children need you. The Earth needs you. The Family of Life needs you. You've got this!

Our Journey Together

No matter where you are in your parenting journey, there is support in these pages for you. The intricate nuances of raising healthy, connected children and the outrageous complexities of navigating the unfolding collapse of the world as we've known it are woven throughout this book with honesty, compassion and a lot of practical tools. Please know that it is never too late to apply these teachings and insights to deepen your connection with your children and to help them turn towards their paths with courage.

This is not simple work. And it's not linear. It is a deeply layered process of discovery into the nature of ourselves, our children, our world and how we all interrelate. It does not move in a straight line. It is not *"Three Easy Steps to..."* It is a twisting and turning, an undoing and redoing, as we seek to emancipate ourselves from our entanglement with the dysfunction of our society so we can allow something more beautiful and Lifegiving to emerge, while raising children with their true human spirits intact.

For these reasons we are going to venture into this work with the support and guidance of the spiral path that is used in Joanna Macy's Work That Reconnects.[1.2] It begins by **Grounding in Gratitude**, then moves to **Honoring Our Pain for the World**, which leads us to **Seeing with New and Ancient Eyes** and then to **Going Forth**. Instead of steps along a linear path, these phases are arranged in a spiral so we can keep coming around to each phase, as needed, in the course of our work. The spiral is a way to orient and empower ourselves during these often disorienting and challenging times.

We'll start by planting ourselves fully in our present reality and acknowledging both the global crisis we're experiencing and the massive paradigm shift that is underway, so we can understand the importance of our roles as empowered New Paradigm Parents. Using the framework of the Work That Reconnects, we'll dive deeper into understanding this big picture we're a part of, exploring the cost of trying to carry on with Business As Usual, the fallout of the Great Unraveling and the magic of the Great Turning.[1.3] *(Chapters 3 and 4)*

Then, we'll enter into the spiral of the Work That Reconnects by centering ourselves deeply in Gratitude. But it won't be your grandma's gratitude *(unless she was a radical, anti-establishment badass!)*. We'll conjure wildly subversive gratitude and gather tools for cultivating life-changing gratitude in our hearts and our households to fortify us all for the journey ahead. *(Chapter 5)*

Once our hearts are filled and we are ready to do some powerful work, we'll move on to Honoring Our Pain by turning towards our emotions. With compassion for ourselves and for our children, we'll learn how to responsibly face our own difficult or frightening emotions about raising children in these troubled times. We'll see what brilliant gifts of transformation these emotions truly are. We'll also gather powerful tools for fielding our children's challenging emotions and teaching them how to metabolize them and hear the messages they carry. *(Chapter 6)*

Then we'll See with New and Ancient Eyes by dreaming into a vision for the future that is both new and deeply rooted in ancient and enduring wisdom; a future in which our children can *thrive!* We'll reflect on the human qualities that this new paradigm will require and explore how we can consciously cultivate these qualities in our children now, so they feel confident as they venture into their futures, actively co-creating a collective future worth living for. *(Chapter 7)*

That's when we'll Go Forth into the nitty gritty of New Paradigm Parenting as we reframe our concept of our roles as parents and rethink the basics of how we care for our children. In the second half of the book, we'll learn to see ourselves in supportive partnership with our kids and will discover more empowering, effective ways to guide our children through their stages of growth while fostering self-worth, capacity and confidence. We'll apply all this to the various stages of your children's experience so you can receive specific support for raising connected babies, toddlers, big kids and teens. *(Chapters 8-14)*

But before we dive in, let me tell you a little bit about myself and how I was called to write this book for you.

2

SEEKING LIFE

*"Do the best you can until you know better.
Then, when you know better, do better."*

– Maya Angelou [2.1]

Coming of Age in a World Gone Mad

I grew up on Cape Cod in Massachusetts in the 1980s in what I considered a "normal" American middle-class white family, surrounded almost entirely by other "normal" middle-class white families. The status quo was strongly in place with a liberal Democrat, Yankee, education-focused flavor. Reaganomics was having its way with our country and my parents were busy making ends meet and doing everything they could to give their three girls the childhoods they thought we deserved. My big sisters were on all the sports teams and had lots of friends. I took ballet and piano lessons and was the baby of the family. We had a nicely manicured lawn, pretty flower gardens and new furniture. We got new school clothes every year, piles of presents at Christmas time and even a couple of family vacations to Disney World. We were encouraged to follow all the rules, get good grades, go to college, start careers, get married and, of course, have kids. The path was laid out for us.

When my oldest sister was 17, and just a few weeks from heading out for college, she was killed in a car accident. I was 9. The path disintegrated. My entire world fell apart.

This tragic loss was my first rite of passage. It was a "coming of age" and spiritual initiation all wrapped up in one, delivered like a freight train and without the benefit of a teacher, mentor or guide. As you can imagine, my living sister, my parents and all the other adults in my life were decimated by this unexpected tragedy. They were consumed by their own shock and grief. No one knew how to take care of the little girl. How would they have known? Our idea of the world didn't include this sort of outrageous disruption.

In many ways, I was on my own to make sense of it all in the spiritual and cultural wasteland of modern-day America. None of the standard stories added up. Not *"Follow the rules and everything will work out alright."* Not *"She's got such a bright future."* And especially not the grating condolences we received from well-meaning loved ones assuring us that, *"God has taken her to a better place now."*

My little child's mind and heart struggled with the big questions: *What was this life all about? What was safe? What was real? What could I count on? What was worth living for?*

I started to pay closer attention. I started to push at the edges of my previously defined reality. As I peered beneath the surface of the status quo, I discovered a seemingly endless sea of hypocrisies, compromises, injustices and imbalances that make up the very bedrock of our modern industrial society and they *broke my heart.*

I was experiencing a pure feeling of distrust, unobstructed by the intellectual thoughts and opinions of adulthood, free of partisan politics and religious ideals. Just the innocent observation of a child that things didn't add up.

How could some people have so much while others were dying of starvation? How could we keep dumping trash and pollution into the environment and act like it didn't matter? Why were all the adults working so hard to be successful but none of them seemed happy? Why did it feel like everyone was lying, from my parents to my teachers, to the people on TV and the politicians?

Growing through my teen years, I couldn't bear the thought of becoming an adult in this lost and depraved society. I just couldn't stomach the façade or understand the value of being alive if it was all going to be a stupid game played at the expense of beauty, integrity, justice and the wellbeing of future generations. For several years, I was convinced that suicide would be my only escape from this life sentence.

> But then *Life* scooped me up, courted me and challenged me to find its magic.

When I truly hit rock bottom, with a complete nervous breakdown and suicidal desperation in my first semester of college, a whisper entered my heart. It was the whisper of *Life*, itself. It came into my being and opened the door of possibility for me, presenting this challenge. It said, *"Life is meant to be beautiful, rich, real, raw and stimulating. It can be, even now, here in the midst of all this pain and confusion. But if you want to experience it, you must shake loose from this path you're on and go out in search of it."*

And so I began my quest for the raw beauty of life, sniffing the trail of radical truth and authenticity. I dropped out of college and hit the road. I ventured beyond the edges of middle-class normalcy and began to peek behind the curtain, so to speak. I came into contact with the poverty, homelessness, addiction, racism and environmental sacrifice zones that are the other side of the middle-class coin. I started to understand how the systems of hypocrisy and corruption functioned to keep everything chugging along for the benefit of the few, the oppression of the marginalized and the complacency of the many.

As I traveled the land and journeyed within, I dove into the study and practice of earth-based spirituality, natural self-care, wholistic nutrition, song and celebration, self-love, natural building, homesteading, organic gardening, healing relationships, community building, alternative education, natural birth and conscious parenting. And I came *alive.*

In studying these systems, I found a precious thread that weaves through them all. *Reconnection:* the process of reclaiming and nurturing our connections with ourselves, each other, Spirit, and the Earth. As this process of reconnection began to heal my own ailments of dissociation, I clearly saw that we are all in this together, as one living Interbeing,[2.2] with an enormous amount of healing to do, tons to transform and infinite possibilities for beauty at our fingertips.

From this depth of awareness arises my commitment to actively participate in the healing of our personal and collective wounds and alienations, to reconnect the separations, to play my part in reweaving wellness for all and co-creating a life-sustaining culture that can be passed on to our future generations.

My Call to Motherhood

Once *Life* had called me back to her, I knew I wanted to be a mother. I wanted to learn how to live well, close to the Earth, and raise children as natural human beings. My first husband and I scoured the country for the right place to raise kids and homestead. We knew we needed to be far from the din of industrialized corporate influence, but we also didn't want to be in the middle of nowhere all by ourselves. After three years of searching, we were fortunate to find a hidden gem for a hyper-idealistic couple with zero practical knowledge about how to raise children or live off the land. It was a small community at the base of enormous mountains, full of natural-birthing mamas and papas and their wild herd of desert babies.

I thought I was in heaven. I was embraced by a whole community of women who taught me how to care for my body through pregnancy and to prepare for a completely natural off-grid home birth. I learned all about the importance of in-arms time and cloth diapering and how to let my baby discover the natural world and be her wild self.

Our goals within this community were all about sustainability. Recognizing how unsustainable the mainstream status quo was, with its endless consumption, its industrial agriculture and its addiction to fossil fuels, we set out to create viable alternatives. We grew our own food, lived close to the land, built our own passive solar houses, used compost toilets, converted our cars to biodiesel and tried our very best to live without money and go "plastic-free." We worked hard to close the loop of our consumption and to live lightly on the Earth.

I had visions of a big happy family of intelligent, grounded children, milking goats and homeschooling, hiking up into the high country and sitting by a fire at night. I dreamed of empowering my children to love life, and to seek connection and adventure. I had a lot to learn.

Lessons in Sustainability

I learned an incredible amount from this community that I lived in for 15 years, through my pregnancy and my daughter's birth and childhood. I learned many ways that we can live and raise children oriented to nature, love and beauty. I also learned about the many ways we unconsciously carried the wounds and illnesses of the dominant society right into our little haven and into our children's lives. It was a gorgeously excruciating infusion of learning that has radically informed and deepened my understanding of what we are meant to do here as parents at this time.

Within this community we all had good intentions and were willing to work hard, physically, spiritually and emotionally. But the intergenerational wounds of this society ran deep within us and we were learning as we went. There's only so much you can do until you know better. And in the meantime, kids are growing, patterns are being laid. Time waits for no one.

Without an intact multi-generational culture, we were at a loss as to how to be parents, how to be married couples and families, and how to be community. We came from various places around the country, a collection of outcasts and oddballs, running from lives that didn't work in search of something better for ourselves and our kids. But we were desperately naïve, idealistic and deeply scarred by the abuses and traumas we had experienced in our own childhoods.

As my husband and I began to try our hand at homesteading and building our own strawbale house while raising a baby, our marriage started to fall apart. The dysfunctional patterns that were laid into our psyches by our parents and society started to play out between us and we didn't have the maturity, skills or support necessary to recognize and work with them. Addictions, insecurities, blame, shame and a general lack of fortitude tore through our lives and destroyed the foundations of our dreams of being a happy, homesteading family. By the time our child was three years old, we were divorced. The dream was dead. Everything changed.

Ironically, right in the middle of this personal unraveling, my homeschooling sixteen-year-old niece came to live with us for a short while because she wanted to learn about sustainability. I vividly remember a sunny afternoon on our land, sitting on a pile of rough-cut lumber that was waiting to be added to our unfinished house, explaining to her how horribly *unsustainable* this all was while my dreams were crumbling beneath me.

I realized that it didn't matter how much food we grew or how energy efficient our home was if our relationships were riddled with dysfunction and we couldn't sustain our marriage. I saw that the least sustainable part of our equation was *us!* Our own woundedness, our mainstream conditioning and patterns, our blind spots and lack of emotional maturity were the things that were tearing it all down. I realized that sustainability goes way beyond physical input and output. There is also a lot of social, emotional, psychological and spiritual work for us to do to heal from the dysfunctions of our society. I realized that we have to do this work for our kids and *with* our kids.

My dream of having siblings for my daughter and homeschooling and working the land all vanished with the divorce, as I had to figure out how to make ends meet as a single mom of a single child. I was crushed and felt like a colossal failure. I doubted my inner vision and felt abandoned by my intuition. There was no work for me in our little town and my grandmother was dying of cancer, so we made a sudden move back to the land of my childhood. For two years, I had to figure out how to navigate life as a working single mother, devoid of community, within the status quo reality of Cape Cod, MA while somehow maintaining my core values around parenting authentically. My child got the commercialized Christmas bug and adjusted to the conveniences of flush toilets and endless electricity. The compromises began. My work as a conscious parent deepened considerably.

After my grandmother passed and I had graduated from the Institute for Integrative Nutrition as a Holistic Health Coach, we had the opportunity to move back to our little mountain town, with a somewhat different orientation than we had before. I started a personal coaching practice and rented a *finished* strawbale house *with* a flush toilet. It was quite lovely.

Our single mom, single child lifestyle worked well for us while she was growing through the elementary and middle school grades at our local experiential education charter school. We were back in community with her father, his new wife and their children, as well as the many other families with whom we shared co-parenting and community life. The challenges and joys of learning and growing together through our wounding and conditioning continued.

After a while, our family grew with the addition of a new husband for me and a new stepbrother for her, who was right around her age. As the two kids entered their early teen years, it became clear that our little community was no longer serving their wellbeing. They wanted more. They craved some real high school experiences and life beyond our little out-of-the-way place. My husband and I saw how limited their options were with their incredibly small peer group. We were also deeply concerned about the high rate of drug use among the local middle and high schoolers and how that was affecting our kids as they navigated difficult choices, peer pressure, dangerous situations and emerging addictions.

So, we did the unthinkable and we moved to the city. All the way up to Portland, Oregon. Life in the city was completely different, and we all learned a lot as we adapted to it. Our daughter loved it and thrived there for almost three years *(until her senior year got cut short by Covid-19)*. Our son grew up a lot in the one year he was there with us and then chose to move back to rural Colorado with more self-awareness than he had left with.

Meeting the Moment, Embracing Complexity

Parenting is nothing if not humbling. All the ideas we have and everything we think we're going to do for our kids are subject to the reality of each child's path. As I've learned this, over my years of motherhood, I've had to let go of my own preferences over and over as I humble myself to my children's paths and learn to accept the opportunities we have (and don't have) available to us at each given moment. I've learned that we need to do our best with what we know and what is offered to us at each stage and phase of growth (mine and hers). Sometimes that looks quite different than I would have imagined or hoped. But it is always perfect in its own way.

More than any ideology or aspiration to minimize my carbon footprint or any other desire I could possibly have, I have come to know that *my most important work as her mother is to cultivate connection, presence, compassion and respect within our relationship and to help her develop the inner resources, self-awareness and capacities that she'll need to navigate her life, whatever it brings her way.* I wasn't able to whisk her away from this dominant society and create a fully viable alternative reality for her, so I've had to learn how to help her see her place in the world as it is, and her role in affecting changes within it.

I've learned how to be honest with her and how to help her hold the complexities of this world in her heart and mind as she develops the capacities and awareness that she'll need to navigate her life in a changing world. She has experienced alternative, experiential education and mainstream public school. She has been fully exposed to corporate and social media and a wide range of earth-based spiritual practices. She has lived in the high alpine desert where there are more cows than people and more stars than you can possibly imagine. And she has learned to thrive in the heart of the city. Most of all, she has learned to think for herself and see beyond the façade and falsehoods of the dominant paradigm. She's twenty-one years old now, well into her young adulthood, and I couldn't be more pleased by the amazing person she has grown into.

My Offering to You

Beyond my personal experience of learning how to parent with consciousness in these turbulent times, I have also worked with, cared for and supported hundreds of children and their families through their own challenges and experiences. For over twenty years I've been engaged in some form of childcare, education or parental coaching, from working in daycares to running afterschool programs, from camp counseling to private nannying. For eight years, during my daughter's childhood, I devoted myself professionally to my private coaching practice. Nearly all my clients were parents struggling to support the physical and emotional health of their families in the midst of these challenging times. What began as holistic health coaching quickly became what I called personal transformation coaching because I found that all my clients' health challenges were deeply entwined with the social, emotional, psychological and material illnesses of our dysfunctional society. My work was dedicated to *personal and cultural transformation as a catalyst for planetary healing.* This book is a continuation of that devotion.

When we lived in Portland, Oregon for three years while my child was in high school, I worked full-time as a nanny. For several months, while looking for a permanent position, I worked as a temp nanny, assigned to a different family almost every day. During that time, I cared for over seventy children between the ages of two months and ten years old and got to really tap into what is going on for parents and their children in these times.

Most mornings, I would commute through rush hour traffic, listening to *Democracy Now!* and hearing in excruciating detail how dire our global ecological, economic and societal situations are. I would often cry or feel outrage about the grievous crimes being committed against justice, humanity and the Earth. Then, when I'd arrive at work, I'd take a deep breath, wipe my eyes and put on a happy face so I could head inside and greet the littles I cared for with good cheer. I knew the moms I worked for were paying attention to the state of the world too, but we didn't want to bring that negativity into the kids' zone. The devastation and anxiety we felt was the elephant in the room, looming just behind our eyes. The inspiration for this book grew out of the cognitive and emotional dissonance I experienced every day during those years – a dissonance I know many other parents are experiencing, as well.

During that period, in my own mothering experience, I was in the phase of helping my young adult children get ready to head out into the world. This was intense in a whole different way. Their other parents and I needed to be painfully honest with them about the world they are inheriting so that we could help them navigate their choices about the future and figure out how to work with anxiety, fear, bitterness, denial and willful ignorance; *our own and theirs.*

As my personal and professional life spanned the spectrum of parenting experiences – from caring for little ones to preparing teens for adulthood – within the political and environmental upheavals of those years (2017-2020), I felt a calling to create spaces of support and reconnection for other parents. I started facilitating Work That Reconnects experiences designed specifically for parents – both locally and online – and I began writing this book. In the last several years, I've had the deep honor of working with parents from all over the world in group programs and through personal coaching, meeting them in their struggles and joys to honestly explore and process the emotions their parenting experience brings up – from the massive global concerns to the most personal household realities. Our work has been focused on cultivating resilience for ourselves and our children. New Paradigm Parenting grew out of this work.

I've found that raising children in these dire times is the scariest thing that *no one* seems to be talking about. It is a secret torment that may invade our sleep or spin around in our minds and hearts in our rare quiet moments. But generally, when we're visiting with friends and family and someone asks how we're doing or inquires about our kids, we tend to keep it light and stay focused on the positives. Rarely do I hear people leading with what's really been troubling them, although I notice evidence of it in their occasional jokes or side remarks. The fear and heaviness bubble up in certain moments. They slip through the cracks and rear their heads every once in a while. And then everyone brushes it off and gets right back to the "bright side," carrying on in the same old way they always have.

This book and the New Paradigm Parenting practices it offers are an invitation to make room for what is really troubling us. To look it squarely in the eyes and let it teach us. To work honestly and bravely with what Life is handing us as parents at this time and to learn *alongside our kids* how to respond to Life with courage, creativity and resilience, so we can be the parents and partners that our children need us to be.

This book offers an anchor, a hand to hold, a shoulder to cry on and some clear suggestions on how to move forward. I wrote it to give parents hope, purpose and direction within these confusing times. To help parents contend with the seemingly impossible obstacles we face through the practice of conscious, courageous New Paradigm Parenting.

My hope is that you experience a bell ringing inside you as you read this book. That you feel the ring of a truth you already knew deep down inside. And I hope that ringing shifts the way you do *everything,* from the way you raise your children to the way you see the world and your place in it. I hope it brings into focus how deeply interconnected we all are and how precious this Earth is; how precious Life is and how precarious this moment is. I hope all this excites and inspires you and that you begin to see parenting as an opportunity for adventurous, meaningful, purpose-driven devotion to Thriving Life for all.

An Invitation to Reflect on Your Intentions

Now that I have shared my hopes and intentions for you as you read this book, I invite you to take a moment to reflect on your own intentions for your experience with this book. Take a moment to check in with yourself, perhaps closing your eyes and taking a few nice deep breaths, and ask yourself these questions:

- What drew me to this book?
- Where do I feel stuck or confused as a parent in these times?
- What do I hope to learn, experience or access?
- How do I want to show up for my learning experience?

(you can write out your answers in a journal or simply reflect on them mentally)

3

GLOBAL CRISIS

"May this new decade be remembered as the decade of the strange path, of the third way, of the broken binary, of the traversal disruption, the kairotic moment, the posthuman movement for emancipation, the gift of disorientation that opened up new places of power, and of slow limbs.

May this decade bring more than just solutions, more than just a future – may it bring words we don't know yet, and temporalities we have not yet inhabited. May we be slower than speed could calculate, and swifter than the pull of the gravity of words can incarcerate. And may we be visited so thoroughly, and met in wild places so overwhelmingly, that we are left undone. Ready for composting. Ready for the impossible.

Welcome to the decade of the fugitive."

– Bayo Akomolafe [3.1]

World in Crisis

Our world is in crisis. On every level and in every way. The moment we find ourselves in is more than just a period of "tough times." It's more than facing a few "big problems" from which we'll eventually recover by returning to some previous version of comfort or normality. We are facing the end of the way we've been operating and a possible opening into an entirely different way of being. We are rapidly careening towards the cliff edge of our accepted collective reality. We are arriving at the moment in which we choose to either sprout wings and fly or plummet to our death.[3.2]

Like an addict who has hit rock bottom, our society is experiencing the cataclysmic consequences of our collective choices and behaviors. I don't see these consequences as a punishment, so much as a revelation and a potential wakeup call. They are the natural results of the way we've been living. They have led us to a moment of crisis in which we're required to make radical changes to continue to live.

Whether personal or collective, a crisis is a critical turning point that requires us to transform in profound ways. Times of crisis show us what is no longer working. They bring us to the end of the line. They undo us. They dissolve everything we thought was solid in our lives. And in so doing, they create space for a radically new way of being to emerge, if we're willing to let it. When we choose to let go of our old ways, we have to traverse the unknown, that in-between space, unlearning what we thought we knew, while something new begins to grow. Crisis invites us to enter the territory of the unknown, with no map, no guide, and absolutely no guarantees.

As we raise children in the midst of this large-scale global crisis, we find ourselves on the edge of the unknown in a *very big* way.

Each of us may sense the intensity of this planetary moment in various ways and in certain poignant moments. But in our daily lives, while we're busy taking care of kids, paying our bills and just trying to make it through the week, it can often feel impossible to maintain our awareness of the true severity of this crisis. Many of us have a tendency to push it out of mind because it's too huge and too overwhelming to consider on top of all our other responsibilities.

This is completely normal, if not inevitable, within our current societal setup. Modern society is designed to insulate us from these considerations by keeping most of us busy enough and comfortable enough to just keep going, day after day, year after year. The momentum of this Business As Usual[1.3] approach has carried us past many red-flag moments along the way in recent generations, and has allowed a large minority of people to skate by in relative comfort. But, as we arrive at the precipice of this global crisis, the insulation and comfort that Business As Usual has afforded is running out, even for the most privileged of families.

This critical moment presents us with a choice and we, the parents of the up-and-coming generation, are charged with making this choice on behalf of our children and all Life. If we want Life to carry on, we have to *choose* it, just like I had to choose whether to continue living in my moment of personal crisis as a young adult. If we want our children to have a livable future, we have to create the fertile ground for a new way of being, and to raise them to be the seeds of an entirely new paradigm. As parents in this time, we are responsible for tending this space of transformation for our world by raising our children to grow towards the new and to *become* the new.

This book, and the New Paradigm Parenting tools it offers, are among the many strands of support being woven into the bridge that will help us move from the reality that is ending to the one that could begin. Walking across that bridge is a choice we each make by aligning with the new and centering it in all our choices, especially in our parenting. This book isn't designed to help you adjust to living in the world as it is, or to help you cope with the stress of living in a crumbling world. It's designed to help you become part of cultivating a new world that supports Thriving Life in a deeply fundamental way.

To have the clarity and strength to leave behind the dysfunctional paradigm that has brought us to this point of crisis and venture forth toward creating a new way of living that can support Life, we have to start by understanding the mess we're in.

The Mess We're In

For the first time that we know of, in the course of modern human history,[3.3] there are legitimate concerns that the basic conditions for Life to exist on Earth will not be in place for the duration of our children's natural lifespans.

Let that sink in for a moment. Take a deep breath and allow yourself to feel that.

The foundational issue delivering us to this moment of existential crisis is the state of the natural environment. Global temperatures have been rising steadily, breaking records nearly every single month. Erratic weather and storms of unprecedented strength and impact have become more and more regular. Catastrophic fires rage through the Amazon Rainforest, Australia, the Western USA, and even the Arctic. The sixth mass extinction is well underway, as species are being lost forever at an alarming rate.

The life support systems that make it possible for humans (and many other species) to exist on Earth are being destabilized. The dramatic loss of biodiversity we are experiencing tears perilous holes in the intricate web of interconnection and reciprocity necessary to support Life as we know it on planet Earth. At the same time, the unprecedented fluctuations in weather, seasons and temperature threaten the food supply and ecosystems that we (and other species) depend on for safety and sustenance.[3.4]

As dire as the global environmental crisis is, it's not the only predicament we're facing. Simultaneously to, and in concert with, the environmental crisis are the political, social, and economic crises. Systems of oppression deeply rooted within our social structures, race relations, economic practices and political systems disenfranchise the vast majority of people on the planet and create nearly insurmountable challenges and conflicts among people. These challenges degrade our ability to respond effectively to the environmental crisis that affects us all. These systems of oppression have woken the ire of people all over the world who are unwilling to tolerate injustice any longer. For decades, city streets all over the world have been regularly flooded with people opposing austerity measures, institutional racism, obscene wealth disparities, authoritarianism, extractivism, continued genocide and other forms of oppression.

The convergence of these multi-fold crises can make it seem like our world is falling apart. In many ways, the systems we have come to think of as the "world" are indeed unraveling. In the Work That Reconnects, we call this aspect of our collective experience The Great Unraveling. Another term for it is Systems Collapse.

Living on the Brink of Collapse

Our children are inheriting a world that has already been profoundly harmed and continues to be harmed by extractive capitalism, industry, colonialism, patriarchy, white supremacy and many other destructive aspects of modern society. The consequences of these abuses are now playing out on a global scale and revealing the impending collapse of many of the systems we rely on to support the status quo: a stable planetary climate, a reliable global food system, a functional economy, and the institutions supporting governments. Considering and accepting the very high probability of a major global collapse of these systems within our lifetimes is not something most of us want to do, but pretending that it isn't happening won't make it go away. This is where we are. At the end of an era. On the brink of collapse.

The word *"collapse"* can trigger images of sudden endings. It can bring up paralyzing fears about a complete and instantaneous termination of life on Earth that we can't do anything about and should therefore ignore with all our might. If we let this resistance and denial get the better of us, it can stop us in our tracks and drain us of our power. But this is not the type of collapse we are experiencing. This collapse is long and complex. It has been playing out in various ways over the course of our lifetimes and will likely continue throughout our children's lifetimes. It has been and will be a defining quality of the human experience for generations as it unfolds. However, within this slow unraveling come countless opportunities for us to adapt and respond with fluidity to the changing circumstances it presents, if we are willing to radically accept it for what it is.

If the word "collapse" seems too dramatic to explain what is happening on a global scale, it could be because you've been afforded certain privileges that have kept you insulated from many of its impacts so far. Collapse is and has been a very real experience for the victims of environmental injustice, genocide, war and poverty throughout the world for decades and centuries. As climate chaos increases, many essential resources will become scarcer and the global economic and political structures we've relied on will likely crumble under the weight of the injustices they've created. Then collapse will become a real part of each and every one of our lives.

The First Nations people of North America who are fighting the oil and gas companies that continue to invade their homes with drilling projects, pipelines and the man camps that come with them have been experiencing collapse for over 500 years. The Indigenous leaders of South America who are ruthlessly murdered to make way for logging and extraction are victims of this collapse. The people of Puerto Rico and all the other places around the world whose homes and livelihoods have been destroyed by climate chaos and have not been able to "bounce back" as they are battered by more and more extreme weather events are in the midst of collapse. Millions of people in the Horn of Africa are experiencing the collapse of their food supply as a result of a years-long devastating drought. Palestinians who are prisoners on their ancestral lands, the people of Yemen who are starving and dying of cholera in the rubble of their war-torn cities and the Rohingya who are pushed from their homes with their babies on their backs while watching their villages burn are all experiencing the catastrophic collapse of the physical, economic and social systems they rely on to sustain life and take care of their children. Even the most "developed" nations are experiencing the collapse of basic economic and social structures as wealth disparities increase at alarming rates and houselessness continues to rise.

Accepting collapse as a major factor in our lives and parenting may seem like an invitation into despair, but our agency and hopefulness for the future must stand on the ground of our radical acceptance of *the whole of reality*. We are here to care for our children and to participate in the *actual world*, the way it *actually is*. Our ability to be resilient in the face of collapse and to care for our children with empowerment, passion and creativity as our world radically changes has everything to do with our willingness to accept collapse as part of our reality. These skills of radical acceptance, resilience and adaptation are also the ones our children will most need as they grow up into a rapidly changing and uncertain future. As we deepen these skills in ourselves, we model them for our children. This is a learning journey we are on together.

When we accept that some, or many, of the systems we've relied on for centuries will collapse in our lifetimes, we allow ourselves to think and act with agency about the choices we can make moving forward. As the Great Unraveling accelerates, I have come to think of it as the collective wake-up call necessary to finally shake loose from our complicity with the destructive and oppressive forces of Business As Usual.

Shaking Loose from Business As Usual

News about these various aspects of the Great Unraveling has been so incessant over recent decades that it often gets folded into what we consider "normal." Reports of catastrophic storms, economic collapse and civil unrest have become so commonplace that they often fail to penetrate the trance of Business As Usual in any significant way. At most, they're seen as inevitable inconveniences that we'll learn to live with or recover from. Often, they are not more than the "shock and awe" background entertainment we've been trained to crave.

The overriding message we receive from our governments, corporations and mainstream media is that, no matter what, we must carry on with what we're doing. We must keep striving for progress. Industry must keep producing and the economy must keep growing. We must create more jobs. Even as the warning signs have become louder and more urgent, Business As Usual has kept chugging right along. It has been obsessive. Determined. Maniacal.

Interestingly, though, as I completed the first draft of this book, in March of 2020, the largest disruption of Business As Usual that we've ever experienced on a global scale began as the Coronavirus (COVID-19) spread rapidly around the world. As factories closed, public gatherings were cancelled, flights were grounded and children were sent home from school, we experienced that *it is possible to pause.* We saw, firsthand, that not everything we thought was necessary actually is!

The living systems of Earth were ready to respond to this collective "anthropause." In the first few weeks of lockdowns, we witnessed stunning improvements in air quality and water quality in particularly polluted cities around the world. Getting a break from human travel and industry allowed many ecosystems and wildlife populations to begin to recover and strengthen. Those first weeks and months gave us some insight into the regenerative power of the Earth and what might be possible if we were able to sustain these massive reductions to our human impact.

The months of quarantine and closures affected us each on many levels in different ways. In addition to the grief of losing loved ones to the virus, many people suffered hardship, economic loss, loneliness, increased abuse, anxiety, hardship or disappointment as a result of these unexpected changes. Simultaneously, these changes opened new opportunities for many people, bringing them closer with their families, dialing down the intensity of their high-pressure lives and allowing them to make career and lifestyle changes. Within the mix of all these blessings and challenges, this large-scale disruption to Business As Usual provided a possibility to see our world through a different lens. It allowed us to reflect on our lives and to re-examine our choices, preparing us, in some ways, to depart even further from what Business As Usual has been.

As the summer of 2020 approached, after months of lockdown, unemployment and uncertainty, an unarmed Black man named George Floyd was murdered by Minneapolis police officers in the United States. As soon as the public saw the video recording of his murder, cities across the US and around the world erupted in outrage. Black lives being taken by white cops has been an intrinsic part of Business As Usual in the United States since its inception. This country that boasts the ethic of "freedom and justice for all" was founded and built on tenets of white supremacy and carries on to this day with racism flowing thickly through its veins.

But, as so many aspects of Business As Usual had been suspended indefinitely, this murder (and the murders of several other Black people that were committed around that time) could not be folded into any semblance of "normal."

Even as COVID-19 had taken a devastatingly disproportionate toll on Black communities and was still an active threat, millions of people of all races flooded the streets to follow Black leadership in exposing the bedrock of racism and injustice that our society stands on for the cruel, dehumanizing lie that it is. Day after day, and night after night, for weeks and months on end, people continued to express their rage and demand justice. Police departments were called to account while statues and symbols of oppression and colonization were torn down all across the United States, breaking a long history of the normalization of racism and genocide in new ways.

Throughout the Coronavirus pandemic, many individuals and factions of government have been pushing for a "return to normal." Many parents, who struggled through the end of that school year, juggling instant online schooling and sudden lack of childcare options with their essential jobs outside of the home or new working-from-home schedules, felt desperate for a return to normal. It's completely understandable. But normal never was. And *normal* is the very thing that has brought us to the precipice of this collective crisis that threatens our kids' futures. Instead of moving backwards for our own sense of comfort, we are being challenged to move forward into something new.

Until recently, many of the individual symptoms of the Great Unraveling have either been isolated to specific regions or been happening just gradually enough that many people can adjust to them. Those in positions of relative privilege or insulation from the specific impacts have been able to maintain a certain amount of denial about the urgency of our situation.

But the pandemic brought the global state of crisis squarely into view. It pushed us all against our edges in many ways, breaking the spell of inevitability that we've been caught in day after day, year after year, generation after generation. It showed us – even if only for a moment – what it could be like to collectively shake loose from the habits of Business As Usual. It gave us a glimpse of what could happen if we were to make different choices on a global scale. This pandemic and the countless other converging global crises we are experiencing are *the consequences* of Business As Usual, and they are our wake-up call to shake loose from it.

What This Means for Us as Parents

As the uncertainty and upheaval of the Great Unraveling increase around us and our children, it can feel almost unbearably taxing to maintain our awareness of these large-scale global issues. But as parents, we can't hide from these realities. Whether we attempt to avoid them or not, they will rear their heads in our own homes and communities, impacting not only our children's futures but their lived experience throughout their childhoods.

Parents and children alike feel the emotional and psychological stress caused by these converging crises. Their encroaching pressure impacts our mental health, our sense of ease, and our hopefulness. No amount of sheltering or denial can keep our children from feeling this pervasive intensity. As much as we may want to, we aren't able to separate ourselves from the troubles of our times or to insulate our children from their consequences.

In addition to feeling the ambient pressure of our world unraveling, we are often also unconsciously drawn into replicating many of the patterns we observe in the greater world within our own households. When these Business As Usual patterns go unobserved and unchallenged at home, they often lead to the symptoms of the Great Unraveling on a personal scale, for ourselves and our children. In our households this can manifest as in-fighting, power struggles, lack of trust, despair and disconnection.

And yet, when we're able to recognize and interrupt these patterns within our households, we can transform them right there, in how we raise our children. Counteracting and rerouting these patterns in our homes is the foundation of New Paradigm Parenting. This form of conscious parenting calls us to face our collective reality head on with honesty and bravery. It calls us to reflect on our own unconscious habits and replace them with conscious practices for cultivating connection and wellbeing. Discovering the transformation we are truly capable of is the big adventure this book invites you to join. It begins with recognizing and understanding the beliefs and stories that may keep us stuck in Business As Usual.

Power Over Paradigm

To successfully change our trajectory, within our homes and in the world, we have to understand the mindset that got us into this mess in the first place. The converging crises of our time are the results and expressions of a very particular collective mindset. These crises stem from a *societal paradigm* that took hold thousands of years ago and radically changed the way human beings behaved in relation to the Earth and to each other.

A paradigm is a framework or worldview made up of underlying assumptions and beliefs that create the conditions for a certain way of being, behaving and understanding the world. It is the story we collectively tell ourselves (and our children) about the world we live in. It is a story told mostly without words, through the way we live our lives. It is the fabric of our perceived reality. It is the blueprint for our shared experience.

The paradigm that has been directing the course of our dominant society for at least the past few thousand years is based on the ideas of separation and supremacy. As reference throughout this book, we're going to call it the Power Over Paradigm, as I've heard it described by one of my most beloved teachers, Woman Stands Shining (Pat McCabe) [3.5] and as Riane Eisler [3.6] explores in her writings. It stems from the idea that human beings are separate from and superior to nature. It's the root of the idea that human beings are meant to have dominion *over* the Earth, instead of participating *with* the Earth and the rest of our relatives in the maintenance of Life.

It's also the idea that a person or group of people can have dominion over another person or group of people. It stipulates a hierarchy of power in every situation, eliminating equality and demanding that there is always someone with *more* power and someone with less; a first place and a second place. It gives free reign to the one(s) with more power to deny the sovereignty, free will and sentience of any being that is not in the dominant position.

The Power Over Paradigm (POP) has been the driving force behind all forms of monarchy, caste systems, empire expansion, religious persecution, slavery, settler colonialism, genocide and environmental degradation the world over. It is the root concept within patriarchy, misogyny and white supremacy. It is the driving force and justification for extractive capitalism and the raping of the land for the "natural resources" humans believe are ours to own and take as we please. It also resides within our minds and personal lives as it creates the basis for our understanding of the world, our economy, our educational systems, our political landscape, our social experiences and even our family dynamics.

The POP has gained its strength by using the physical and psychological violence that it substantiates to manipulate us into believing that power is something that can be taken by some and denied to others. That is a lie. Actual power exists in *every* aspect of Creation. Each being and every person is a channel for the Power of Life that moves through us. Each being is endowed with their own sovereignty and personal authority to engage with the Power of Life. For hundreds of thousands of years, before the onset of the Power Over Paradigm, human beings experienced power through their connection and relationship with each other, the land, the natural world and the cosmos. This natural power passed through lineages for countless generations as cultural narratives, practices and skills that served Life. Strands of this legacy live on in communities around the world that have been able to resist complete assimilation into the POP.

Domination is a lie that we have been tricked into believing. This trick has been played out over centuries and reinforced by intergenerational trauma through brute force and highly sophisticated indoctrination. Through brutal methods of violent coercion, torture, genocide, forced displacement and assimilation and the interruption of our intergenerational cultural education, we have been tricked into forgetting that we have our own access to the Power of Life and that it's our free-will choice whether to give it away or not.

Throughout history, POP forces have overtaken traditional earth-based cultures by using tactics of unconscionable violence that had been unthinkable within the cultural contexts of the societies being invaded. Flouting all traditions of integrity and dignity, POP forces often attack the most vulnerable members of the community, burn food supplies and dwellings, and then round up and relocate people, separating them from their land and often from their own families, thus disrupting the natural conduits for cultural and personal power.

After these initial phases of military violence, the POP seeks to assimilate the survivors into their worldview by separating children from their parents, traumatizing them into an ongoing state of fear, forbidding the use of their traditional language and cultural practices and indoctrinating them through forced POP "education." Once this indoctrination takes hold, the people tend to perpetuate this paradigm on their own by replicating cycles of abuse, applying pressure to one another to comply with social norms and raising their children to see the world through the lens of the hierarchical power that justifies domination and oppression.

This same process has happened to cultures in every part of the world throughout the course of modern history. Your own ancestors were likely dominated in such a way. Your own ancestors may have also participated in inflicting this domination on others. In *The Chalice & the Blade,* Riane Eisler describes the process like this:

> *"Directly, through personal coercion, and indirectly, through intermittent social shows of force such as public inquisitions and executions, behaviors, attitudes and perceptions that did not conform to dominator norms were systematically discouraged. The fear conditioning became part of all aspects of daily life, permeating child rearing, laws, schools. And through these and all the other instruments of socialization, the kind of replicative information required to establish and maintain a dominator society was distributed throughout the social system."* [3.6]

The Power Over Paradigm has now forced its way into almost every nook and cranny of the planet. Through its insatiable greed, it has created a global economy based on privatization, extraction and pollution, destroying the lives and cultures of countless people, killing off many species of our plant and animal relatives, devastating ecosystems across the planet and even destabilizing our global climate.

Because the dominance in this paradigm is primarily seated in the white, Euro-American, wealth holding male identity, those who don't share those identities are disproportionately harmed by the proliferation of this society. Although there are many forms and layers of hierarchical dominance playing out in various countries throughout the world, those who generally suffer most at the hands of this societal scourge are Indigenous people across the world, Black and Brown people, people of the Global South, "poor" people and "poor" countries, non-human species, natural ecosystems and women (to some extent, even if they hold white privilege and/or wealth).

However, it's critical to note that *everyone* suffers at the hand of this twisted mindset and its effects on our society and planet – even those who hold the most power. No matter how insulated or privileged a person is or has been, none of us are immune to its devastating effects and it is our shared responsibility to interrupt and dismantle it in every way we can – in our own minds, in our homes and in our communities.

> *"It is my experience that the world itself has a role to play in our liberation. Its very pressures, pains, and risks can wake us up – release us from the bonds of ego and guide us home to our vast, true nature."*
>
> – Joanna Macy [3.7]

Breaking Down to Break Through (the POP goes pop!)

Fortunately, the Power Over Paradigm is neither *actually* dominant nor sustainable. Its violent shows of force and rapid growth have made it *seem* powerful while it's had its run. But in the long lineage of life on Earth – even within the much briefer span of human existence – it has had a *very* short run. And it is quickly coming to an end.

The inevitable collapse of the POP and its Industrial Growth Society is rapidly approaching for reasons that are easily observable:

- They require perpetual growth but exist within a finite biosphere.
- They consume resources much faster than those resources can be replenished.
- They destroy the life support systems and materials necessary for their maintenance (water, air, land, ecosystems).

This way of living simply cannot be sustained. From within the context of the POP, which regards the world as a collection of lifeless matter and positions itself as the only way of being, this impending collapse may feel cataclysmic. It may feel like the end of the world. However, as we zoom out to consider the situation from a wider vantage point, we may see that the POP and the Industrial Growth Society are only aspects of our reality (not the entirety of it) and that their collapse may open new possibilities.

Advances in modern science over the last century have shown us what many ancient and enduring spiritual traditions have known for millennia: that our world is more than a collection of lifeless, mechanical parts and resources. It is alive and intelligent. It is relationships and movement. It is a symphony of *"dynamically organized and intricately balanced systems."*[3.8]

Living Systems Theory[3.9] explains that these interrelated living systems include cells, organs, organisms and ecosystems, as well as communities, nations and societies. Living systems are naturally self-organizing and responsive. Through exchanges of energy and information (feedback), living systems can maintain balance (homeostasis) in the midst of dynamic circumstances. In response to feedback, living systems can also adapt by growing toward greater complexity. This is resilience. When feedback is blocked, the balance is thrown off, which can cause a living system to lose its coherence and unravel. This is collapse.

In either case, when the feedback loop indicates that a living system will no longer be able to go on as is, it changes radically. Whether through adaptive resilience or collapse, the living system lets go of the old norms and structures that no longer serve its survival. This allows for entirely new norms and structures to emerge. In some cases, the new that emerges is unrecognizable in the context of the old. Even though the unraveling experience can be painful and scary, it is a form of Positive Disintegration[3.10] because it dissolves the structures that kept the system stuck and makes way for the intelligent, self-organizing principles of Life to create a better system. As the POP reaches the end of its viability, it may break down to break through in this way.

"It helps us to recall that the life living through us has repeatedly died to old forms and old ways. Positive disintegration is integral to the evolution of living systems. We know this dying in the explosion of supernovas, the relinquishment of gills and fins in moving onto dry land, the splitting of seeds in the soil."

– Joanna Macy and Molly Brown [3.11]

Throughout the history of Life on Earth, moments of crisis have catalyzed the emergence of radical transformation. For this reason, I see these signs of crisis in our world as messengers, communicating that we are finally arriving at a time when significant change is possible. This transformation is not being dictated by humans. The intelligence of Life itself is guiding the process, bringing us back into alignment with Natural Law and into its next expression. I feel it already happening. I believe we are on the cusp.

The true and enduring paradigm on Earth is the Thriving Life Paradigm.[3.12] True Natural Law is grounded in sovereignty, free will and mutual thriving. Within the Web of Life, each being has its own original instructions (or natural way of being) that fits into and coordinates with each of the other beings' natural ways in a manner that enhances life. No one being has legitimate authority to dominate any other being and each one is dependent on all others. Life is built in a spiral, not a straight line or a pyramid.

> *"The Law of Life is not open to negotiation or compromise. Mother Earth's Authority is absolute, all other false 'authorities' will bow to Hers in the end. It can be no other way..."*
>
> – Woman Stands Shining (Pat McCabe) [3.12]

Our logical brains may try to convince us that humans are an exception to this law. We may believe that the forces of the Power Over Paradigm are "too big to fail" or that human beings have already caused too much damage to the Earth. We may look at the scientific evidence and conclude that our own demise and the destruction of life-sustaining ecosystems around the planet is now inevitable. However, it is exactly in moments like this, when *everything* is on the line, that miracles are known to happen.

Our job as parents in this time is to align with the positive transformation that is already underway; to see and understand collective change as a Great Turning, and to learn how to *turn with it*. New Paradigm Parenting is a way to do just that in our everyday lives, while we support and prepare our children for a radically different way of being human beings on planet Earth.

> *"Another world is not only possible, she is on her way. On a quiet day, I can hear her breathing."*
>
> – Arundhati Roy [3.13]

4

SEEDING A NEW PARADIGM

"When asked if I am pessimistic or optimistic about the future, my answer is always the same: If you look at the science about what is happening on earth and aren't pessimistic, you don't understand data. But if you meet the people who are working to restore this earth and the lives of the poor, and you aren't optimistic, you haven't got a pulse. What I see everywhere in the world are ordinary people willing to confront despair, power, and incalculable odds in order to restore some semblance of grace, justice, and beauty to this world."

– Paul Hawken [4.1]

Right alongside Business As Usual and The Great Unraveling exists a groundswell of healing transformation, a mycelial movement of ordinary people responding to the needs of the world with fierce love and resilient allegiance to the wellbeing of the Whole. In the language of the Work That Reconnects, we call this movement The Great Turning.[1.3]

The Great Turning is the story of a massive paradigm shift that is already well underway and is happening on millions of fronts as people all over the world choose to realign themselves with the power of Life. It is just as real, and perhaps even more powerful than, The Great Unraveling and Business As Usual. It operates side by side with, and simultaneously to them. It's what gives Paul Hawken optimism about the *"ordinary people willing to confront despair, power, and incalculable odds in order to restore some semblance of grace, justice, and beauty to this world."*

The Great Turning describes the worldwide transition from the Industrial Growth Society to a Life Sustaining Society.[4.2] Orienting ourselves firmly within this third story gives us the opportunity, as parents, to consciously and actively work toward a future that could sustain Life for our children and future generations of all species.

> *"You never change things by fighting the existing reality. To change something, build a new model that makes the existing model obsolete."*
>
> – Buckminster Fuller [4.3]

Our Radical Paradigm Shift

To transform our paradigm into one that could support a Life Sustaining Society, everything we have come to take for granted, all our societal assumptions and modes of operation, will have to be questioned and radically restructured. The shift needed now has to go way beyond reducing our CO_2 emissions or approving policies within our current governmental structures. It has to happen at the level of paradigm.

As we witness the Power Over Paradigm take hold on a profoundly global scale and, through its dominance, threaten the very existence of Life on Earth, it's crucial that we become able to identify this paradigm within ourselves and our lives so we can consciously dismantle it in our own minds and hearts to make room for a new, Thriving Life Paradigm to emerge.

This paradigm shift has to be rooted in a radical transformation at the very core of our beings, in the way we see ourselves and exist within the Web of Life, the way we live and the way we raise our children. Fortunately, our children come into the world without the biases and beliefs of the POP. They come ready to learn the ways of their people. Since cultural paradigms are passed from generation to generation, mostly through subtle daily interactions between children and their caregivers, parenting provides a perfect opportunity to contribute to radical cultural transformation.

As people raised within some version of Business As Usual, we often unconsciously perpetuate the POP in the way we parent. Unless we consciously examine this paradigm and the way it has affected our own worldview, it's natural to recreate it in our homes. Even when we try hard to avoid being overbearing or authoritarian, we often simply re-arrange the positions of power within the same old paradigm and wind up digging ourselves in deeper. Power struggles between parents and children, competition between siblings or friends, loss of connection, feelings of purposelessness, challenges with self-worth, depression or anxiety, as well as unhealthy or dangerous teenage rebellions are common symptoms that arise within our households when this paradigm pervades.

By restructuring our relationship with power, restoring our sense of empowerment, health, love and mutual respect, reconnecting with the Power of Life and aligning ourselves with the Thriving Life Paradigm, we can raise children who feel naturally empowered, healthy, loved and respected. Parenting in this way can heal the wounds that have been passed down to us and give our children a much more solid foundation from which to grow and create positive changes in the world. It all comes from what we were taught as kids and what we perpetuate as we raise our kids. Once we understand what is going on, we can re-establish our relationship with natural power and raise our kids to live in a life-sustaining way.

The Power Over Paradigm does not dominate the future. It won't have the final word. As we align with the power of Life and let it move through us, we begin to see clearly that we are actively creating the conditions of the future each day with our choices and that our children will continue to create the future with their choices as they grow. We are not bound to continue to create the same conditions over and over. We can create different possibilities and different outcomes by making different choices now and raising children who see the world in a new way, starting from the beginning.

When Life whispered to me at the depths of my own despair, that is what it told me. And it showed me that the future of my own life was not set in stone. It empowered me to engage in a dynamic relationship with Life instead of succumbing to the confines of the future I thought was inevitable. As we collectively align with the Great Turning, Joanna Macy encourages us to work toward creating the future we truly *want*, instead of the one we think is most likely.[4.4] As long as Life is still living, the Sun is still rising, flowers are still blooming and we still have children to care for, there is a possibility for Thriving Life to be restored for humans and all our non-human relatives here on planet Earth.

> *"Every person alive today is part of the dream of the ancestors. We are the fulfillment of prophecy. Now, it is time for us all to step into our role as ancestors of the future and dream the next seven generations into being. In doing so, we must recognize that giving them life is not enough. We must also work to provide them with a world that is capable of sustaining their lives. This is the work of our time, the work of our lives...Together, we must turn from our stories of domination and destruction and begin to write a new story based on cooperation and conscious co-creation of a more humane and sacred way of being."*

– Sherri Mitchell [4.5]

Thriving Life Paradigm

The essence of this "new paradigm" is a radically mutual support of Thriving Life for *all* aspects of creation. This is actually not *new* at all. This mutuality *is* the very Design of Life and is the way that Life has been sustained on Earth since its very beginning. The paradigms within which Indigenous human beings from all over the world have operated for hundreds of thousands of years have all been rooted in this awareness of Mutual Thriving.

The true and underlying cause of the Great Unraveling is that the Power Over Paradigm has been working against the Design of Life. Natural Law dictates that things are either working well for everything/everyone or they're not really working at all and will eventually need to be reconciled. Robin Wall Kimmerer explains and describes this phenomenon, that *"all thriving is mutual,"* in several exquisitely poetic, scientifically backed and Indigenously rooted essays in her book, *Braiding Sweetgrass*.[4.6] There is no way around or out of this mutuality. *All* of Life is bound together, inextricably, in brilliant interconnectedness.

The abusive, oppressive, extractive Business as Usual approach that has dominated the lifetimes of recent generations may have appeared to "work" for some people. But its apparent success has always been at the grave expense of "others" (marginalized people, other species and ecosystems worldwide). This is why its dominance has been a short-lived and tenuous illusion that is rapidly careening towards its expiration date. The few can only feast off the sweat of the many for so long. In a Living System, balance is bound to be restored, one way or another.

So, for human beings to continue living on Earth we will have to radically change the way we're living and bring ourselves into alignment with Life itself. What is new about the Thriving Life Paradigm at this time is *the choice* we can make to align ourselves with it intentionally from this moment forward. As the descendants of victims and perpetrators of colonization and as children of the Industrial Growth Society we can allow Thriving Life to guide us to a new path forward, towards the possibility of a viable future for all.

Living into the Unknown

Whether we'll be able to pull off a massive global paradigm shift and whether that will save the world from the brink of destruction or not is beyond our control. But the outcome is not nearly as important as the ways these understandings transform how we live in the present moment. Our choice to plant seeds of a Thriving Life Paradigm in the way we raise our children is about honoring the Life that still exists and the ways that the Earth is still nourishing us, even as Her systems are threatened. We owe it to the children we care for and that which gives them Life to teach them how to honor and care for Life to the best of our ability. It's not only what the world needs; it's what *they* need to understand their place in the world and their value as caregivers and lovers of Life. Even in the midst of the environmental and societal breakdown we are experiencing, children raised within this paradigm learn how to thrive. Like flowers rising out of cracks in the concrete, they bring something new and beautiful to the world; something desperately needed.

As Joanna Macy encourages us to work for the future we *want*, she is clear that there is no guarantee what the outcomes of our actions will be. We don't know whether our choices will "save the world." The future is, after all, uncertain. But, as Rebecca Solnit explains brilliantly in her book, *Hope in the Dark*,[4.7] within that uncertainty exists great possibility. Working toward the future we *want* frees us up from being bullied by our fear into aligning with a bleak image of the future just because it seems more likely. It empowers us to withdraw our commitment to despair or apathy. If there is even a shred of possibility for humans to come into balance with our world, we need to strive for it with everything we've got. Nothing less than the very lives of our children and future generations are at stake.

As we venture into this unknown future – day by day, year by year – our children are growing up and it's part of our job to somehow prepare them for that future. This can feel utterly daunting when we have no idea what kinds of skills they'll need, what the economy and food supply will be like, what jobs may or may not be available to them and what conditions may exist for them in 20 or 30 years.

In my work with progressive education professionals, I've been introduced to the approach of *cultivating qualities and capacities* rather than teaching specific skills or concrete information. Instead of relying on the memorization of old, outmoded information, this approach encourages critical thinking and problem solving. This approach teaches children *how* to learn and fosters their ability to respond and adapt to the circumstances they encounter. It builds confidence and capacity and encourages innovation.

As we raise our children on the cusp of a new and changing world, this approach is essential. Instead of raising them to plug away at Business As Usual and succeed in the "game of life," we need to raise them to be resilient, adaptable, creative, compassionate and responsive people who could, in their growth, even change the course of our collective future with their brilliance.

> *"The eyes of the future are looking back and they are praying for us to see beyond our own time."*
>
> – Terry Tempest Williams [4.8]

Tending to the Lineage of Life

As living parents, we are the potential ancestors of great grandchildren we will never meet, but whose very lives are dependent on the choices we make today. The world they are born into, the cultural realities they will experience, what is possible for them and *what is not* will all emerge from the lives we live today and how we raise our children.

It is a commonly known cultural precept of many tribes indigenous to Turtle Island (North America) to consider the effects that each action and decision will have through the next seven generations. In intact cultures such as these, ancestors and descendants are very real members of the community. Most (if not all) natural human cultures around the world have functioned for time immemorial in living relationship with those who came before and those who are to come after. A sense of responsibility, reciprocity and care for these relationships imbues intact human cultures. This awareness is a reminder that our ancestors and descendants are within us just as we are within them. It helps us remember that we are radically interconnected and dependent on one another.

The lack of this awareness of intergenerational mutual causality in our modern worldview doesn't make it any less real. Counting back seven generations from today lands us in 1815, right in the middle of the Industrial Revolution. It's easy to see how the choices made by the people of that time continue to have a profound effect on our lives. The industrialization of our lives, including factory work, urbanization and mechanization have radically altered who we are as human beings and how we relate to the Earth. The Industrial Revolution's reliance on stolen land, stolen resources, colonization, genocide and slavery cut an unfathomably deep wound right through the center of our collective humanity. It is still being cut and it is still bleeding. The extractive capitalism and expansion mindset that accompanied and fueled the Industrial Revolution has allowed the Power Over Paradigm to spread like wildfire and defile almost every corner of the world with toxic chemicals and industrial waste that still poisons our earth, air and water. These effects will continue to persist for generations from now.

The fact that intergenerational awareness is not part of the Industrial Growth Society is not happenstance. It is by design. It is, in fact, the only way that this model of human society could flourish. If we were consciously aware of and paying heed to the accumulated wisdom of our ancestors or able to consider and feel the effects of our actions on the ones yet to be, we wouldn't be able to participate in the Industrial Growth Society. It is only because our natural connection with the continuum of Life has been severed and distorted that we can live this way.

Joanna Macy brings our attention to this topic by saying, *"The technologies and economic forces unleashed by the Industrial Growth Society radically alter our experience of time... [They] depend on decisions made at lightning speed for short-term goals, cutting us off from nature's rhythms and from the past and the future, as well. Marooned in the present, we are progressively blinded to the sheer ongoingness of time. Both the company of our ancestors and the claims of our descendants become less and less real to us."* [4.9]

In Martín Prechtel's school, Bolad's Kitchen, he encourages his students to strive to become *"people worth descending from."* As a parent of children who will hopefully grow to care for and love the children of the future and be part of the continuum of life, I invite you to sit with that phrase for a moment and feel into it for yourself. What does it mean to become a person worth descending from? What does it mean to have something worthy of passing down to future generations? What would it take to be an ancestor that is worthy of praise and gratitude at this pivotal time on Earth?

> *"We live in a kind of dark age, craftily lit with synthetic light, so that no one can tell how dark it has really gotten. But our exiled spirits can tell. Deep in our bones resides an ancient, singing couple who just won't give up making their beautiful, wild noise. The world won't end if we can find them."*
>
> – Martín Prechtel [4.10]

Our Innate Human Wisdom and Purpose

Deep in our bones resides the beauty of our innate humanness, like a dormant seed waiting patiently for the proper conditions to sprout and grow. Martín Prechtel calls this patiently waiting seed the Indigenous Soul.

In an interview with Derrick Jensen for Sun Magazine he says, *"We are all still human beings. Some of us have buried our humanity deep inside, or medicated or anesthetized it, but every person alive today, tribal or modern, primal or domesticated, has a soul that is original, natural, and, above all, indigenous in one way or another. The indigenous soul of the modern person, though, either has been banished to the far reaches of the dream world or is under direct attack by the modern mind."*[4.11]

Even through the countless generations of conquering and being conquered and the devastating losses of cultural knowledge, languages, and traditions that helped us remember how to live in beauty and balance with the Earth, this innate humanness lies hidden within each of us. It contains the original instructions of what it means to be human on planet Earth. It is older than any specific culture and more enduring than any empire. It is the blueprint for our natural way of being.

When this precious seed sprouts, it takes on many unique and varied forms, according to the times, conditions and location of its sprouting. Looking beyond the Industrial Growth Society, we can find evidence of its sprouting and flowering in the countless, vibrantly diverse Earth-based cultures of the world, both throughout history and still resiliently persisting to this day. Each one expresses this same brilliant humanness in its own culturally specific and unique way. Some of the commonalities expressed in many different intact cultures include beauty-making, humility, reverence and life-giving reciprocity. Elaborately gorgeous clothing, crafts, song, dance, language, prayer, social/familial structures, education, land stewardship and traditional foods are some of the various expressions of the innate human wisdom that can be found in intact human cultures across the world, throughout time immemorial.

Creating the conditions for this glorious humanness to sprout again in our lifetimes is not about recreating or appropriating any particular culture. It is not about going back to the past. It is not about adopting the forms and practices of someone else's culture. It's about authentically reconnecting with the sacredness and brilliance of being human on planet Earth. It's about shaking loose from the false concepts we carry about humanity and creating space for a healthy humanity to grow from the fertile soil of the Thriving Life Paradigm.

One of the main tenets of the Power Over Paradigm is that human beings are the pinnacle of Creation. It asserts that human beings are exceptional in every way. That we singularly possess intelligence. That we are the only beings with souls. That we have a right to rule over the Earth and gratify our own needs to our hearts' content and without consequence. The rest of the Earth (and even the Universe) is just a backdrop to our journey of exploration, innovation, progress and accomplishment. The mountains and oceans are the raw materials and vehicles upon which we grow our fortunes. This paradigm is really *all* about humans, but it also relies on human self-hatred and disempowerment.

As the consequences of the Power Over Paradigm pile up and some of us become aware of how humans and our industry have caused such a great degree of suffering and destruction, the self-hatred part of the paradigm magnifies. It's common to hear people describe humans as a plague or a cancer on the Earth. Misanthropy, the hatred of humankind, runs rampant among people who acknowledge the damage that has been caused by humans. It particularly breaks my heart when I hear this sentiment coming from young people. As teens and young adults start trying to make sense of what is happening to the world, it's understandable that they would draw the conclusion that humans are inherently flawed.

Underlying (or overt) Judeo-Christian precepts of original sin and other cultural narratives about the "human condition" and "human nature" corroborate these conclusions. When presented with the limited evidence that our narrow concept of time permits and the overwhelming self-hatred that the Power Over Paradigm employs to keep us powerless, it all makes perfect sense. But this perspective suffocates our Indigenous Soul by failing to recognize that we are a sacred and intentional part of the Design of Life, with an essential and beautiful role to play among all the other beings in Creation.

Look into the eyes of any newborn baby and it's clear that human beings are not fatally flawed. The possibility for renewal and reconnection to human brilliance is one of the greatest miracles and opportunities of being a parent. Each human born onto the planet comes with this glorious bundle of original humanness tucked right into their very core. Humans are amazingly beautiful, creative, caring, built for connection and love, courageous and adaptable, perceptive and profoundly self-reflective creatures.

According to countless cultures outside the scope of the Power Over Paradigm, human beings are here to lovingly care for the Earth and our fellow species. In many traditional narratives, humans are considered the "younger siblings" in the Family of Life. We have not been here as long as most other animals and plants and we are utterly dependent on the rest of the Family of Life for our survival. A human baby is perhaps the most vulnerable creature on Earth. We wouldn't survive past a few days of infancy without the constant care of our elders for years, in addition to the nourishment, shelter, warmth, medicines and other support offered by our non-human kin. The nobility and preciousness of humanness is deeply bound by humility. It has to do with being close to the earth, as in the word *humus,* the organic matter that gives soil its life. Being in service to the Earth is where our true greatness lies. Not in lording over the earth. Not in being the pinnacle of Creation. But in being deeply entangled within and in service to the vast and complex Interbeing of Life.[2.2]

I've learned from Martín Prechtel that, in reciprocity for all these gifts, we can offer our humble gratitude with gifts of beauty we make with our hands or with our words, in prayers and song. The exquisitely elaborate and culturally diverse expressions of intact human cultures in every part of the world throughout extended history are examples of this human reciprocity. I see these expressions as evidence of human worth and value in the world and reminders of our intended contribution within the Family of Life – a contribution we can learn to give once again. This sacred reciprocity practice is a path towards restoring our human integrity that we can walk with our children as they grow.

> *"Conscious parenting is activism and activism is hard. Activists are cycle breakers. Breaking cycles requires deep change and that takes time. So, activists need a lot of patience. It can be deeply painful. So, we need the ability to bear great pain. It is often exhausting. So, we need to be good at loving ourselves and taking care of ourselves. Conscious parenting is activism. You are changing the world."*
>
> – Vivek Patel [4.12]

Parenting as Activism

In this book we engage parenting as a form of activism. Or, more correctly, what Bayo Akomolafe has termed *postactivism*.[4.13] Postactivism invites us to shake loose from preconceived notions and paradigmatic conditioning. It urges us to decentralize our rigid human authority and open our awareness to the many other forms of intelligence and movement that are dynamically shaping reality in each fluid moment. It reminds us that *"we are 'in deep', and we must account for the fact that how we even see the problem is part of the problem."* [4.14] Postactivism is deeply based in inquiry and sacred reflection. It is a response to our living world which recognizes that when we approach activism unconsciously, distorted by the mindset that created the problems we seek to "fix" we generally wind up recreating the problems again in a different way.

The "work" of this book is not to figure out how to escape the crises of our times or how to raise perfect kids or save the world. It is not about "getting it right" or finding the solution. New Paradigm Parenting is about becoming deeply familiar with the reality in which we are raising our children and responding to it authentically. When speaking about postactivism, Bayo Akomolafe says that it's not really about thinking outside the box, but that it's about *"touching the box."* I take this to mean a process of awakening to more fully understand the circumstances in which we find ourselves.

It's true that we need a new way of seeing, or a new model as Buckminster Fuller expresses in the quote shared earlier in this chapter. But "thinking outside the box" as a way of escaping our circumstances is actually the same kind of thinking, dressed up in a different outfit. I recognize what Bayo Akomolafe says about "touching the box" in what happened for me when I tried to leap into sustainability in my early 20s without really understanding what I was trying to leap away from. This experience made me aware of the box of my own conditioning, and that of my peers. It showed me how that conditioning came through in our parenting and marriages, undoing the very things we cherished most. It showed me that the real work is coming to understand the ways in which we were programmed and the wounds we carry so we can heal from the inside out. Slowly, deeply, thoroughly.

In this way, our work here is to comprehend the dynamic, pivotal, powerful, precious, precarious, complicated, unfolding, changing reality in which we're raising our kids. There is a much greater intelligence at play here than human intelligence. Life is unfolding, adjusting, responding to all that has been done and is being done on all levels. We are in the midst of it. We are not in the lead, nor do we need to be left behind. As we choose to align ourselves with Life and teach our children to live in that alignment, we do our small, but important, part to shift the tides of consciousness.

Grounding in this deep awareness gives us the fortitude to take meaningful action for profound change and healing in the way we parent, actively break cycles of disconnection, disempowerment and abuse. Breaking these cycles and healing the trauma that we have inherited is difficult work. It takes patience, practice, discipline and humility. There is no right way to do it. It may be exhausting and confusing at times and there will be unexpected challenges around many corners. You may not get the pats on the back or confirmation of your good work for years to come. That's what the creation of masterpieces is all about.

Of all the endeavors you engage in through your life, there will be nothing more important than raising the little humans in your care, to the best of your ability, in a way that will allow their innate human brilliance to take sprout and grow. None of your greatest accomplishments will have more value or influence on the world than the human beings you raise.

New Paradigm Parenting is a life's work. It is legacy work. This kind of parenting is, in itself, a profound form of activism that has incalculable effects on the future of our world. It is the greatest gift we can give to the world in service to our lineages and future generations. Children raised with dignity and respect, nourished by love, empowered to enact their Life-serving purpose on the planet can grow into adults who can see, feel and think beyond the Power Over Paradigm, allowing the Thriving Life Paradigm to emerge through them and contributing to a Life Sustaining Society.

The Great Remembering

a poem by Jo delAmor

We are the children of the Great Forgetting…
Amnesiac orphans, separated from the clan of life by lies.

Lies, told and carried through countless generations
Poured from the lips and actions of our mothers and fathers
Right into our own tender hearts

Lies, bundled up by our teachers and heroes
And handed to us like suitcases made of bricks
For us to carry and pass on to our children and theirs

False stories about the shameful sin it is to be human
That we are essentially flawed
That it is human nature to conquer and destroy

False stories about our dominion over the natural world
That we are intrinsically superior
That it is a human right to colonize and consume

Our own sacred memories were buried and twisted
As these lies have been enforced with violence and brutality
At first, overt, as they stole our children
And raped the trust right out of us.

And then, generation by generation, this brutality mutating
Into an insidious lust for validation in the slave master's game…
Tricking us to want what kills us…
To want what kills our children
and the very possibility for life to continue.

Self-absorbed, lonely, depressed, desperate and hungry…
We have forgotten how to feed life
And how to receive nourishment from life.

We have forgotten the simple delicious dance of the gifting way…
The way of giving the song of our lives in praise
To the glorious web of existence…
The way of dropping our seeds on the fertile ground
And rejoicing as they sprout and nourish our relatives.

My heart longs to put down this burden of forgetting
To rejoin the clan of life and remember the dance.

In graceful moments of quietude,
When the din of motors and motor-mouths and motor-brains
Gives way to the subtle, beautiful, inexplicable, gentle knowing
Of the voice that still sings deep down in my bones…

I begin to remember the magnificent legacy of human existence…
The majesty of our true human nature.

I hear the exquisitely intricate languages of original peoples
Steeped in thousands of years of intimacy with the living world
Conversing with stones and weather…trees and ancestors…
Rising in song and prayer and laughter

And I whisper… "I am here…daughter of the
Great Mother and Father of all of Creation…a relative in the web…
Long lost sister of the Sacred Hoop of Life."

And I find myself molting the justifications I inherited…
Shedding my ability to go along with the lies anymore.

Shedding my tolerance for the violence of
Bulldozers ripping the Earth in the name of progress
Gears grinding, diesel engines pumping toxic fumes
Into clear blue sky.

Shedding my willingness to play the game of chasing dollars
To buy sustenance stolen from the belly of our Mother
By the jaws of industry and trucked across her precious body
To save me the trouble of learning my local foodscape.

Shedding my patience for so many years spent distracted
By the illusion of our personal achievements
While the survival of our grandchildren hangs precariously
Over the precipice of melting ice caps and privatized water.

I find myself longing to just lie down beside the creek and listen
For years and decades and eons
Until I remember how to hear her song.

Until it sings through me and my cells remember
What my soul never forgot…
Releasing this notion of separateness
And letting roots grow from my body,
Snaking their way through the cool, moist soil
And sending tendrils of new life reaching up toward the sun
In praise and reverence.

I find myself rising with my siblings
The wayward human prodigal children of existence
Turning back toward LIFE
And begging for remembrance
Ready to heal and learn
And reweave the BeautyWay
On behalf of ALL of Creation

And I feel the birds and trees
And insects and creepy crawlies
And the Great Central Sun
And the Earth Mother herself
Celebrating our return
Eager to share their songs with us
And teach the dance of the Gifting Way once again

So that we can become the parents
Of the Great Remembering.

PART TWO: Moving Through the Spiral

5

GROUNDING IN GRATITUDE

"To be thankful for the water that quenched my thirst is to remember the moment in which I felt parched. And when I remember, I cannot help but express gratitude to the one who thought it not robbery to attend to my needs, however large or small. In that moment of thankfulness, I remember the sensation of thirst and am grateful for the one who has poured water into my cup.

– Rev. Yolanda Pierce [5.1]

Grounding ourselves deeply in gratitude provides a powerful source of steadiness and buoyancy to support us through the dynamic and often challenging terrain of New Paradigm Parenting. It helps us remember how precious this life is, how amazing it is to be human beings on planet Earth and how outrageously fortunate we are to have the honor of tending to and caring for young ones at this pivotal time in our world.

It is a time-honored tradition of the Work That Reconnects to always begin with gratitude. But it's not just for the beginning. Since the work is nonlinear and follows the movement of the spiral, it reminds us to return to gratitude again and again, as often as we need to. Gratitude is the ground from which everything else sprouts and to which everything else returns. By returning to gratitude again and again we practice reconnection. I invite you to welcome gratitude into your parenting work as fully as you can and let it sustain you through all the ups and downs you'll experience.

The form of gratitude needed for New Paradigm Parenting extends far beyond the typical practice of maintaining a cheery attitude about "the way things are." Instead, it roots us deeply into the outrageously generous gift of Life, itself, so we'll have the strength to challenge and change the way things have been done in the Power Over Paradigm and open ourselves fully to Thriving Life.

> *"The corporate revolution will collapse if we refuse to buy what they are selling – their ideas, their version of history, their wars, their weapons, their notion of inevitability."*
>
> — Arundhati Roy [3.13]

The Subversive Nature of Gratitude

As we begin our exploration into gratitude, I invite you to gather up all your preconceived notions and prior experience with gratitude practices and put them on the shelf for a moment. We're going to take a look at how gratitude is typically used within the construct of the POP. And then we're going to venture together past these frequently prescribed forms of gratitude to an entirely different, deeper, lifegiving gratitude that has the power to subvert and dismantle the conditioning of the POP. This exploration of gratitude can be one of our first practices of "touching the box" or reflecting on how the dominant paradigm influences and informs the way we feel about the world.

Gratitude is typically thought of as a lovely, pleasant, polite or pious thing to engage in. Something your grandmother may have taught you as part of your etiquette training, or perhaps something you learned in your place of worship. The true nature of gratitude, however, is wildly subversive to the status quo of the Power Over Paradigm because it directly challenges one of its foundational precepts: *that you are never enough.*

Author Harriet Brown posits, *"If tomorrow, women woke up and decided they really liked their bodies, just think how many industries would go out of business."* [5.2] This is because so many of the corporations and industries that make up our economy are fueled by women's discontentedness with themselves and their appearance. And, of course, it's not just women and our bodies. It's everything and everybody.

The Power Over Paradigm convinces us that we all have to struggle and compete for a piece of the pie, that we are never good enough, that we should spend our whole lives and all our energy trying to accumulate *more* things, *more* prestige, *more* clout and, ultimately, *more power*. The entire economy of the POP is based on discontentedness and scarcity. Radical gratitude, based in the abundance of Thriving Life, therefore, has the power to bring the POP to its knees, toppling the empires of oppression and exposing the lies they were built on.

In the Power Over Paradigm, the world is seen as a collection of lifeless material that is ownable and exploitable. The people and countries that have claimed ownership of the most stuff are the ones that wield the most power. Those with less are forced into the position of striving to become like those with more. Countries are ranked into positions as though they were racing each other to some future destination. Everything in the world is seen as a commodity: land, food, water, all the "resources" of the Earth and all the products we make from them. Our bodies, our presence, our ideas and our time are mere *commodities* to own and wield power over. The shortage of any of these things and the compulsion to constantly accumulate more of them is what keeps the Industrial Growth Society cruising along.

Within the confines of the Power Over Paradigm, gratitude is often used as a tool to force complicity and complacency. We're trained to *"keep calm and carry on."* We're taught we should be grateful for what we have and maintain a cheery attitude about the slice of the pie that we're allowed. This form of gratitude is designed to help us cope with the world the way it is and to stay in our lane. Another way to put that is that it's designed to keep us in our place in the pyramid of power, grateful that we're not on a lower rung and clinging to the privileges or benefits that come with our position. If we speak up about the injustices and wrongs of the system or express frustration with the way things are, we're often shamed for being spoiled or having a bad attitude. Many of us are even told that our bad attitude could make bad things happen, and that it would be our own fault if we lost some of our "good luck." In this way, the POP has distorted our natural desire for righteousness and safety to secure our compliance and pressure us into a contrived state of gratitude even when we have the feeling that some things are terribly wrong.

In the POP gratitude is also, at times, equated with winning. People tend to express gratitude for the stuff they have, the power they've gained and the opportunities they've been afforded. In this way, our expressions of gratitude can take the form of a list of assets or begin to look like Scrooge's pile of coins. When we equate gratitude with wealth and fortune against a backdrop of scarcity, it can skew our perception of the costs of these privileges and create a rigid sense of protection over and attachment to our personal bounty. Again, this form of gratitude keeps us locked into the worldview of the POP, as we continuously seek to improve our lot in life so we can increase our tenuous sense of gratitude.

For those who have been oppressed and abused by the systems of the dominant society, an invitation to express gratitude can feel like a slap in the face and an appeal to forget all the harm that has been done. For those with *growing awareness* of the injustices of the POP, this narrow form of gratitude may bring up feelings of guilt and grief about the cost of the privileges they've experienced. It can become confusing and painful to try to feel grateful for opportunities made possible by a system that is destroying Life itself and putting other humans in perilous harm. All these feelings invite us to move beyond the confines of the POP and to tap into a deeper sense of gratitude.

Gratitude based in the Thriving Life Paradigm is not about the stuff or opportunities we get as a result of our place on the pyramid. It's not about the pyramid at all. Thriving Life gratitude is about the miracle of Life. Sometimes you may experience this form of gratitude within the framework of a luxury provided to you by your place in the pyramid. Perhaps you've been granted the opportunity to pursue higher education, study abroad, travel, learn and connect with beautiful people and beautiful places on the planet. And perhaps you feel gratitude for these experiences even though you are aware of the costs of these privileges. Or perhaps you feel gratitude for the strength and resilience you gained by growing through different forms of adversity caused by the oppressive structures of the POP. It's okay to feel the gratitude and the grief at the same time. Sometimes they are mixed up with each other. This depth of awareness is an opportunity to pay attention and go deeper.

As we move beyond the limited expressions of gratitude within the POP and open to Thriving Life Gratitude, we can call on radical acceptance to guide our way through the challenging terrain. Radical acceptance is a form of presence and deep surrender to the Great Mystery. It is a willingness to *be with* "what is" on all levels. All the beauty and all the pain, all the privileges and all their costs, all the wounds and all the opportunities for healing. It is a spiritually mature awareness that there is much more to this whole collective experience than we could ever fathom. That there is a sacredness that calls us back towards life and shows us the way to dismantle, transform and heal the atrocities of the POP.

Reverence for the Sacredness of Life

Over generations and centuries, the conditioning of the POP has degraded our relationship with sacredness and reverence. We've been robbed of our simple ability to appreciate Life, as it is given, for the miracle that it is. This strategy has been used so we'll perpetually lust after what is being sold to us, whether it's a product, a religion, an idea or an illusion of safety. Through this trick, we are made to think that those who hold societal, religious or political power are somehow *more* powerful than the Life that flows naturally through and around each and every one of us.

Radical gratitude can cut right through this lie because it's awake to the vibrant, precious, powerful aliveness of the world that is available to each of us in every moment. It's about appreciating the value of what is given and about cherishing each part of our lives. It allows us to turn our attention – which is the real seat of our personal power – to the inherent value, worth and aliveness of the so-called "commodities" of our world: the land, food, water, time and connection with others. Authentic gratitude is a form of reverence that reactivates a long-dormant sacredness within every part of our world. With this simple, radical practice, we not only enliven and nourish ourselves, but we also put the brakes on the relentless drive for *more* and do our part to dismantle the unjust power structures of this dying paradigm.

> *"Teach the children... Show them daisies and the pale hepatica. Teach them the taste of sassafras and wintergreen. The lives of the blue sailors, mallow, sunbursts, the moccasin-flowers. And the frisky ones–inkberry, lamb's-quarters, blueberries. And the aromatic ones–rosemary, oregano. Give them peppermint to put in their pockets as they go to school. Give them the fields and the woods and the possibility of the world salvaged from the lords of profit. Stand them in the stream, head them upstream, rejoice as they learn to love this green space they live in, its sticks and leaves and then the silent, beautiful blossoms. Attention is the beginning of devotion."*
>
> – Mary Oliver [5.3]

Practicing this type of radical gratitude is about reveling in the pure bliss and joy and awesomeness of Life. To feel grateful for the Sun that warms our faces and coaxes the seeds to stir in the soil. To appreciate the Earth beneath our feet and the rain that falls from the sky. To feel satisfied by the food that nourishes our bodies and helps us stay healthy. To cherish the time we have with our children and our other loved ones. To notice and appreciate beauty. To be moved to create beauty as an act of reciprocity, and for no other reason.

We reweave our relationship with sacredness, reverence and authentic gratitude by consciously directing our attention to the precious aliveness around us and within us. As we choose to do this over and over, we train our minds and hearts to *appreciate*. This is how we plant our feet firmly in gratitude. This is the ground to which we can return over and over to recharge and fortify our resilience and our creativity as we raise our children to sustain and cherish Life.

There are millions of opportunities for this type of awe-inspiring gratitude in every moment of our lives. We could melt into a giant puddle of juicy reverence at any moment if we paused to *really* grok the miracle of breath, the workings of the musculature and intelligence of our human hands, the countless synchronicities, connections and near misses that have kept us alive thus far, or the outrageously complex reciprocal relationships between air, water, temperature, gravity and motion that create a livable biosphere here on Earth.

As we engage gratitude to support our New Paradigm Parenting, we can practice weaving this awareness into our little moments. We can notice how sweet and soft that little two-year-old hand feels in ours. We can see the spark of discovery in the six-year-old's eyes. We can savor the rare moment when our teenager says something honest and vulnerable to us. Bringing our full presence to these little moments has the power to soften the anxiety, stress and overwhelm we may feel. It lets Life come through and reminds us what we are truly here for. This practice of noticing the little blessings helps us stay grounded in gratitude and bolsters our strength and resilience even in the difficult, scary or uncomfortable moments. It allows us to hold *everything* in our awareness at the same time and fully experience the connection, value and beauty inherent in parenting. It gives us access to the magic and power of Life. We are caring for Life, after all, as we raise little humans. It's amazing and beautiful – and such a blessing!

If you're having a hard time connecting to the "sacredness" of all this, or if you just want to tap into it a little more deeply, I invite you to take a moment to remember and meditate on the first time you held your child. If you are a biological parent, it was likely within moments of birth. If you are an adoptive parent, it was likely a culminating moment after a long and intentional process. Take a few deep breaths and bring yourself back to that moment in time by remembering who you were then, what you knew and what you didn't know, how you felt, what struggles and challenges you went through to get to that moment, what fears may have arisen for you and/or your partner, and what complications, if any, you experienced. And then remember what happened inside of you when you felt the warm tender weight of this brand-new human being in your arms for the first time. When you saw the way this little being moved. When you first looked into their eyes. This is the unexplainable, precious sacredness we're talking about. This is the miracle of Life. Every single human being started out like this: vulnerable, dependent on love and care, carrying the magic of this miracle, brimming with potentiality. This is the improbable but utterly continuous blessing bestowed upon us generation after generation. This is what we are charged with being present to and caring for each day.

"Walk as if you are kissing the Earth with your feet."

– Thich Nhat Hanh [5.4]

Ecstatic Appreciation and Lessons in Resavoring

Halfway through my daughter's first year in college, she had an assignment to write about sense of place. She shared this excerpt of her writing with me:

> "I remember when I was growing up my mom and I would take a lot of trips. We would drive back into the San Luis Valley through Poncha Pass and dip into this vast bowl. The Sangre de Cristo mountains that were my backyard would be glowing and bright golden pink. My mom would always let out a grateful sobbing gasp and hold her Italian hand up in the direction of the mountains. I, being 10 years old and so used to the mountains, would roll my eyes and say "Mom, you see the mountains every day!" She would ignore my irritation and with teary eyes she would just look at them in awe."

In this assignment, she goes on to write that it was only later, after living away from these mountains for some time, that she really began to understand the gratitude I was expressing and how that same kind of gratitude and depth of appreciation came over her, as well. Now, when she returns to the mountains for vacations from college and has to leave them again, she *feels* them in her heart.

The way we revel in the blessings of Life while our children are growing up has a huge influence on how they will grow to see and experience the world. My child would often roll her eyes and complain when I gasped at sunsets or praised the snow or even when I told her I loved her. She would say something like, *"I know, Mom...why are you making such a big deal about it?"* But, because my expression of gratitude and reverence was genuine, it nourished her in foundational ways and showed her a way of being in authentic connection with Life. It created a baseline of awareness, presence and appreciation that lives within her and is growing more and more as she becomes a young adult. It cast a field of connection that she can always come back to.

I realize this form of expression may be hard for many of us. In our industrial society, most of us haven't exactly been raised to go gaga over Life. Maybe we've even been criticized for our enthusiasm at times. Maybe it feels like it would be embarrassing to show that much of ourselves. Maybe this kind of expression sounds like it would have to be contrived. Maybe your kids' eye rolling makes you feel self-conscious. Or maybe it's just not your style to express in that way. But whatever form it authentically takes – without forcing it – your vibrant love and appreciation for Life is something that your kids actually *need* to experience and witness. By expressing your gratitude out loud, you give them permission to do the same and help them understand the magnitude of the miraculous beauty and outrageous gift that Life is.

Otherwise, how will they know how mind-blowingly precious this Life is? How will they know how to care for Life? How will they know how important it is? How will they know how to see, listen and respond?

Even though my daughter went through a period of eye rolling during her adolescence, we've shared this love of Life together since she was a tiny being. Before, after and even during the eye rolling phase. When she was three and four, and we lived on the wild coast of the Atlantic Ocean, I used to bring her to the beach all bundled up in the middle of winter. When we were leaving the house, she would often resist a bit, saying she didn't want to go, but as soon as we got walking on the beach, she would lose herself in wonder and awe, searching for the magical spiral moonsnail shells that were our special treasures to find among the seaweed.

The same type of thing would happen in her older years when we lived back in the Rocky Mountains. She hated the idea of going on a "hike", but as soon as we got out into the woods, she would light up with this sense of magic and discovery as we found countless beautiful fairy realms and she created and decorated fancy dwellings for these invisible beauties. We've always celebrated and enjoyed the snow and snowboarding together, finding cool new beautiful places and traveling across wide-open landscapes.

We've also always enjoyed cooking, making delicious meals and eating them together. Throughout her elementary school years, we had a near-daily after school ritual of getting popsicles and spending a nice, long, relaxed moment eating them while talking about the day. I used to challenge her to a contest to see which one of us could eat our popsicle the slowest, savoring every lick and enjoying it to the fullest. Sometimes when she was enjoying a treat on her own, she would eat it *really* slowly and say she was "resavoring" it!

Modeling and practicing this depth of appreciation with our kids when they're young helps them feel resourced. It gives them an enduring sensory connection with their world and nourishes their sense of belonging. As a nanny, I cared for a little boy from the time he was ten months old until he was two and a half. We were in Portland, Oregon where there are gorgeous flowers all year round and everywhere you go. Every day, as we went out for walks, we reveled in the beauty of the flowers. We noticed new ones, pointed out all the different colors and stopped to smell them every chance we got. After a year of not seeing each other, his mom sent me a picture of him smelling flowers and told me that he still stops and smells every flower he sees. Because he was so young and it had been so long, he probably didn't remember me very well, but he was still savoring the beauty of the flowers, like it was the most natural thing to do.

It's important to practice this sort of embodied reverence in the "good" moments of our lives as much as we're able so it becomes a natural part of our experience that we can tap into and use in the "bad" moments. Because this form of gratitude is not conditional on winning or having stuff, it's available to us in every moment, even the hard ones. It can help us through challenging times and resource us when we're depleted or in crisis. It can be accessed somatically. It can be tapped into mentally. It is a practice that can permeate all moments and aspects of our life.

When you're in pain, anxious, struggling, frustrated, having to deal with a major challenge or crisis, you can find something small and beautiful that is connected to the ever-present vibrancy of Life and tune into it. It could be a sensation in your body, your breath, a color, a scent, a memory, a vision, etc. It won't make the challenge go away but it will help sustain and strengthen you while you tend to it. It will give you a lifeline to the power of Life. It may even orient you to that bigger, deeper power in such a way that helps you overcome and move through the challenge you're facing with a truly lifegiving empowerment. Gratitude in this form is a powerful tool for you, as a New Paradigm Parent, and for your children as they navigate the ups and downs of their own life paths.

As parents, we've got to experience ecstatic gratitude like Life depends on it. Not just our own lives. All of Life! This ecstatic expression is where gratitude really gets its subversive juice. This is where it gathers the power to shake down the towers of apathy and arrogance that the POP is built on. This is the magic necessary to free us from the flatness they try to sell to us. It awakens the power of Life and opens the channel that each one of us has within us so that this power can flow directly from Source and contribute to the great shifting tide of a new paradigm blossoming, as we practice *coming back to life.* [5.5]

Embracing the Journey

Your life as a parent and your kids' lives are probably not going to be like you imagined they would be. Your kids may not experience many of the things that you thought were quintessential parts of childhood. They may face challenges, stressors and opportunities that you could never have imagined. You aren't living the *idea* of parenting. You are *actually* parenting. You are living the very real experience of intimately sharing the growth and learning process with a brand-new human being in a time that has never existed before with Mystery and unprecedented circumstances around every corner.

Grounding in gratitude means ditching the fantasy and dropping into the real, daily experience and connection of family life, with all its messiness and imperfection and all its completely unplannable moments of splendor.

Right now, wherever you are in your parenting journey, however old your kids are, you can choose to soak in the moment. To embrace it fully. Even if you haven't gotten a full night's sleep in months. Even if you never get to finish a sentence in an adult conversation. Even if you're busy making ends meet and stressing about the bills. Even if you got in a screaming fight with your tween or had to bail your teenager out of some kind of asinine trouble. No matter where you are on the journey, there are blessings right at your fingertips, waiting to be received. Every stage of growth has its own priceless treasures. And none of them last very long. There is wisdom in the old adage, *"The days are long, but the years are short."*

I know the days feel long sometimes and it's hard to stay grounded in gratitude and presence. This "job", after all, comes with a lot of external and internal pressure, high stakes, no training, lots of obstacles and is constantly changing. On top of that, most of us have to do it while we're working at least one other job. And just when we get the skills from one stage mastered, the kids have moved on to the next stage! Meanwhile, our overactive Power Over Paradigm conditioning is always urging us to strive for the best, think ahead, over-plan, strategize and compete. All sorts of ideas about getting into the "best" schools and all the "right" programs and throwing the "best" birthday parties and buying the "right" stuff start swirling around in our heads and pulling us away from being grounded in the present moment with our children.

Practicing gratitude and presence can help us flip the script on this old paradigm conditioning and embrace our parenting journey as a paradigm-shifting adventure. When we release the ideas of how parenting *should be* and we become present to what it *actually is*, we can stay connected to our children's real needs and help them be themselves, authentically. Presence, gratitude and radical acceptance are a New Paradigm Parent's best friends. They allow us to be in the moment with our children at each stage of their growth, getting to know them again and again as they change (because they do change, all the time). If you follow their lead and let yourself learn from them, they'll guide you and surprise you.

When I was out and about at the playgrounds and toddler classes in Portland with the little boy I nannied for, I saw moms of little ones all the time. They often looked harried, and I would hear them complain about not getting time to themselves or having an endless pile of chores at home or about the weight they wanted to lose. I would see them getting flustered with their little ones. And it would break my heart. It's true that toddlers take *a lot* of energy and attention. It's also true that caring for a toddler can be really hard and that support and self-care are critical. But those years fly by more quickly than you can blink an eye. If you resist the experience or resent the hard work, you're likely to miss the endless wealth of opportunities for cultivating connection and building essential loving boundaries, trust and wellness into the very foundation of your children's lives and your relationship with them.

So, soak it up. Enjoy it. Have fun. Radically accept the moment you're in. Laugh often. And savor this precious experience! Most importantly, don't lose your sense of humor. It's a wild, strange experience and it's often ridiculous. Laughing at ourselves and our situations and finding the joy in the little stuff can carry us through. This is the preciousness of life.

Cherish this time and take good care of the relationships and connections you are cultivating with your kids. These are your people. If the roots of love and trust are nourished in these early years, these young ones may become your most powerful and beloved allies for the rest of your life. Don't let all the other nonsense get in the way. Don't worry too much. Give parenting your all, like it's the most important thing in the world, because it is. But realize that there is no "perfect" way to do it and that it's all utterly perfect, just the way it is.

So, exhale deeply and arrive in the moment.

Cultivating Gratitude in Your Household

Gratitude is the fertile ground necessary for healthy family life, and it's one of the most important skills your children will need for maintaining their mental health as they grow. Cultivating this form of radical gratitude within your family dynamics strengthens your relationships, your resilience in the face of challenges and the quality of your joy in times of blessing. It starts in your own heart and consciousness as you work with the awareness we explore in this chapter. It extends to your children as you embody and model it for them. When you are coming from this level of deep acceptance and presence, it is much easier to respect your children and their unique life paths. It also makes it easier to teach them how to value and respect themselves, the life they've each been given and all the ways in which they are provided for.

Starting from a very early age, we can teach our children to notice and appreciate all the little wonders of the world and the kindnesses bestowed upon them. Instead of just training them to *"say thank you,"* we can teach them how to pause and notice. It is about savoring the moment and expressing appreciation. You can show this to them in many, many ways every day as you express gratitude and make space for them to do so as well. Enjoying a good meal together, learning new things together, and spending special time together reading, playing, cuddling, looking for rainbows, stopping to smell the flowers and investigating the bugs are all ways to build this presence and appreciation into your children's daily experience.

Expressing our gratitude directly to our children for all the wonder and beauty and helpfulness they bring into our lives is important too. Let them know when they do something helpful or bring a smile to your heart. Let them know they are valued and appreciated. As children grow up within this practice, they begin to understand that every moment is an experience of give and take. They see and understand that their joy and comfort is provided for by others and that they can give joy and comfort to others as well.

Your household will be so much sweeter if you actively practice reciprocal gratitude with your children and other family members. As your children develop the practice of noticing the blessings in their lives, it will be much easier to communicate with them, establish reasonable boundaries and extend generous amounts of trust and freedom to them as they get older. Building this practice into your family when your children are little will make your passage through the tween and teen years infinitely more pleasant and smooth.

Part of this practice is to live our lives in such a way that our kids experience and become familiar with contentment. From an inconceivably early age, our children are bombarded with highly sophisticated marketing to rope them into becoming lifelong consumers. They are taught to *want*. They are pressured into wanting what they don't have and into constantly upgrading what they've already gotten. Corporate advertisers have long understood the value of marketing to children, who not only have a *major* influence on the spending habits of their parents, but also hold the promise of lifelong brand loyalty. With a powerful knowledge of child development and psychology, these companies create advertisements that manipulate our children's minds and distort their perceptions of reality and their relationship with desire...before they even start talking!

To some extent, this has and is being done to us adults as well, although the sophistication and intensity of media and marketing have increased significantly since any of us were kids. It's important to realize that we are being manipulated by the same profit-hungry corporations and endlessly striving mindset of the Power Over Paradigm as our children. Whether or not your family has a lot of money, it has a relationship with *want*. How you live your life, what you covet, what you are jealous of, what you thirst for and how you respond to the pressures of the market all influence your children. The pleasure you take in the blessings you have and your sense of satisfaction with the parts of life that are not commodified influence and guide your children, as well.

Unfortunately, no amount of "soaking up the moment" can really compete with the force and intensity with which the corporate agenda influences our kids. So, in addition to modeling contentment, it's important to bring our active attention to counteracting the conditioning of capitalism by speaking about it honestly and explaining the choices you're making in age-appropriate ways to your kids as they grow up. You can share with them this practice of radical gratitude and conscious choice-making as an act of resilience and civil disobedience to the forces that are harming our planet.

Drawing honest and understandable connections between consumer choices and their consequences can help our children comprehend their own power and responsibility as consumers and help them see themselves as *more* than consumers within the context of the world. This isn't a smooth or easy process. Your children will likely want to *fit in* with all their might and will buck against anything that is not status quo (especially if they are surrounded by status quo peers). You will probably have to make a lot of compromises along the way as you navigate their desires and your own entanglement with consumerism. But, as you engage this practice and conversation over the years, you and your children will learn a lot. You will likely find your own unique balance with sovereignty and choice when it comes to what you want and how you relate to the gifts of Life with gratitude and appreciation.

As adults, we are the ones who set the tone for our children by the things we do and the things we *don't do.* If you want to foster a sense of gratitude in your household, it is well within your means to do so.

PRACTICES FOR GROUNDING IN GRATITUDE

Now that we have a sense of why cultivating gratitude is essential to parenting in the midst of global crisis, let's talk about how to make it actually happen! When introducing a gratitude practice into your family, be extra sure you're coming from a genuinely grounded place and modeling gratitude authentically. Kids can sense inauthenticity from miles away and often resist new things that feel artificial or that are being imposed upon them. The suggestions below will work best if they are introduced as fun ways to connect with each other. Your attitude and flexibility will also make a big difference. These ideas will work best if you can engage in them humbly and fully, with openness and adaptability to what works for your family. So, please take these suggestions below and play with them. Allow your family to adapt them into something alive and thriving that works for your unique family constellation.

Grounding in Gratitude: Open Sentences for Co-Parents and Kids

Open Sentences are a time-honored, beloved practice used in the Work That Reconnects.[1,2] They give us the opportunity to share from our hearts and to be deeply listened to.

You can use the following open sentences (or invent new ones) to explore the concepts introduced in this chapter with your co-parent(s) and kids. You and your partner will each take a turn reciting the beginning of the sentence and then speaking spontaneously from your heart to finish the sentence during your allotted time, while the other partner listens. When you are the listener, center deeply in your own emotional grounding so you can hold a warm, loving presence while the other person shares. As the listener, you should *just listen*, receiving what is shared without commenting, interjecting, comforting or trying to fix anything that your partner expresses.

When using this practice with your children, remember that they have incredible insights and imaginations that truly *need* to be heard. Being received deeply by their parents validates their intuition and vision. It strengthens their sense of courage and calls forth their inner resilience. Using open sentences with your kids is an excellent way to practice listening attentively to your children and getting to know them more deeply as they grow. Using this practice with your co-parent(s) is a great way to cultivate connection in your shared parenting experience.

Set a timer and pay attention *the whole time*, without commenting or interrupting, as the speaker shares from their perspective. For very little ones (3-6 years old), you may want to start with 30 seconds. For older kids and adults, you can set the timer for 1-2 minutes. Let them know that they can take the whole time and that they can say anything that comes to them.

Open Sentences to use with your co-parents:

1. My favorite parts about being a parent are…
2. Some of the best little moments of parenting I experienced in this week (or month) have been…
3. Some of the things that I love and enjoy most about my children are…
4. The things my children and I really enjoy doing together are…
5. My children motivate and inspire me when they…

Open Sentences to use with your kids:

1. Some interesting and wonderful things that happened today were…
2. I feel really happy and peaceful when…
3. Some of my favorite things about nature are…
4. I can feel that I am loved because…
5. The most magical experience I've ever had was…

Pass the Thanks

Create or choose a beautiful object that can be passed between family members to express gratitude to each other. It could be a beautiful stone, a super cute stuffed animal, a paper flower or something that can be worn like a pretty pin, clip or necklace. Choose something that would be appreciated and enjoyed by everyone in the family. Introduce this idea of passing the thanks as a fun game and a way to share love and appreciation all around through the family.

When the person who has the object feels grateful to another person in the family, they can pass the object to them and express their gratitude. Decide on a plan of how often the object might be passed from one to the other depending on the size of your family and the flow of your lives *(daily, weekly, etc.)*. Challenge each other to notice feelings of gratitude for one another and to keep the object moving around the family in a fluid way. If you have multiple members in your family, challenge each other to give the object to someone new each time.

Gratitude Check-in

Taking a moment to reflect on gratitude and express it to each other is not necessarily a brand-new idea, but if it's not already part of your daily flow, you can start weaving it in to cultivate deeper gratitude in your household. Again, it's important to let this practice be fluid and authentic. If it feels imposed, stale or rigid, kids will quickly wiggle out of it.

If your family eats a meal together every day or once a week, you could open the mealtime conversation with a question like: *"What was the most interesting, awesome or special thing that you experienced or noticed today?"* Then, give everyone at the table a chance to say their cool thing from their day. If this becomes part of your family practice, you all may get in the habit of keeping your eyes out for very cool things and remembering them so you can bring them to your nightly or weekly gratitude check-in.

Be sure to model this by noticing and sharing your own expressions of gratitude in an authentic way. Let this time of sharing be open and fun. Be careful that it doesn't become too pious or carry heavy expectations of the "right" ways to answer that question. Practice really listening to each other and receiving each other's expressions. If mealtime doesn't work well for your family, you could weave this practice into other times in your family flow, such as your bedtime ritual or your end of school/workday check-ins.

6

EMBRACING EMOTION

"If you're listening, if you're awake to the poignant beauty of the world, your heart breaks regularly. In fact, your heart is made to break; its purpose is to burst open again and again so that it can hold ever more wonders."

– Andrew Harvey [6.1]

"I always feel better after I cry. You know? Lighter."

This is what my seventeen-year-old daughter said to me as she helped me clean up the kitchen at midnight after a long, difficult and deeply emotional conversation. It was the kind of conversation that I've found you have to just lean into. The kind you have to see coming and decide to prioritize over cleaning the kitchen quickly and getting to bed at a reasonable hour. The kind led by feelings that *need* to be addressed with all the respect you would give to a queen or a goddess, had she turned up unannounced on your doorstep at 10:30 pm.

That night, my child was feeling all the typical emotions and stress that come with approaching the end of high school and preparing to pass through the threshold from childhood into adulthood. She was feeling everything that fledgling young adults have felt for generations.

And, on top of all that, she was feeling the intensity of becoming an adult in a world unhinged. She was scared. She was confused. She was angry. She was overwhelmed.

She told me all these things that night. She told me how confused she was and how she doesn't know what to trust, or if there is even anything *to* trust and whether there even really are such things as "facts" and "truth." She told me how angry she was at me and how hard it has been to be my child and have to talk about "intense things" and the state of the world and to have to acknowledge how everything is connected when she just wants to be a "normal" kid.

This was a night in early 2020, before the onset of Covid-19 and before her senior year was abruptly cut short by state mandated lockdowns, when "normal" still felt like a possibility to her. The feelings she was having this night were set off by concerns I had expressed earlier about a certain social media app she was using. Through her teenage years, she had been free to use her phone and to access the Internet at her own discretion. I didn't control or limit it. But I did talk openly with her about it and try to educate her about things to be aware of and precautions to take. Most of the time, she was quite open to talking about it. That night, she didn't want to hear it. The intensity of the world and all the complexities she was navigating were weighing on her too heavily. After I expressed my concerns, she went to her bedroom and began to brood.

A couple of hours later, I popped into her room to say a quick goodnight, hoping to get to bed early. As soon as I saw her, I realized she was upset. I could feel this was a moment to pause and lean in. I asked if I could come in and if she wanted to share what was going on for her. She did. I did my best to listen and not to get defensive. When my defensiveness began to arise, I tried to notice it and reorient to a deeper presence and to the essential thing that was going on. *She was having feelings.* Strong feelings that were bubbling to the surface and demanding attention.

As she spoke and I listened, she began to cry. All the stress and pressure she had been carrying broke through and flooded out of her in tears. I sat with her in loving presence. I acknowledged how hard it is to be a teenager right now and validated the specific stresses she expressed. I let her feel what she was feeling, all the way through, without trying to stop or fix it.

Emotional Fluency

Becoming fluent in the language of emotions is an essential aspect of New Paradigm Parenting. As we honestly face the realities of our times, there is *a lot* to feel, for ourselves and our children. Emotional fluency is about learning how to honor emotions. It's about learning to understand how they speak to us and through us, how to maintain a high quality, emotionally safe space for your family and how to express emotions in ways that create healing instead of harm. Since these skills and kinds of awareness are not commonplace within the dominant paradigm, all this may take some extra attention and effort to develop.

As you work on cultivating this emotional fluency, you'll discover that it's a powerful way to partner with your children and the living world. Embracing the full spectrum of our emotions (even the really hard ones) and learning how to process them healthfully allows us to move through our lives in resilient and creative ways. Acknowledging our children's feelings and allowing room for them to safely express themselves lets us form deeper bonds of respect and trust with our children as they grow. Modeling healthy ways of being with and moving through complex emotions is a powerful way of supporting our children's development and preparing them for their adult lives within a complex world.

To cultivate emotional fluency in your household, you don't have to have all the answers or to behave perfectly all the time. You just have to be willing to be a student of emotional fluency alongside your children and to commit to doing your best to learn from each moment. This is an ongoing, lifelong practice of discovery that you'll do in *partnership* with your children. It is not a destination or some sort of static knowing that you can first attain and then impart to them.

As emotions arise or conflicts and tensions increase, you can pause and ask yourself:

- *"How can we be fully with this moment together, in love and respect?"*
- *"How can we increase trust, closeness and connection through the way we navigate this situation?"*

You may find that approaching things in this way interrupts ingrained old-paradigm patterns and habits of emotional reaction. Just pausing and acknowledging the moment as an opportunity for learning and connection can allow the emotions to truly express themselves and be understood. As you grow along this learning journey, you'll find that it requires being alert and willing to move slowly when needed.

Feelings As Messengers

Typically, in our modern world, we're not encouraged to acknowledge our feelings. In our society, feelings are generally considered a nuisance, at best. We're often told to power through, get over it, toughen up, focus on the positive, stick to the facts and numb ourselves into compliance. But the feelings that arise through us carry information that is critical to our personal and collective wellbeing.

I've come to understand that feelings are messengers. They're intelligent. They provide us with essential feedback about our relationship to our world and the path we're on. They provide the opportunity to pause, self-reflect, course-correct, deepen our understanding and heal what needs to be healed. Much of my coaching work with parents is dedicated to helping them learn to listen to and trust their own feelings.

Our human bodies are highly sophisticated instruments that are integral parts of the vibrating, pulsing, living Interbeing of Life.[2.2] They're designed to keep us connected and informed about the state of our world. The emotions that arise within our bodies tell us what's working and what's not working in our lives and the world around us. When we're attuned to their messages, we're guided to care for ourselves, others and our world. When we're cut off from them, don't feel safe enough to express them or don't know how to read and understand the feedback they're sending, we're unable to respond. We literally can't be *responsible* human beings, fulfilling our roles as caregivers and creative stewards of Life, without acknowledging and responding to our feelings.

This is one of the greatest tricks of the Power Over Paradigm. When we are cut off from our feelings, we are extremely easy to control. We can be manipulated into committing unthinkable acts of violence against Life. We can be tricked into giving away our whole lives and our precious time and energy to a system that destroys us and our children and the possibility of future generations. We can convince ourselves that it's okay to defile drinking water or enslave and oppress other human beings or invest our money in fossil fuel development because it turns a good profit.

Severed from our ability to safely feel, we can also convince ourselves that we deserve the abuse we're receiving or that humanity is flawed and meant to suffer. Without the intelligent guidance of our feelings, it can be easy to lose sight of the preciousness and sacredness of Life. This is one of the most powerful ways that the dominator society maintains its grip on us.

Joanna Macy describes the "colossal anguish" people feel at the devastation of the natural world as "a great public secret." It is something we are conditioned not to talk about or to acknowledge in any way. In her books and work, she outlines the enormous consequences of avoiding these painful feelings and how important it is to allow ourselves to *fully feel our pain for the world.*

> "The refusal to feel takes a heavy toll. Not only is there an impoverishment of our emotional and sensory life, flowers are dimmer and less fragrant, our loves less ecstatic, but this psychic numbing also impedes our capacity to process and respond to information. The energy expended in pushing down despair is diverted from more creative uses, depleting the resilience and imagination needed for fresh visions and strategies."
>
> – Joanna Macy [6.2]

Metabolizing our Emotions

To serve our children well and give them the skills they need in this time of crisis, we have to develop our capacity to embrace, understand and process the emotions we have about the world. We need to acknowledge the realities that our children are growing up within and metabolize our own emotions about them so we can face the challenges with courage and agency and teach them to do the same.

We begin by giving *ourselves* permission to feel. It may feel scary to "go there." I get that. We spend our whole lives trying not to fall apart; trying not to fall into the depths of despair. But despair is not great sadness. Despair is what clings to you when your feelings are blocked. Despair is what consumes you when you spend all your energy trying to turn away from your feelings, trying to hold them down and keep them out of sight. It's the pervasive depression and "free-floating" anxiety that has become all too common over the last couple of decades. It's what clogs us up and gives us the sense that we're not *really* living.

As we begin to allow ourselves to truly feel, while learning how to understand and respond to our feelings, we will move through *and beyond* our hardest emotions. We'll finally be able to break loose from the grips of the despair that has been trailing us all along.

Picture a small mountain creek at the end of winter. Throughout the autumn and winter, leaves and branches have been falling into the creek bed. The water level has been very low, and the creek is mostly frozen over. There's very little movement happening. Just a mess of debris clogging the way. And then, the spring sun comes and begins to melt the heavy snows on the mountain peaks. The melted snow races towards the creek bed and begins to flow down. As the snowmelt increases, the pressure builds, the banks overflow and there is a rush of water moving with speed and force down the steep slope of the mountain. Everything that had collected in the creek bed throughout the winter gets washed away – branches, leaves, fallen trees, even large boulders – and the creek runs clear. Dancing, singing and sparkly in the sunlight, the creek is full of life. This is what happens to us when we let our emotions move through us naturally and freely.

It isn't enough to mentally acknowledge that we are having a feeling. For the world to speak to and through us, we need to *actually feel* our feelings and allow them to move through us like rushing water, like the forces of nature that they are. Martín Prechtel teaches and talks about the importance of "metabolizing" our emotions by deeply feeling and expressing them.[6.3] He reminds us that when natural, healthy, connected people experience the loss of something or someone dearly beloved to them, they *grieve.* Actively. Wildly. Pouring out all the love they feel for that precious lost being until they are disheveled, spent and emptied out. That active grief is a gift of love given to that lost beloved. It helps them surge onward. It feeds Life. And it renews the griever. In the emptiness that remains, the griever often feels the depth of their connection with all Life.

In these moments, after true emotion has moved through us, we feel lighter, like my child said after her cry. We see more clearly. In that open space, we are more available to receive what the world needs to tell us. This is the way it works for all our emotions; the ones we categorize as "negative," like grief and anger and the ones we categorize as "positive," like love and joy. When we allow our living emotions to move through us and to express themselves as wildly as they need to, this inevitably transforms us. It is this process of transformation that I am referring to when I write about *metabolizing emotions.*

> *"There is a brokenness*
> *out of which comes the unbroken,*
> *a shatteredness*
> *out of which blooms the unshatterable.*
> *There is a sorrow*
> *beyond all grief which leads to joy*
> *and a fragility*
> *out of whose depths emerges strength.*
>
> *There is a hollow space*
> *too vast for words*
> *through which we pass with each loss,*
> *out of whose darkness*
> *we are sanctioned into being.*
>
> *There is a cry deeper than all sound*
> *whose serrated edges cut the heart*
> *as we break open to the place inside*
> *which is unbreakable and whole,*
> *while learning to sing."*
>
> *– Rashani Réa* [6.4]

Cultivating Emotional Safety in Your Home

Clearing your own emotional backlog by *feeling* and *metabolizing* your emotions in healthy ways allows you to provide your children with the one thing that they need from you more than anything else: *emotional safety.*

The sense of emotional safety we create for our children when they're young will be one of their most essential resources as they grow into adulthood. We can't protect them from all the harms and hardships of the world, but we can cultivate an emotionally safe space for them to process and contend with the difficulties they experience. To be strong and resilient in this challenging world, our children need to feel emotionally safe with us. They need to know that it's safe to feel and express all their feelings with us. They need to feel our unwavering presence. They need to know that our love for them is courageous and unconditional, even when times are hard.

Our children are going to be sad and scared, frustrated and disappointed at different times in their lives. They're going to get hurt and have their hearts broken. They may struggle with depression or anxiety. It can be extremely unsettling for parents to see our children suffer and struggle. Sometimes the emotions our kids express may even throw us off our center by triggering our own fear, anger or deep grief. Within the Power Over mindset, parents often attempt to maintain a sense of control by trying to fix, stop, dismiss, deny or defend against uncomfortable feelings that their children express. If we try to shut down their emotional expression or we become overwhelmed with our own emotional flurry in reaction to it, they'll get the message that it's not safe to express their emotions to us.

When big feelings arise, here are some simple steps we can take to respond to them in an emotionally safe way:

1. **Respond with presence:** When your children are experiencing challenging emotions, your response will make all the difference in the world to them. Responding with presence and respect lets them know that it's safe to express and explore their emotions with you. Instead of brushing them off or trying to fix away their problems, you can acknowledge that they are having an emotional experience that is worthy of your attention. If they want to share, you can pause what you're doing and listen

compassionately. If they're not ready to share, it's important to respect that and let them know you'll be available when they're ready.

2. **Name the feeling(s):** Emotions usually come all swirled up together with ideas, stories, projections and sensations. It can be difficult to know what's what in all that mess. When your child is upset, you can help them identify and name the feeling(s) that are arising. This can help your child clarify what's going on for them and drop into their emotional center. For example, *"Taylor is such a jerk"* can transform into *"I feel really sad about being left out"* or *"My stomach is in knots, and I can't sleep"* can transform into *"I feel scared and worried about the nearby wildfires."*

3. **Validate the feeling(s):** Having their feeling(s) validated by a loving parent gives a child permission to really *feel* them. This is an opportunity to let them know that you see their feeling(s) as a legitimate response to what's happening in their lives (even if you don't initially understand or relate to them). You can say something like *"I see that you're pissed off about that. It's totally understandable"* or *"I know it's really sad and scary for you to have to face this right now."*

4. **Support *feeling* the feeling(s):** This is the time to let them really emote and allow the feeling(s) to move through and express themselves in whatever way they need to, even if its messy. If you're able to stay calm, centered and honestly witness their pain without trying to stop or fix it and without encouraging them to run away from it, they will have the chance to *feel* it and metabolize it. Whether it's something as small as what another kid said to them on the playground or as large as grieving the loss of one of their peers to suicide, it is essential that they *feel* it and that they feel supported by you while they do.

5. **Reflect on the feeling(s):** Emotions are often carrying very specific messages about something that needs to be understood and

addressed in our lives. Once the emotion has moved through and you sense that most of the energy has been discharged, you can open a conversation with your child to explore what messages or insights may have been exposed through this process. You can start with the simple question: *"What can you see now that you weren't able to see before?"*

An emotionally safe household is not something that springs into existence in a moment of emotional crisis. It's something that is cultivated and maintained on a daily basis, in all the little interactions and communications that happen between family members. It's an environment where *all* feelings are welcomed as valid, and no one is shamed or chastised for their emotions. It's an environment where family members take responsibility for their own feelings, without deflecting, projecting or entangling with one another. It's an environment where family members are able to reflect on their feelings and the information they carry, talking openly with one another about what they're learning.

The best way to cultivate an emotionally safe space for your kids is to model emotional fluency with your own behavior. By being emotionally honest and making room for *all* the feelings to exist with respect within your household and relationship, you let them know that all emotions are okay.

Again, this doesn't mean you have to have it all figured out or always be perfectly well-behaved. It means being authentic and willing to learn as you go. When your own feelings arise, you can show them how to identify a feeling and name it, by saying out loud, *"I'm feeling grumpy"* or *"I'm feeling sad today."* You can model the other steps as well, by giving yourself permission to feel the feelings you're having and reflecting on the messages they bring. You can adjust the intensity and depth you share with them in age-appropriate ways as they grow, being mindful about the amount of sharing that fosters connection and trust, without causing overwhelm.

If you've laid this groundwork, then you'll be able to guide them through their experience more easily when they encounter challenging feelings. If they haven't seen you model emotional authenticity, they may be less receptive to your guidance when they're in the thick of it.

Creating Healing Instead of Harm

How we express our emotions can create healing, or it can create harm. Families can be the center of this emotional healing. Unfortunately, they can also be the center of emotional harm.

In the Power Over Paradigm society, many families are riddled with emotionally harmful behavior as family members treat each other far worse than they would ever treat a stranger. When people aren't emotional fluent in the ways we've explored in this chapter, emotions can be overwhelming and confusing. In a society that forces us to repress our emotions most of the time, it's easy for them to boil over when we're at home where we feel less inhibited.

It's common for families in this society to perpetuate and reinforce unhealthy emotional patterns, baggage and "bad habits" generation after generation. Emotionally unhealthy family dynamics can include lashing out at each other when we feel upset, laying guilt trips on one another, judging or shaming each other and being overly entangled or codependent with one another. Emotional and psychological abuse are also primarily experienced within our families of origin. People often excuse this type of behavior by saying it's because they feel "safe" to be their true selves with their family members. But I would argue that it's not safety that they feel. It is more likely that they just feel less inhibited, and they assume that they are less likely to be punished for their behavior if it takes place within the privacy of their own homes. If they truly felt safe, they wouldn't need to project and attack because they could actually be honest and vulnerable with one another.

Emotional safety and emotional fluency take a lot of work in this POP society. In addition to using the process outlined above for responding to emotions in an emotionally safe way, it is important to learn and teach our children how to distinguish feelings from judgments. This helps to create a family environment in which each person truly takes responsibility for their own feelings. In this environment, there's space for someone to feel sad or angry *without projecting it onto anyone else*. In this environment, it's also possible for family members to feel and move through their emotions without entangling other family members. Everyone acknowledges that everyone has all the feelings sometimes and everyone in the family does their best to be compassionate with each other.

In a similar way, it's also important to distinguish our feelings from our behavior and to take responsibility for the impact of our behavior. As a parent, you can model these skills by naming your feelings as they arise. Then you can acknowledge how that feeling may be affecting your behavior while bringing yourself into accountability for the impact that behavior might be having on others. *"I'm feeling really grumpy today. I'm sorry for being short tempered with you and not wanting to joke around. It isn't about you, at all."* A simple communication like this creates room for the feeling, and it interrupts the assumptions and projections that happen when we unconsciously react to each other and take things personally. It releases the other people in the family from becoming ensnared in guilt-laden, defensive or codependent reactions to the natural emotion you are having.

When we take responsibility for our own feelings, listen to them deeply and learn from the messages they carry, we are healing and growing. When we support each other and receive support from each other in loving and respectful ways, we're cultivating wellness in our relationships and family.

Dealing with our Triggers

Working on your emotional fluency can bring up lifelong patterns, personal triggers, intergenerational wounds and old traumas that will need to be felt and released. Carving out some adult time for yourself (or with other parents who are doing this work) can help. If you have experienced significant personal trauma or are struggling with your own emotional stability, you may want to reach out for the support of a skilled therapist.

Our relationships and experiences with our kids can be really triggering, frustrating, scary and even downright infuriating at times. An important aspect of emotionally fluency is understanding where our emotionally charged reactions come from and how to work with them. Particularly charged emotions are often caused by repressed feelings, rejected aspects of ourselves and our own unresolved trauma more than they're caused by the qualities and actions of our children. When we aren't triggered, it's possible to feel grounded and stay responsive even in extremely intense emotional situations. When we are reactive, rather than grounded and responsive, it's usually an indication that there's something going on beneath the surface that needs to be addressed.

When you feel your emotional temperature rising and that emotional charge getting activated, it's your signal to pay attention to see if you can find out what's causing the trigger. Ask yourself what the situation or interaction is bringing up for you. *Is it pushing buttons set in place by your own upbringing? Is it highlighting a gap between your expectations and reality? Does it remind you of an old wound or bring you into proximity with a personal or intergenerational trauma? Does it shine a light on some of your own perceived shortcomings or aspects of your children's personalities or behaviors that you judge, or wish didn't exist?*

If allowed to go unexamined, these emotional charges can severely interfere with our ability to connect deeply with our children and to cultivate emotional safety within our relationships with them. They can cause us to lose our tempers, become overly controlling, cling to our children unreasonably, project our fears and expectations onto them, distance ourselves emotionally from them, resent them, judge them, envy them, blame them and many other emotionally unhealthy parental behaviors that are, unfortunately, quite common in our POP society. For deeper support in developing your own emotional fluency and understanding how to work with your own personal triggers, I highly recommend reading and working with *The Darkside of the Light Chasers* by Debbie Ford.[6.5]

In alignment with that work, whenever I talk about healing and becoming more emotionally healthy, I am referring to *becoming whole*. I never mean healing as an attempt to erase or avoid the "bad" or "unwell" parts of ourselves, but instead to learn to understand them, embrace them and work with them in a way that supports wellness and connection. Since our children have a tendency to bring it all up for us, parenting is a huge opportunity to work on this in our lives.

The invitation here is to transmute the pain into strength and clarity; to metabolize it into beauty; to grow through it into resilience. Life will continue to be difficult, and we will continue to be "imperfect." We can't erase the "bad" things that happened in the past or prevent all the pain that may happen in the future. We can't keep our children from having painful experiences. But we can practice and teach resilience. Through emotional fluency, we can teach them to dance with it all, so they can learn and grow and adapt, as necessary, to continue to move towards greater health, wellness and connection.

The Emotional Dissonance of Parenting

A social media post I saw from Extinction Rebellion[6.6] pointed to the *"grinding cognitive dissonance of living in a society where the gap between what science says needs to happen and what people are actually doing looms large."* Whether we realize it in every moment or not, this grinding cognitive dissonance is weighing on each of us significantly and causing many layers of pain, suffering and anxiety. For parents, this suffering is magnified a millionfold and the dissonance is much more than cognitive. It is emotional. How can we hear the daily reports of irreversible climate chaos and the rapid breakdown of Earth's life support systems and carry any semblance of sane hope while we're looking at our precious little ones?

We find ourselves torn between our awareness of the devastation of the world and our desire to just focus on raising our children with hope in our hearts. We're caught between the big picture collapse and the little moments of triumph. Learning to walk, winning a game, making a beautiful drawing, playing in the river. We want to fully support our kids' ability to grow and learn and be playful children. But we also know that their future and their very lives are at stake. Living on this emotional pendulum can be utterly exhausting. When we try to keep it all hidden and under control and we're not able to metabolize our emotions, this dissonance can wear us down.

It can be very scary to be raising children given the state of the world. It's perfectly okay to be scared. And to feel confused or anxious or even to feel dissociated and apathetic. These are all normal, healthy responses to this very unhealthy situation. Joanna Macy's teachings on this have been deeply helpful for me. She assures us that our fear, anxiety or depression is not some personal pathology. Something is not "wrong" with us. Instead, something is *right* with us. If we're feeling those feelings in response to this world gone mad, then that means we're still capable of feeling for and with our world. Instead of judging ourselves for having these feelings, we can start to listen to them and allow them to help us adjust our life paths and parenting accordingly.

Joanna Macy teaches that each so-called "negative" emotion has a flipside that tells more of its story. She says that *"our sorrow is in equal measure love. We only mourn what we deeply care for."* [6.7] This is the same essential teaching that Martín Prechtel shares about the profoundly intertwined nature of grief and praise.[6.3] When we understand this deeply, we know that our grief is born out of our love. We grieve because our hearts recognize the preciousness of the subject of our sadness. Understanding our grief through the lens of love can inspire us to protect and care for the beings, places or systems that are being threatened or lost. Instead of falling into despair, it can move us to put our love into action.

Likewise, Joanna Macy shows us that the other side of fear is courage. To even acknowledge our fear in a fear-phobic society is an act of courage. She says that the other side of anger is passion for justice. When we work with our anger skillfully, it can motivate us to stand up and fight for justice. And, as to our feelings of numbness, apathy or emptiness, which are natural responses to these times of trouble, they can bring us to our knees in humble openness. When we allow ourselves to admit that *we don't know* and that we have reached the end of our ability to feel, we create the conditions under which new feelings and new understandings can arise. If we can bring our presence to rest inside that emptiness, we may find that we are ready to begin anew.

Resourcing Ourselves

As parents, we can use our understanding about the flip side of painful emotions to access the strength within them as we resource ourselves. Many of the parents I talk with and work with through my programs express that they feel guilty for bringing children into the world the way it is. They wonder if it was a selfish decision to put their children in this position and add to the impact of humans on the planet. They say that if they knew then what they know now, maybe they wouldn't have chosen to become parents. They fear that their children's future will be full of suffering. They are overwhelmed by how difficult and complex it is to raise children with all the confusing influences of this destructive society that they can't seem to keep at bay. They worry about how to talk to their children about what is happening in the world. They're scared that they won't know what to do.

All these feelings arise out of our intense love for our children. We are genetically hardwired with an overpowering love for our children and an interminable desire to protect them at all costs. Along with this hardwiring comes a profound parental intuition that lets us know when their wellbeing is threatened. Many parents I know are motivated to care for the world *because they care so deeply for their children.* This intuition, and the love from which it flows, are your greatest internal resources as a parent in these tumultuous times. Learn to listen to them exquisitely and respond to them with sincerity and determination.

In addition to staying connected with these internal resources, it's essential to resource ourselves by carving out time to process and metabolize our own adult emotions in a way that doesn't negatively impact our children. Some of the ways you can create this adult space and time to *let yourself really go there* and feel everything you're feeling are by journaling, spending time embraced in nature, processing with a trusted friend or counselor, participating in group work or through ceremony, ritual, or prayer. By making time for this regularly, you give yourself the opportunity to metabolize and digest the *big adult feelings* you're having without projecting them onto your children or impacting them with an inappropriate level of intensity. Each time, on the other side of this emotional work, you'll likely have a more distilled analysis of what's going on for you and an ability to be more present, open and transparent with your children in ways that match their levels of development and personalities.

Engaging in group work and/or establishing a strong network of adult community support is an important way to resource ourselves. Reading this book for your own personal self-inquiry may be a good start, but ultimately, this work is too much to carry all by yourself. Human beings are meant to live collectively. We are deeply interdependent, social creatures and require mutual support to truly thrive. Even in the best of times, parenting is meant to be held within the arms of community. If you're raising children with a partner, please invite them to share in this work with you. Then reach beyond your own immediate family to connect with a small group of other parents you know and interact with on a regular basis to process and digest this work. Creating this type of community to tend to our emotions with other parents allows us to release, transmute and refresh ourselves so we can return to our lives and parenting with more presence and connection to our power.

As our children grow up, they need to witness us working with and responding to our emotions effectively so they can experience and imbibe this model of mature emotional intelligence. They need to learn from us how to process challenging or intensely heavy emotions, because they will have a lifetime of them too. As they get older, you can share more and more with them about your process. As you develop your own skills for metabolizing your emotions, you can help them learn how to metabolize theirs so they can orient their lives in courage, agency, passion and love.

Honoring Their Big Feelings

If you think it's challenging to be a parent right now, try being a kid. No, really. Our kids are growing up in situations that we can't even imagine. As you respond to your children and reflect on their personal experiences, remember to always take that into account. Everything that you can understand through your own childhood experience should be given a wide berth of compassion for all the ways in which things are so much more intense for them now.

In a time when school shootings and active shooter drills have become commonplace (at least in the United States), our young people are dealing with existential stressors that most of us can only begin to comprehend. They also have the stress of coming of age when online sexual predation and cyberbullying can invade every moment of their lives through their handheld devices and every picture or comment they post on social media can be weaponized against them at lightning speed and captured for "all eternity" in the chronicles of the Internet.

Imagine trying to make sense of the world when facts have become obsolete, and you can find online "experts" to reinforce any possible perspective from white nationalism to flat earth theory with an apparent legitimacy that rivals anything coming out of the mouths of our supposed political leaders. Or trying to get excited about your future when all signs point to climate collapse. How are young people supposed to make sense of all this? How are they coping?

These are some of their attempts at coping that I notice:

- Apathy
- Anxiety
- Depression
- Self-loathing
- Self-harm and suicide
- Reckless disregard for life
- Fierce competition and debilitating stress
- Arrogance, privilege, hate and intolerance (that arise from a sense of fear and scarcity)

Some of these harmful coping mechanisms and the intense emotions our kids express may be scary or triggering for us. They may even stir up our own childhood trauma. Or we may also find that we don't fully understand or relate to the feelings that they're having. Those are our own emotions to process and work through and should not be projected onto our kids.

As we strive to create an emotionally safe place for them, it's incredibly important that we *make space for them to have their own emotions and their own process.* If we're able to be a grounded, loving adult presence in their lives, we can help them navigate the levels of healing and emotional work they need to move through, no matter what they're facing.

Helping Them Navigate

Everyone will have moments of feeling grumpy, sad, angry, giddy, excited, scared, anxious, uncertain, apathetic, etc. These, and any other possible feelings, are all okay. Do not disparage, dismiss, ignore, belittle or make fun of your children's feelings. They are real. They are important. They carry essential messages that can help your child find their way in the world and give you direct guidance into how to parent them more effectively.

As you develop emotional safety and trust in your relationship with your kids, you can help them be present with their emotions and learn to understand the flipside or fuller story of each of the emotions they are feeling. Through this process, we may be able to help them develop their emotional maturity, their empathy for our suffering world and their courage and fortitude to navigate their own path in it.

Especially when kids are little, their emotional expressions may reveal that they need rest, food or water – or that they're getting sick. They might signal a stage of growth or a hurdle they're overcoming. Your children's feelings may provide vital information on something you're doing or not doing (like paying attention) so that you can course-correct. Or, as they grow older and their lives become more complicated, their feelings might point to some hurt or obstacle they've experienced in their world beyond your awareness. When children feel respected and safe to express emotions in your presence, they can share more of their life with you, and you can be the supportive partner they desperately need to navigate a world they are only beginning to grow into.

When your children get upset, try to notice and respond to the feeling they are having instead of the behavior. If they are frustrated, angry or disappointed and acting out in some way, you can talk to them about the feelings they are having by saying something like, *"Are you feeling frustrated?"* or *"I understand. That's really disappointing."* Then you can connect with them about how to let the feeling be there, how to feel it and how to express it in a way that won't cause harm to themselves or others. These moments are excellent opportunities to support your children in connecting with their own inner knowing and intuition as they learn to listen to the messages that their feelings are sending and learn from them.

Sometimes your children won't know why they're feeling what they're feeling. That's okay too. On some level most of us (and our kids) are feeling a significant amount of subconscious empathic stress as we pick up on the suffering of the world. This causes quite a lot of unexplained angst, distress, anxiety and confusion. We can hold presence and respect even for these feelings that are beyond our direct understanding and don't seem to be connected with anything in our personal lives. We can use the same practice of acknowledgement, validation and *feeling* the feelings even when we don't understand them.

Growing up in a suffering world within systems that do the opposite of what they claim to do can be upsetting and disorienting for kids. To establish secure mental health and find their own orientation in the world, children need the adults in their lives to be honest with them and to provide an environment where it is safe for them to be honest. If your children feel that it's not emotionally safe to be honest with you or that you are withholding honesty from them, they will hide away certain parts of themselves to preserve some semblance of emotional safety in your presence.

As your children grow and ask you questions about their world, you have an opportunity to be honest with them to the extent that they can understand at each stage of their development. If you've been doing your own work to metabolize your emotions and you are tuned in to your children, it will be much easier to figure out what is appropriate to share and in how much detail. As children grow, they'll need to explore the same concepts over and over, learning them more deeply as their ability to comprehend and the context of their experience deepens. So, if you're engaged with this process, you'll have many chances to help them understand their world.

Many parents are worried about how to handle difficult conversations with their kids that might bring up big feelings. For example, one of the big, anxious questions I hear parents asking in my programs these days is *"How do I talk to my children about the climate crisis?"*

My response is: on an ongoing basis throughout their lives in all the little moments, at every stage and in every turn, with loving honesty and the respect that they deserve as fellow human beings who are sharing this experience with you and the rest of humanity. Speak to them honestly when they ask questions, when they notice things, when they hear something about the changes in the environment or learn a lesson in school that needs more depth, when they express fear or confusion or sadness, or when you make decisions grounded in your sense of responsibility and care for our world. Share it all with them, moment by moment, as they grow, in language that they can receive. And keep it up throughout their lives.

This is the same approach necessary for talking with our kids about racism, economic inequality, sexuality and any other large-scale concept that will be a reality in their lives. Many parents try to wait until the "right time" to talk about aspects of the world that they deem inappropriate for children or fear may bring up big feelings. Meanwhile their children are learning about these topics from the moment they are born through the media, education and peers. As they grow up, they'll have all sorts of feelings about these important aspects of their world, and they will need an emotionally safe space to process them. If you avoid having honest conversations with them until they're "old enough", they'll get the message that it is not emotionally safe to process them with you.

Parenting Through Hardship

If embracing emotions and cultivating emotional fluency in your household seem like processes intended for only those who have easy, spacious lives with plenty of time and resources, I assure you that they most certainly are not. In fact, I don't know many parents who would categorize themselves that way. Everyone I know (myself, included) has raised their children through adversity and hardship. I'm pretty sure that even the wealthy, highly privileged parents that I nannied for while living in the city saw themselves as under duress most of the time. It's the nature of parenting that it's all too much, too fast. The kids are growing up faster than we can learn how to care for them. We are inundated with expectations and responsibilities and never feel that we're doing enough. Unexpected challenges are almost predictable, except you never know when they're coming or what they will be.

However, no matter what our socio-economic situation is or how much stress we are experiencing, our children need us to keep their welfare in focus and to prioritize it in every moment while they are growing. As a parent, you need to do what is necessary to create conditions for your child to thrive. If you are having a marital crisis or going through a divorce, if you're panicking about money or health care, if you are ill or someone close to you is ill and needs care, if you've experienced a great loss of someone very dear to you, if you are the victim of abuse, if you struggle with mental illness or have to work several jobs to make ends meet or any other hardship imaginable *the children in your life still need you to center their wellbeing.*

Just as our kids can feel the state of the world whether they fully understand it or not, they also feel the state of our households and our lives. They feel all our stress and struggles on some level. That's okay. We don't need to pretend that everything is fine, and we don't need to create a completely stress-free environment for our kids. Even if we could, that's not what being human is about. Centering their wellbeing, however, is about acknowledging and respecting their experience, keeping them in the loop to the extent that is appropriate and prioritizing their care. During times of hardship, it's especially important to communicate with them respectfully and to listen closely to what they need in order to feel safe and thrive.

When we prioritize this primary responsibility and put our children first with emotional intelligence, we are often guided through our hardships with greater healing and clarity. Your child's wellbeing can become a barometer for the conditions of your life. As you tune in to what they need, you may understand what needs to change or what support systems need to be created for them to feel safe and supported and free to grow and learn in a healthy way. This may require some creativity or extra courage. It may require asking for help or setting up special resources for them. And, if you allow it to, it may even entirely change your life, *for the better.*

As I write this, one of my greatest mothering sheroes comes to mind. She is ten years younger than me and was my niece's best friend. I met her when she was in high school shortly before she became pregnant at the age of seventeen. She was unprepared to be a mother, to say the least. The father, a teenage boy, was completely negligent and emotionally abusive. She suffered the scorn that teenage mothers receive in our society and struggled to care for her beautiful little girl. Eventually, she met another young man who wanted to be with her and help her raise her baby. They had a second child together and tried to realize their dream of living close to the land in a cabin in the woods, but things got worse. He was also abusive, and she struggled with debilitating mental illness for years. Through it all, she worked hard to center the wellbeing of her two sweet daughters, making difficult choices to keep them safe and provide loving, creative space for them.

After years of struggle, she could see that this situation wasn't serving her girls and that it was up to her to change it. She mustered the courage she needed to file for divorce even though many of the people in her life had been telling her for years that she couldn't care for her daughters on her own. Once that toxic relationship was out of their living space, she and her girls began to thrive. She found her creative spark and began performing in community theater. She created her own house cleaning business to make ends meet. She came out as a lesbian and began to inhabit her own skin and feel her worth for the first time in her adult life. She kept the cabin in the woods, is living her dream of off-grid, close-to-the-land coziness and is putting herself through nursing school. Her girls love her and are close with her. They are bright, beaming beings and are incredibly fortunate to have her example of courage, emotional maturity and fortitude to guide them in their lives.

Throughout my child's life, I've felt the responsibility to center her wellbeing through the various hardships we've navigated and to be mindful about the choices I'm making for our lives and how they will affect her growth, development and self-worth. I'm sure that I haven't always made the best decisions or done things perfectly. I've been learning along the way, for sure. But, by orienting my life around the priority of her wellbeing, our lives have been saved many times over. Through this orientation, I've learned many lessons, healed many wounds and been granted many opportunities I would otherwise have missed. And as a result, she has grown into a powerful, self-reflective, mature young adult – a person I'm proud to call an ally in this crazy world.

As you venture through your experience as a parent, you'll have to navigate many personal and collective hardships. There is no way to avoid them. *But do not allow them to make you forsake your children.* When the chips fall, make sure your children are in the center. What is good for them will ultimately be good for you and will likely be the healthiest choice available to you. They are relying on you for a reason. Responding to their vulnerability and dependency on you may be exactly what's needed for you to discover what truly serves Life.

PRACTICES FOR EMBRACING EMOTION

As you do your own work to deepen and strengthen your emotional fluency, you can introduce your kids to some new awareness and practices and incorporate them into your family flow.

I encourage you to take small steps with this at first and be sure to prioritize your own emotional development so you can lead by example. Be careful not to force these practices or impose heavy expectations on your family. Embrace the process of developing emotional maturity like any other learning process that takes time and consistency. In the same way that your kids will learn how to cook, play an instrument, or develop their capacity to do homework, this process will involve many small steps over time. For it to work out well, it has to be rewarding enough for them to want to keep going, so your two most important jobs are to stay devoted to your own emotional development work and to create an emotionally safe space for your kids to develop their emotional fluency at their own pace. Emotional fluency is an essential skill for kids to learn as they grow towards and into adulthood, so stick with it through all their phases and stages! The practices suggested below are activities I've found to be effective with my own and many other families. Please play with them and adapt them to your family, as needed.

Embracing Emotion: Open Sentences for Co-Parents and Kids

Please refer to the instructions for Open Sentences in the practice section of Chapter 5: Grounding in Gratitude.

Open Sentences to use with your co-parents:

1. When I think about the state of the world our children are inheriting, I feel...
2. When I consider the flipside of my _____ (choose a challenging emotion) I understand...
3. Times or situations in my life when I felt emotionally safe and supported were...
4. Ways that I can improve my own emotional tools, skills and support systems are...
5. Some ways I can create a more emotionally safe space for my children and support their emotional development are...

Open Sentences to use with your kids:

1. The things that scare or worry me the most are...
2. What I find confusing about this world is...
3. When I feel like I can't share how I'm feeling I...
4. I feel safest to express my emotions when...

Emotional Barometer for the Family

This visual emotional barometer gives you a simple way to stay tuned into the emotional temperature of each of your family members. It creates space for a wide range of emotional experiences and allows them to be present without stigma or judgment. When you introduce this tool to your family, be sure to acknowledge that *all* the emotions represented here are normal, natural and inevitable. At some point, we will all feel these feelings and they're *all* ok.

The basic setup for this tool is a hanging chart representing a wide range of emotions and a movable icon or symbol for each family member. The icon can be a picture of the person or some animal or special symbol that represents them. Each person can move their personal icon to the area on the chart that represents how they are feeling.

When you share this tool with your family members, you can create a plan and certain agreements for how you will use it together as a family. Be sure to really listen to your kids and include their input as you develop the plan. You can start by looking at the collection of emotions represented. Are any missing? Do all family members understand what each emotion means? For younger children, this could be an opportunity to help them understand the various emotions represented.

Then, you can decide how you'll use this new tool. You may want to decide on a certain time of day that you'll check in with the chart and move your icon. Perhaps at the end of the school or workday? Or in the morning? Maybe you want to decide to just move your icon whenever a new feeling arises.

It's important to make agreements about how you will respond to and use the information that the chart expresses. I recommend including an agreement that grants permission to not have to talk about your emotion if you don't want to. You can come up with an agreed upon question for checking in about it, such as *"I see you put your icon on _____ today. Do you want to tell us about how you're feeling?"* If the family member doesn't want to talk about their emotion, it's essential to respect their choice and just let the awareness of the emotion be present. If this agreement is respected and the family member is held in love without interrogation, emotional safety for all family members will grow. As emotional safety develops over time, it may allow for more and more actual sharing.

We can help to dissolve the stigma around certain emotions by being honest with our family about how we feel and by allowing our children to be honest about how they feel without rushing into judgment, panic, worry or solutions. If your child puts their icon on *lonely* or *sad* or *irritated*, you can show them that it's okay to feel that way by giving them space to talk about it *if they want to* and letting them know that their feelings are totally natural.

The chart below has a collection of emotions that I curated based on what I feel is most relevant and relatable for parents and kids in these times. As you make your own chart, feel free to elaborate and/or modify this collection in whatever way feels most appropriate for your family. You can draw up your own chart or find a printable version of the chart below on my website at www.RadiantBalance.com.

If you hang your chart on the fridge or other magnetic surface, you can create a set of magnets with the icon or picture for your family members on each one of them. If you hang it on a corkboard, you could use pins for the icons. Another option is to laminate both your chart and icons and use double sided tape or poster putty to stick the icons to the chart.

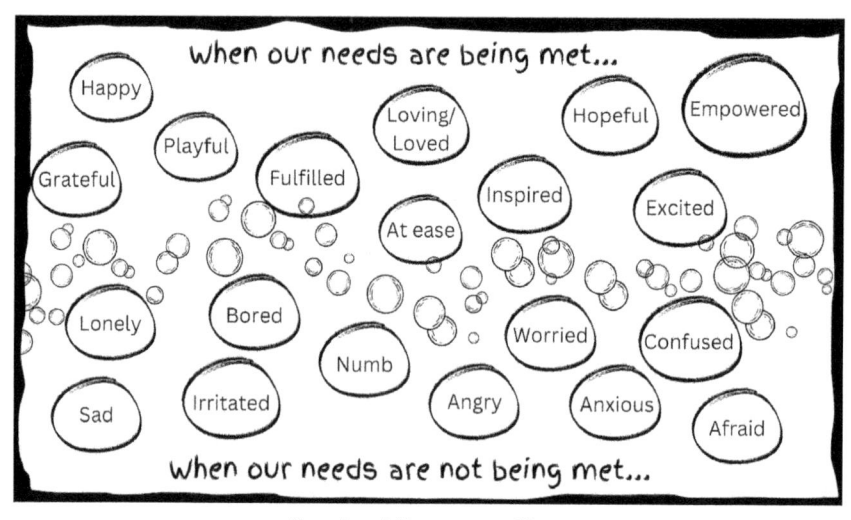

Emotional Barometer Chart

The Deck of Unmet Needs

To take the Emotional Barometer to the next level, you can acknowledge that often our most challenging emotions are a result of unmet needs. Using the list below you can create a stack of cards to accompany your chart, putting the emotion on the front of the card and the list of possible unmet needs on the back (a printable version of these cards can be found at www.RadiantBalance.com).

These cards can help identify which unmet needs might be causing the emotion. If the family member with the challenging emotion is open to exploring the underlying causes of their emotions, you can look through the list together and listen to what they have to say about their possible unmet needs. Then you can work together with them to figure out how their needs could be met in a healthy way. Even when your kids aren't open to exploring this with you, they may look at the cards on their own (maybe when you're not looking). Just the presence of the cards and the introduction of this concept of unmet needs can be helpful for kids as they mature and learn how to understand their emotions.

Unmet needs cards:

- Bored – meaning, celebration of life, challenge, creativity, discovery, growth, learning, stimulation, inspiration
- Lonely – connection, affection, belonging, closeness, companionship, trust, warmth
- Sad – closeness, love, companionship, confidence, competence
- Irritated – sleep, nourishment, time alone, respect, to be understood, choice, freedom, autonomy, order, ease
- Numb – connection, meaning, purpose, safety, understanding, spontaneity, inspiration
- Angry – justice, safety, to be understood, respect
- Anxious – safety, stability, rhythm, assurance, protection, love, understanding, trust, nurturing, confidence

- Afraid – safety, security, stability, support, understanding
- Confused – communication, honesty, clarity, respect, integrity, presence, inclusion
- Worried – understanding, certainty, agency, safety, security, trust

Rituals for Transitioning

Holding space for big emotions and challenging feelings requires dropping into deep presence with our kids and opening up in vulnerability together. This can be really beautiful. At times, it can feel heavy or intense. After an intense conversation or emotional processing, it can be helpful to use a simple ritual to transition back into the everyday household rhythm or into the bedtime routine. This will allow for a sense of release and closure; a sort of exhale. Even if the whole situation isn't resolved or fixed, releasing the energy and consciously bringing your session to a close can be a way to allow ourselves and our kids to be okay with the unresolvable and the unanswerable in this complex world.

Some examples of simple rituals that you and your kids could use for this transition are:

- Lighting a candle
- Sharing a mantra
- Singing a song
- Praying
- Shaking it out or another somatic practice
- Telling a joke or doing something funny together

7

NURTURING NEW PARADIGM QUALITIES

"In a very real way we are writing our own future, the future of our world, on the hearts and minds of our children. Let's think deeply, love selflessly, and act intentionally to write messages of peace and goodness and generosity of spirit on the hearts and minds of our children, our messengers, our hope for a better tomorrow."

– L.R. Knost [7.1]

Messages to the Future

As we come to terms with the intensities of the world our children have been born into and feel all the feelings that realization stirs in us, we can begin to see our place in the world with new eyes. We can begin to see that, as parents, we're planting seeds for the future in *every* moment of our children's lives. We begin to understand that the impressions they develop about the world and who they are within it will inform who they become as adults. These impressions will shape what they think is possible, and how they choose to show up in the world. We see that we really are writing the future, as L.R. Knost says, *"on the hearts and minds of our children."*

Moving beyond the Power Over Paradigm and into the cultivation of a Life Sustaining Society will require raising children who grow into adults with a commitment to collective wellness and mutual thriving. Creating a future in which our children can *thrive*, along with the rest of the Family of Life, will call for a completely different way of thinking and behaving than that of the dominant paradigm. It will require a deep healing of wounds and dismantling of lies. It will require raising human beings who are supported in that healing process and who know how to carry it on for themselves and their relatives. It will require children who are rooted in their ability to engage healthfully with the living world in ways that are not driven by fear, scarcity, trauma or patterns of woundedness. It will require creating conditions of wellness for our children and cultivating the qualities and strengths in them that will inspire them to truly care for the Earth, each other, and themselves.

The Power Over Paradigm has obscured our perception of the world. It has polluted our minds and hearts as much as it has polluted the water, soil, and air. But it has not destroyed the beauty and brilliance in our souls or in the Soul of the World, which is still resiliently alive and waiting to blossom, again and again. The magic of Life still exists and will emerge in more and more fullness as we bring ourselves into alignment with it. As we dream into the vision of this new Life Sustaining Society, let's consider the human qualities that would sustain life, justice and wellness for all so we can nurture them in our young ones.

What the World Needs Now...

Love, sweet love! Of course, that's what the world needs, and *has* needed for a long time. And not *just* a sweet love. It needs a love that is also fierce, intelligent, fully inclusive, restorative and powerful. It needs a love that has many facets and grows from many specific qualities and orientations that we can consciously cultivate in our children. With these qualities firmly rooted in our children, they'll have the necessary capacities to actively co-create a collective future worth living for.

I'm sure the list below doesn't cover every possible quality necessary to support the emergence of a Thriving Life Paradigm for humankind. But, as I dream into this potentiality and reflect on the children I've cared for, these are the qualities that come to my mind and heart. When I look at this list as a whole and imagine a generation of children within whom these qualities flourish, I see a world in which all beings can thrive. I know, from direct experience, that even here in the midst of this dysfunctional society, it's possible for us, as parents, to influence the development of these qualities in our children. The more of these qualities our children develop, the more resiliently they will navigate their lives and the more healing they will bring to the world.

Qualities necessary for a Thriving Life Paradigm:

- Wonder, Awe, Reverence and Gratitude
- Loving Connection, Empathy and Compassion
- Belonging and Kinship with the Family of Life
- Respect, Consent, Equity and Justice
- Reciprocity, Cooperation and Collaboration
- Humility, Vulnerability and Emotional Fluency
- Curiosity, Critical Thinking, Creativity and Innovative Problem Solving
- Courage, Confidence, Self-worth, Honor and Dignity
- Honesty, Authenticity and Self Expression
- Resilience and Adaptability
- Joy, Humor and Playfulness

"If I had influence with the good fairy who is supposed to preside over the christening of all children, I should ask that her gift to each child in the world would be a sense of wonder so indestructible that it would last throughout life, as an unfailing antidote against the boredom and disenchantment of later years, the sterile preoccupation with things that are artificial, the alienation from the sources of our strength. If a child is to keep alive his inborn sense of wonder without such a gift from the fairies, he needs the companionship of at least one adult who can share it, rediscovering with him the joy, excitement, and mystery of the world we live in."

– Rachel Carson [7.2]

Wonder, Awe, Reverence and Gratitude

As children of a magnificent, miraculous Universe, our most natural and authentic state is awe. I love that Rachel Carson wishes she could call on the fairies to preserve this inborn sense of wonder but recognizes that, in lieu of fairy magic, the companionship of an adult who is willing to experience wonder and awe alongside the growing child is what's really needed. We are those adults being invited to practice awe and swim in wonder as our children grow. A person in awe is connected to the Source of Life, the sources of our strength, and not one easily manipulated by the power plays of the dominant paradigm.

As we explored in our Grounding in Gratitude chapter, teaching our children how to live in a practice of radical gratitude and reverence is a powerfully subversive way to detach from the Power Over Paradigm. It is also a brilliant way to deepen our connection with Life. As our children experience appreciation for the ways in which their life is sustained, they learn how the sustenance of Life works and can find their role in the great Web of Life more easily.

Loving Connection, Empathy and Compassion

Children are full of love when they are little. They love their parents and siblings to the moon and back. When that love is returned and children are raised in a loving environment, with encouragement for positive connection they become capable of growing that love far beyond the edges of their immediate families. Prosocial human beings that are comfortable with loving connection are essential to the cultivation of a Life Sustaining Society.

As our children grow, it's also important to foster their natural tendencies toward empathy and compassion. Most of the children I've worked with display an amazing ability to feel for others and a desire to help. As caregivers, we can notice this natural tendency as it arises and encourage our children to act on it, supporting their longing to contribute to the wellbeing of others and helping them develop this practice as they grow up. As we heal from the damages done by the Power Over Paradigm, we need a generation of people who are willing to put themselves in each other's shoes and help each other grow into a more equitable and mutually beneficial way of living.

Belonging and Kinship with the Family of Life

Hyperindividualism, one of the most seductive and dangerous lies of the Power Over Paradigm, attempts to convince us that each one of us is separate from others and that we should put our own self-interests above all else. This lie works in direct opposition to one of the most basic aspects of human emotional and mental wellbeing: Belonging. Human beings are intrinsically social and collective beings. We need to belong to each other.

Raising our children with a strong sense of belonging helps them see themselves as part of a larger constellation of relationships. Feeling a sense of belonging and kinship, not only in their nuclear family, but in the long lineage of past, present and future humans, and with all living beings in the Family of Life, orients them deeply in collective awareness and collective responsibility.

Respect, Consent, Equity and Justice

From a very young age (even 1 or 2 years old) children can learn that they have autonomy over their own bodies and other people have autonomy over theirs. We can teach children that each person has a right to their own choices and that, as we make our choices, we need to consider how they affect others. Teaching our children how to ask permission before touching another body or before taking something out of someone else's hand helps our kids grow into adults who respect themselves and others. It's essential that we model the importance of consent by respecting their little bodies, asking permission before touching or moving them or taking something from their hands. This awareness of consent can protect our children from those who may seek to harm them and keeps our children from being harmful to others.

Centering the understanding of privilege and the dismantling of oppression in your parenting will help your children see the world through the lens of equity and justice. As we attempt to plant the seeds of a new paradigm in the hearts and minds of our children, we need to reframe our orientation to power and agency so we can grow a culture in which *all* are empowered. This work is *particularly* important if you and your children are part of a dominant, privileged class or sector within a society that has grown from the genocide, enslavement and/or disenfranchisement of others (there are many different versions of this societal dominance around the world, but two very notable examples are being white bodied in the USA or Australia). Raising our children to understand that we have inherited an unjust system that needs to be fixed is critical to a future of equity and justice.

Reciprocity, Cooperation and Collaboration

In our Grounding in Gratitude chapter, we explored reciprocity as an expression of gratitude for the Earth and towards other people. As we raise our children with this practice, we can teach our children to see themselves as part of a team. Whether the team is a single parent and a single child, a whole big family, a classroom, a neighborhood, or the full Family of Life, we're always interacting with others. This orientation to working as a team helps our kids learn how to bring their gifts to the collective generously and to graciously receive the gifts of others in the collaboration and cooperation necessary for a Life Sustaining Society.

Collaboration and cooperation are exciting skills to practice and bring into focus throughout your children's lives. Since these skills haven't been well supported by the Power Over Paradigm, you may find yourself having to stretch and learn alongside your children, as you discover (or rediscover) how to work with others, honor their gifts, receive their input and find ways to communicate. As we work together to cultivate a Life Sustaining Society with high quality collaboration, we'll experience the magic of synergy and co-creation and see that the whole is truly greater than the sum of its parts.

Humility, Vulnerability and Emotional Fluency

As we move beyond the Power Over Paradigm, we begin to understand that true power doesn't come from force and dominance, and that putting on a tough image doesn't get us very far. True power is a connection to the Source of Life that comes through our intuition and emotions. As we explored in the Embracing Emotions chapter, we can help our children maintain and strengthen their access to these inner channels by teaching them that it's okay to be vulnerable and express their feelings.

You can create a safe environment for expression in your own home by modeling humility and vulnerability and by holding a respectful, loving space for your children when they express their vulnerability. As they get older, you can also teach them skills for regulating their energy, staying tuned in to their intuition and inner guidance and expressing their emotions effectively to others. These are the skills necessary to become healthy adults and the leaders we need to guide us into a functional way of living.

Curiosity, Critical Thinking, Creativity and Innovative Problem Solving

Our world is full of seemingly unsolvable problems, and we basically have to create an entirely different way of living if we are going to survive the collapse of the Power Over Paradigm. In this pivotal moment, we're in need of some very creative problem solving. Fortunately, our children come into the world with a natural propensity for curiosity, critical thinking and creative problem solving. If we encourage these natural gifts, rather than suppress them (the way conventional schooling often does), there is no telling what remarkably innovative responses they may have to the situations in which we find ourselves.

As our children learn and grow, we can stand beside them in wonder. Instead of giving them the answers and showing off what we think we know, we can stimulate meaningful inquiry by guiding them through the discovery process. We can suspend our "knowledge" momentarily while they wrestle with a new thought and delight in what they come up with.

Courage, Confidence, Self-worth, Honor and Dignity

Our children's lives are not going to be easy. They will encounter many obstacles and many forces that seek to diminish them and make them feel powerless. One of the central tactics of the Power Over Paradigm is to rob its subjects of their honor and dignity. Every single one of us descends from human beings who, at one time, maybe very long ago, *knew* that they were brilliant, beautiful, sacred members of the Family of Life. People like this are wonderful stewards of a Life Sustaining Society, and they are not easy to control. As the forces of oppressive empires and colonization ravaged the surface of the Earth, they stripped the people of their honor and dignity in every way they possibly could.

For our children to grow beyond the constraints of this dominant paradigm and create a future that feeds Life, they will need their natural honor, dignity and self-worth intact. Fortunately, these attributes are natural endowments of every little human being and can be cultivated and encouraged as they grow. Teach your children that they are needed in this world. Teach them that they have a purpose and that their lives matter so they can move forward with the courage and confidence required to meet the moment.

Honesty, Authenticity and Self Expression

Along with self-worth and dignity comes the ability to be yourself, honestly and authentically. Each of us comes into life with our own special gifts, our own way of seeing and understanding, our own particularities that make us who we are. The world needs each of us, exactly as we are. It's in this diversity of perspective and expression that we really thrive. Diversity makes every system stronger. When we're not hemmed in by the prejudices and boxes of an oppressive society, we can steward and care for Life much more beautifully.

There are countless ways that the Power Over Paradigm tells our children that they need to hide parts of themselves and fit into one of the pre-programmed boxes that has been designed for them. From institutionalized racism to relentless genderization and forced compliance with a consumer economy and political ideologies, our kids are inundated with expectations and fabricated answers to the questions of who they are. As parents, we can consciously create space in our homes and families for our children to blossom as the authentically individual human beings that they are.

Resilience and Adaptability

We can't even begin to imagine how much change our children will have to navigate in their lifetimes. All we know is that things are not going to continue on as they have. The Earth simply doesn't have the resources to keep sustaining an extractive capitalistic human society. So, one way or another, everything is going to change, and our kids will have to be resilient and adaptive if they are to make it through and be of any use to the world. This is why it's essential for us to teach our children how to deal with challenges and hardship gracefully and healthfully. Everyone knows that facing and working through real life challenges is character building, but modern parents often have a hard time staying out of the way enough to allow their children to build character in this way.

Even if we have plenty of money, we should not bend over backwards to create a fantastical childhood of constant pleasure and gratification for our children. It doesn't serve them at all. In fact, it interferes with their growth and development and creates an unnaturally insatiable appetite for ease. As part of a healthy childhood that prepares a person for the rest of their lives, a child should have to learn how to wait, give others a turn, make mistakes, fall down and get hurt, experience disappointment, and get bored. That doesn't mean we should intentionally create suffering for our children. And it doesn't mean we shouldn't let our kids have plenty of fun. But if we insulate them too much from the normal discomforts of life and try to make every day and every moment a magical theme park adventure, we are impeding their healthy development and stunting their resilience.

Joy, Humor and Playfulness

Even as our children must struggle and learn from their struggles, they also need to have some fun! A sense of natural joy and playfulness and an ability to see the humor in any situation may be the qualities that help our kids the most. When we feel connected to the living world and see our lives as important, but small, parts of a grand unfolding, this sense of joy comes easily. Humor and lightheartedness are essential to resilience. Without an appreciation for irony, mystery and playfulness, we would all be brought to our knees before even making it through the gate. Being able to laugh at ourselves, try things out and fail and notice the ironic humor in how life unfolds helps us make it through the more difficult moments we'll have to face. Feeling joy and carrying joy in our hearts are also essential practices for caring for and sustaining Life.

"We are the middle children of History, coming of age at the crossroads of civilization, a generation rising between an old world dying and a new world being born. We are the 'make-it or break-it' generation, the 'all-or-nothing' generation, the crucible through which civilization must pass or crash."

– Joshua Gorman [7.3]

Young People Taking the Future into their Own Hands

Children are often able to see the simple truths that adults have been conditioned to ignore by the abuses of the dominant paradigm. Although we're talking about how this paradigm shift will affect the future, it is not a future-tense endeavor. We're right in the middle of it. It has already been happening for decades, *at least.* Time and time again, over all these years, it has been guided by the young people of the day. As children come of age in a world full of hypocrisies and injustices many of them will be guided by their natural empathy and curiosity to seek ways to help. If we encourage and nurture the new paradigm qualities we explored above as they grow, they'll be more equipped to keep their authentic humanity intact and follow through on their natural impulses to care for the world.

Young people from around the world, in different times and situations, have assessed the situation they were born into and said, *"This won't do!"* As they've grown toward adulthood, they've seen beyond the lies and rationalizations of the adults in power. They have understood the consequences of this Power Over Paradigm and have been unwilling to go along with its program.

Young people have been the major catalyzing force in many of the movements challenging the Power Over Paradigm around the world.

In the US Civil Rights and Anti-War movements of the 1960s, Tiananmen Square, the South African Anti-Apartheid movement, the Arab Spring and any other uprisings, protests and movements, young people have been fighting for their future. Now, in addition to trying to shift political tides towards peace, freedom and justice, young people are fighting for the viability of a future for Life on Earth. As some of the youth of today begin to understand that they may not inherit a livable planet as a result of the decisions of past and present politicians and industry leaders, they are doing everything they can to turn the tides of our corporate-political-industrial machine.

In 1992, when she was only 12 years old, Severn Cullis-Suzuki gave this speech at the UN's Earth Summit in Rio de Janeiro:

"I am only a child, yet I know if all the money spent on war was spent on finding environmental answers, ending poverty and in finding treaties, what a wonderful place this earth would be. At school, even in kindergarten, you teach us how to behave in the world. You teach us to not to fight with others, to work things out, to respect others and to clean up our mess, not to hurt other creatures, to share, not be greedy. Then, why do you go out and do the things you tell us not to do? Do not forget why you are attending these conferences, who you are doing this for. We are your own children. You are deciding what kind of a world we are growing up in. Parents should be able to comfort their children by saying 'Everything is going to be alright, it's not the end of the world, and we are doing the best we can'. But I don't think you can say that to us anymore. Are we even on your list of priorities? My dad always says, 'You are what you do, not what you say'. Well, what you do makes me cry at night. You grown-ups say you love us. But I challenge you, please, make your actions reflect your words. Thank you."

– Severn Cullis-Suzuki [7.4]

Since Severn Cullis-Suzuki spoke those words, countless youth activists and leaders have been working on this same issue in a variety of different ways. Young people from tribes and countries all over the world are begging our political and industry leaders to stop the destruction of the planet. They are putting their bodies on the line in physical confrontations, they are writing inspiring songs and poetry and delivering powerful messages of truth and urgency to audiences around the world, they are inventing next level solutions to many of our practical problems and some of them are even suing their governments.

In 2018, Autumn Peltier, a 13-year-old First Nations Anishinaabekwe girl, addressed the UN General Assembly on the issue of water protection.[7.5] In her young life, she has become known as a "water warrior" and has been recognized globally for educating the world about the sanctity of water and advocating for universal water rights. Xiuhtezcatl Martinez, now 23-years-old, has been speaking, writing and performing on behalf of the environment since he was just six years old. [7.6] He is one of 21 young people who filed a lawsuit in 2015 against the United States government for violating *"the plaintiffs' rights by encouraging and allowing activities relating to greenhouse gas emissions that significantly infringed upon their right to life and liberty."* [7.7] In 2018, Greta Thunberg, a 15-year-old girl from Sweden, seized international attention and inspired millions of students and their families to participate in "Fridays for Future" school strikes with her extremely straightforward statements and demands for world leaders to treat the climate crisis as the emergency it is.[7.8]

I cry every time I hear (or even read) the words spoken by Severn Cullis-Suzuki in 1992. I am often moved to tears by Xiuhtezcatl's songs and Greta's speeches. I cry because what they say is so true. And because it feels crazy and heartbreaking to me that the children of the world have to be the ones to bear the burden of the misdeeds of their elders. But our children have been born into the world just the way it is, with all its beauty and all its wounding, and they want to respond. They *were born* to respond. And we're here to help them. We certainly don't need to pressure our children into becoming international youth activists or hold them to the standards of these very public figures, but we can look at their examples to understand that it's possible for children to respond to the world in meaningful ways. Children are naturally intelligent, loving, creative and passionate. And each one comes with their unique gifts to offer the world. As their parents, we can ask ourselves what support, information, experiences, resources and encouragement we can provide to help them respond in the ways they are called.

While working for a small nonprofit in 2015, I had the great pleasure of organizing and chaperoning an extraordinary learning adventure for seven high school students from Colorado to attend the Bioneers Conference[7.9] in California. A few years earlier, I attended the Bioneers conference on my own and saw the incredible Youth Leadership Program they have. I dreamed of bringing a group of youth to the conference to connect them with this global awareness and have the empowering experience of working with other youth to tend to the needs of our world. We had a limited number of spots available for the trip, so I asked any students who wanted to attend to write an essay to apply.

One of the essays I received was from a senior in high school whom I had known as a member of our community since she was just a little girl. In her essay, she expressed a deep level of skepticism that anything could be done about the problems of the world. She had grown up hearing about the impending apocalypse and watching documentaries full of doom and despair. She was burdened with a sense of futility about the future. She couldn't see a path forward for herself, post-graduation. She said that her desire to attend the conference was a kind of measured, last-ditch curiosity to see if there was any hope at all.

During the conference, she and her classmates were on fire! They devoured the information at every plenary and poured through the schedule to figure out how to attend all the afternoon workshops that inspired them. Throughout our time there, we held continual group discussions to digest and explore everything we were learning together. At the end of the conference, this young woman told me that she finally saw how she could contribute to the healing of the world, no matter what field she was interested in pursuing or what skills she wanted to develop. She said she realized that the world needed people who were dedicated to caring for the world in all fields and all walks of life.

When New Paradigm qualities are cultivated in young people, the natural human spirit that is so alive in them can come through even more strongly. That doesn't mean that every freedom fighter and youth activist had perfect parenting. It also doesn't mean that if you nourish these qualities "perfectly" in your children, they'll "save the world" with their activism. This is not an all-or-nothing scenario. It is an invitation to make way for the power, possibility and potential of young people who are informed and supported. It inspires awe to behold young people who have the confidence to be courageous and the critical thinking skills and creativity to address some of our biggest challenges and who deeply care about our world and feel a responsibility to Life and future generations. Whether our children's care for the world plays out on the international stage for all to see or in small, personal, less seen ways, these qualities will guide them and support them in contributing their unique gifts to the world.

PRACTICES FOR NURTURING THE NEW PARADIGM

We can nurture the New Paradigm every single day, in every moment of life with our kids. The practices below are designed to support that experience for you with a few creative ideas. Hopefully, these ideas inspire and spark even more ways of nurturing the new in your daily life. When we embrace parenting as an opportunity to seed future generations with the capacity for wellness, joy, creative problem solving and compassionate care for self, others and the world, it becomes an inspiring and enlivening experience.

We aren't here just to feed and shelter these kids and crank out another generation of citizens. trained to maintain the status quo. We're here to heal the wounds we've inherited, to transform our collective relationship with the world and to open pathways into a future in which all beings can thrive. When we approach parenting in this way, it makes the whole experience way more interesting and worthwhile!

The practices below have proven to be fun and transformative for many families and can help you to get the ball rolling in this direction. As always, please play with them and adapt them to fit your family. And please invent your own ways of nurturing these new paradigm qualities in your family, as well!

Nurturing the New Paradigm: Open Sentences for Co-Parents and Kids

Please refer to the instructions for Open Sentences in the practice section of Chapter 5: Grounding in Gratitude.

Open Sentences to use with your co-parents:

1. The messages I want to write on the hearts and minds of my children are…
2. The Thriving Life Paradigm qualities that are vibrantly alive in my household and children are…
3. The Thriving Life Paradigm qualities that I want to put more energy into cultivating in my household and children are…
4. If I were feeling joyful and playful about the future, my grandest vision of the best possible world for my children to grow into would be…
5. Some things that my children and I can do to actively contribute to the Great Turning are…

Open Sentences to use with your kids:

1. For every person and animal on the Earth to be healthy and happy, we would all have to…
2. My favorite thing about cooperating with others is…
3. I know I can make it through challenging times because…
4. Some ways that I'll be able to help the world when I'm older are…
5. Some ways that I can help the world right now are…

New Paradigm Game

This simple game provides an opportunity for your kids to learn about each of these words and qualities, while exploring how they can help the world. You can adapt and expand this game into more complex forms or keep it relatively simple. Be sure to adjust your approach to this game according to the ages and abilities of your kids so you are truly meeting them where they are and giving them something meaningful and engaging for them.

You can make your own cards to represent the New Paradigm Qualities using the kid-friendly definitions below or find a printable version of them at www.RadiantBalance.com

Begin by asking the child to describe an issue or conflict that's happening in the world or one that's happening in their personal life. Let your child share what they understand and feel about the situation. Listen to them and let them really share their perspective.

Then, ask them to pull one of the cards randomly out of the pile and read the quality and the definition aloud (or read it for them if they need help). You can take a moment at this time to see if they need any help understanding the definition. The definitions below are kid-friendly ways to talk about these qualities and get your conversation started. Of course, please elaborate on them with your own insights and to meet your kids as they are!

Once they have a clear understanding of the quality, ask them to express how that quality could help in the issue or conflict they were just talking about. They could draw a picture to express it, act it out or just share their thoughts and ideas. After they have the chance to explore how that quality could be helpful in shifting or healing the issue, you can explore how they could cultivate that quality in their own lives. Ask them what kind of help or learning they might need to grow that quality in themselves and make it stronger.

You can repeat this process by choosing other cards to discuss how those qualities would affect the same issue. Or you might choose to identify a new issue to explore. If you are playing this game with more than one child, make sure they all have a chance to describe an issue, pull a card, share ideas, ask questions and express themselves.

New Paradigm Qualities:

- Wonder: a sense of curiosity and interest in things that you don't fully understand.
- Awe: a feeling caused by experiencing something that is very surprising, beautiful, or amazing.
- Reverence: a feeling of great respect mixed with love and awe.
- Gratitude: the feeling of being thankful; gratefulness.
- Loving Connection: feeling loved by others and loving them back; a sense of belonging and sweetness.
- Kinship with Life: feeling that all living beings on Earth are our relatives.
- Empathy: a sense of understanding and really caring about what someone else is going through.
- Compassion: a feeling of sharing another's suffering that leads to a desire to help.
- Respect: honoring, valuing and showing consideration for someone else or ourselves.
- Consent: permission or approval; deciding what is okay for us and what is not.
- Equity: fairness in the way people are treated.
- Justice: the upholding of what is fair, right and honest.
- Reciprocity: giving and receiving, back and forth.
- Cooperation: being helpful and supportive to other people.
- Collaboration: working together with others to get something done.
- Humility: knowing that you're a small part of a very big world.
- Vulnerability: showing your real feelings, sharing what's challenging you and asking for what you really need.
- Emotional Fluency: knowing how to express your feelings honestly without blaming other people for them.

- Curiosity: wanting to learn or know more about something or someone.
- Critical Thinking: thinking about all the parts of a situation and see how they connect.
- Creativity: the ability to make or think up something new, original or imaginative.
- Innovative Problem Solving: finding creative, new ways to solve old problems.
- Courage: being able to face your fears or do something that could be difficult or dangerous.
- Confidence: knowing that you can do hard things and are a good person.
- Self-worth: valuing yourself and knowing that you deserve to be treated with respect.
- Honor: a personal standard or principle that you live up to by doing the right thing.
- Dignity: a sense of honor and self-worth that inspires you to act with honesty, generosity and courage.
- Honesty: telling the truth and living by the truth.
- Authenticity: being fully honest and genuine.
- Self-Expression: freely showing your real and unique emotions, thoughts, style, ideas and personality.
- Resilience: the ability to make it through challenges and come out stronger or wiser than before.
- Adaptability: being able and willing to learn and grow as your situation changes and new information becomes available.
- Joy: a feeling of great happiness and pleasure.
- Humor: being able to see what's funny in the world, in ourselves and in our situations.
- Playfulness: having fun with the world, our lives and our situations.

Study Young Changemakers

This practice is an invitation to embark on a learning journey together with your children to explore some of the inspiring changemaking work of young people throughout history and right now. Help your kids see how young people have been working for Thriving Life for a long time, in many ways. Be sure to include changemakers from a variety of different races, national origins, cultures, genders and other identities. Try to discover young people working in a variety of different fields and modalities. Look for changemakers who will inspire your kids and who will be relatable for them.

You can begin by learning more about the changemakers mentioned in this chapter and then follow the curiosity of your children to learn about new ones. You can watch videos of these young people speaking or performing, watch documentaries or read articles about them, and look for projects and movements that center young people, such as the Sunrise Movement and Generation Waking Up.

Taking Action as a Family

This practice is an opportunity to actively participate in the massive paradigm shift that will support Thriving Life for the future generations of all species. Begin by talking with your kids about how all our little choices make up our lives and contribute to the world we live in. Invite them to imagine with you what choices your family could make to support Thriving Life for all and make the future better for coming generations.

Ask yourselves…What changes could we make? What new activities or actions could we engage in? What could we learn or teach or give? What could we let go of?

Get out a big piece of paper (or a whiteboard) and heartstorm[7.10] a bunch of ideas. When you're heartstorming, all ideas are included without judgment. Write it all down. Include teeny choices and huge ones. Gather all the ideas you can.

Once you've got a good collection of ideas, consider how these choices could contribute to the Great Turning and feed Thriving Life. How could they help you as a family to become really good ancestors for the ones yet to be? As you explore these questions, you may discover some ideas don't really fit or need to be adjusted or filled out. This is the time to make those changes and trim down your collection of ideas.

Once you've got a solid collection, choose just 3-5 choices or actions that your family can commit to and put them on your calendar. Be realistic about timing and pacing and set yourselves up to actually follow through with them.

You may discover that you have way more than 3-5 really good ideas. That's awesome! Making choices to support Thriving Life is an ongoing, daily, lifelong endeavor. Save your list somewhere accessible (and add to it as new ideas come up). Then, when your first group of actions has been implemented, return to your list to choose a few more and add those to your calendar.

As you make this a regular part of your family life, you teach your kids that their choices matter and set them up for a lifetime of empowered change-making and care for the Earth.

Some ideas of little and big choices I've seen families make together:

- Cut back on-screen time and spend quality family time outdoors connecting with nature.
- Change some of the products you buy and use to natural products with less packaging, instead.
- If you are a settler (or a descendant of settlers) living on unceded, occupied land, find out who the Indigenous caregivers of that land are (if you don't already know), learn about their history and their current reality. Find out what projects they're working on and what needs they have at this time, and then contribute your support to them in the ways that they express would be helpful (donations, volunteer hours, supplies, etc.) [7.11]

- Participate in an action to block some of the harm that is being done to the planet and/or her people – a protest, letter writing campaign, educational campaign, etc.
- Volunteer your services or donate to people in need. You might bring sanitary supplies or food to people experiencing houselessness, volunteer at a soup kitchen, help your neighbors, contribute to a community initiative, etc.
- Have a handmade/low-trash winter holiday where all presents are made by hand and present wrappings are natural or reusable.
- Grow a garden and/or raise some animals to provide some of your own food and deepen your relationships with your more-than-human kin.
- Learn an ancient craft. Choose something that humans have been doing for generations that's connected to the Earth and creates beauty (like spinning, weaving, making friction fire, making natural clay pots, etc.)

A Mother's Day Message

from ALisa Starkweather

"You want to honor mother today?

Remember this day was originally a mother's voice to halt ceaseless wars, bloodshed, and tyranny. Honor, then, the values of compassion, vulnerability, kindness, truth (the real kind), courage, grace, empathy, generosity, justice, connection, gratitude, honor, respect, dignity, wisdom, wonder, magic, humility, caring, holding, giving, restoring, gentleness, strength, intensity of feelings, creativity, deep knowing.

Take action. Honor rest and the body. Connect with the earth, not forgetting you are her child, and you are relatives. Honor the feelings – joy, grief, fear, anger – all of them important messengers of direction and healing. There is so much to be – especially now. Most especially right now.

Happy Mother's Day to me means a world where we take seriously confronting misogyny, racism, misanthropy, xenophobia, apathy, whiteness (as a systematic oppression), addictions, lack of self-care from the inside out. Happy Mother's Day means that we take seriously what we are leaving for the children – taking care of all children in our global decisions, and to stop fighting among ourselves.

This is the time to melt our hearts and be decent humans for the children. And all of this – all of what is here can hold love that is of fierce nature. That is a mother's love." [7.12]

PART THREE: New Paradigm Parenting

New Paradigm Parenting is the gift that we can give each day to our children and to the world. It exists in all the little moments and the myriad choices we make. It is cultivated in the environment in which we choose to raise our children and the sense of connection, belonging and safety we foster in them. It's expressed in the way we answer their questions, challenge them to rise to the moment and make space for them to try something new, fail and try again.

In some ways, this New Paradigm Parenting work might seem small or even insignificant. In the face of the dominant paradigm and corporate culture, it can sometimes feel like our efforts as parents aren't making enough of an impact. But these formative moments are where culture and paradigm are created. Every little choice we make is huge in the lives of our children and the way they understand the world. You'll see the spark of this gift come back to you, sometimes in mysterious ways or unexpected moments. You'll hear your own words come out of their mouths at some point, even those words you thought they were ignoring. You'll see their choices and their inner voice guided by the path you held for them as they were growing up. And the people they become will be the adults of the future.

In the previous three chapters, we moved through the first three phases of the spiral of the Work That Reconnects: *Coming from Gratitude, Honoring Our Pain for the World* and *Seeing with New and Ancient Eyes*. The rest of the book is dedicated to the fourth phase of the spiral:

Going Forth. This phase of the spiral is all about action. This is where you gather up all the energy, compassion, insight and inspiration you've generated along the spiral so far and carry it into your daily life. It is about taking empowered action.

The following chapters include a collection of guidance for New Paradigm Parenting in many of the very specific aspects of parenting that I've studied, experimented with and practiced over the past two decades – and counting! Although each child is unique and each moment in our parenting experience will contain nuances that can't be predicted, I have observed some near-universal needs and patterns of connection that can help us navigate our care for children at this crucial time. In the following chapters, I share many of these observations and specific ways to foster wellness and strengthen resilience in our children from the very beginning and as they grow. These chapters are full of practical tools and personal stories to help you apply those reflections to your own parenting experience and weave this Thriving Life paradigm right into your daily life as a New Paradigm Parent.

As you work through the ideas, concepts and practices in the rest of the book, you can always spiral back through the first three stages of the spiral as often as you need to by referring back to the chapters on Grounding in Gratitude (Chapter 5), Embracing Emotion (Chapter 6) and Nurturing New Paradigm Qualities (Chapter 7). You can also tap back into the paradigm shift we're participating in by revisiting the chapters on Global Crisis (Chapter 3) and Seeding a New Paradigm (Chapter 4). Parenting is not a linear process, so it is natural to spiral through these concepts again and again as your children grow and you deepen and evolve your New Paradigm Parenting practices.

8

OUR ROLE AS NEW PARADIGM PARENTS

"And a woman who held a babe against her bosom said, 'Speak to us of Children.'
And he said:
'Your children are not your children.
They are the sons and daughters of Life's longing for itself.
They come through you but not from you,
And though they are with you, yet they belong not to you.
You may give them your love but not your thoughts,
For they have their own thoughts.
You may house their bodies but not their souls,
For their souls dwell in the house of tomorrow, which you cannot visit, not even in your dreams.
You may strive to be like them but seek not to make them like you.
For life goes not backward nor tarries with yesterday.
You are the bows from which your children as living arrows are sent forth.

The archer sees the mark upon the path of the infinite, and He bends you with His might that His arrows may go swift and far.
Let your bending in the archer's hand be for gladness;
For even as He loves the arrow that flies, so He loves also the bow that is stable."

– Khalil Gibran [8.1]

Throughout our lives we gather ideas of what parents are and what they should be through the lens of the Power Over Paradigm. We pick up these ideas from our parents, of course. What they did. What they *didn't* do. We also pick them up from our friends' parents or other relatives and from depictions of parents on TV and in movies. As we raise our children, we unconsciously play out the roles and styles of parenting that we've observed throughout our lives. It's completely natural.

However, as New Paradigm Parents seeking to interrupt the old paradigm and create the possibility for a new paradigm to sprout up within the hearts and lives of our children, it's essential for us to bring these unconscious tendencies squarely into our consciousness attention.

Conscious cultural transformation requires us to start looking for and noticing the ways in which we may be replicating the old mentality and methods of Power Over Paradigm parenting, to examine them and to intentionally work on transforming them. We are stretching into new parenting terrain, giving our children something that we didn't receive so that they may have a future that we can hardly imagine. It can be a messy process, at times. It will involve some trial and error and, most certainly, many unexpected blessings along the way.

If you think about it, it's easy to see that we're basically just children who happen to have been here on Earth a little bit longer than the children we're raising. We respond to the world in similar ways and have similar needs. We were also raised in this "world in crisis" and have experienced some of the very same challenges and wounds that our children are experiencing. We're all in this together, doing our best and learning as we go. We're not experts at life. We don't have all the answers. We're not authority figures here to police and control the children in our lives. We are neither infallible nor beyond reproach.

We're just people who have been given the precious gift and opportunity to care for young human beings in need of love and ready to learn. If we can acknowledge and embody that definition of what it means to be a parent, we can *be* a gift to the children in our lives, and our children can become a gift to the world.

Parenting is so much more serious, more important, more exciting and more interesting than we've been taught to think it is. It is a Sacred Calling to *save the world*. When I say "save the world" I don't mean to protect us from all danger or to keep the world the way it is and preserve the comforts we've been trained to rely on. I mean that it's an opportunity to participate in weaving wellness back into the world by reclaiming our sacred human calling to be caregivers, nurturers, and nourishers of Life. It's a chance to love the world by healing the wounds we've inherited and by raising our children to be connected, lifegiving human beings.

It's an opportunity to be a conduit through which Life's sacredness can flow across time. It invites us to channel the wisdom of past generations and to be called forward by the inspiration of those yet to be. It's a chance to reawaken what it means to be a human being on Earth in beauty, reverence, and integrity. As we raise our children with this intention, we get to learn about all this right along with them.

Each day, with each decision and interaction, we're all co-creating our shared future. Our children and how we parent them are huge parts of that co-creation. Neil Postman said that *"Children are the living messages we send to a time we will not see."* [8.2] With Khalil Gibran's passage at the beginning of this chapter, we see them as "living arrows" that are sent forth from our bows. What a relief it can be to let ourselves be bent like the bow and then let go in trust. To trust the arrow, the archer, the air, and the destination. We are a small part of a much bigger story but if we do our part well, hold steady and don't cling to our arrows or burden them with unnecessary impediments, we can play a vital role in their successful flight to the *"house of tomorrow."* As we bend gladly in the archer's hand, let's consider what they will carry into that time beyond.

In a single generation of intentional parenting, we can change the trajectory of our children's lives and, with it, our collective future. As we consider what we'll give our children (or from what we'll free them) in this generation, I invite you to think about what can be lost or gained in the course of a generation. In the history of empire expansion, colonization and assimilation, many communities have suffered outrageous losses of language, culture, home, sense of purpose and orientation within a single generation. One generation of children stolen from their parents and sent to boarding or residential school where they are stripped of their original language and lifeway changes the course of a cultural lineage significantly.

Conversely, one generation of parents dedicated to reconnection and deep healing can change the course of their family or community lineage by planting and nourishing seeds of perspective, memory, vision and hope. There's abundant evidence of this in the growing movements of revitalization of Indigenous communities, languages and food systems right now across Turtle Island (North America). We can also see evidence of the considerable healing and revitalization that can happen in one generation when we reflect on the profound effect that the Civil Rights movement of the 1960s had on the African American communities of the United States. Or by observing the difference in how women were seen and functioned within Western society between the 1950s and the 1980s. One generation can make a profound difference in the lives, hearts and minds of the children raised within it.

You are one of the stewards of this generation of young people being raised on the brink of a possibly unlivable future. Previous generations have taken us here, step by step, one generation at a time, for better and for worse. The closer we get to systems' collapse, the faster it seems we're galloping. Those of us caring for children now have the urgent calling to take responsibility for pulling in the reins and changing our collective direction by raising children who can think and function beyond the Power Over Paradigm. We can choose to slow down and repair the damages done, learn from our lessons and plant seeds of collective wellness in the hearts and minds of our children.

Our World is at Stake. Nothing less.

The preciousness and sacredness of vibrating, pulsating, colorful, complex Life is calling us to respond. As parents, we are uniquely positioned to respond in a way that will outlive our own time by raising children who know how to listen, learn, and respond to their living world.

> *"When a child comes into your life, it is time to relearn life, not teach them your ways."*
>
> – Sadhguru (Jagadish Vasudev) [8.3]

Counteracting Indoctrination

To pull this off, we have to become aware of the conditioning we've received within the Power Over Paradigm, how it plays out within us and how our children are also being indoctrinated into this paradigm in countless ways from the moment they're born. This brings us back to the practice of "touching the box," as Bayo Akomolafe says.[8.4] With this awareness we can better understand the often-hidden context within which we're living and parenting. Through this practice, we begin to recognize where we have choice in our lives and parenting. As we consciously exercise that choice, we can create new possibilities and understandings for our children.

The "box" of the Power Over Paradigm is supported and perpetuated by stories and patterns that are so deeply woven into what we know as society that it's almost impossible for us to see them. Many of these stories are lies that have been told so often and for so long that it's extremely difficult for us to realize that they are untrue. The Power Over Paradigm is based on concepts of supremacy and upheld by force.

The Power Over Paradigm claims that:

- Some human beings have the right to wield power over other human beings or animals, plants, and the Earth.
- Our world is made up of a bunch of non-sacred, non-living matter.
- We're separate from each other and from the Earth.
- Power lies in the hands of the few.
- Those with the most money and the most capacity for violence are the most powerful.
- Everyone else is powerless and the best they can do is try to climb the ladder and claim a little bit larger piece of the pie for themselves.
- Humans are greedy and violent by nature and that there's not enough for everyone, so we're bound into struggling and suffering.
- This way of understanding the world is the only way.
- We couldn't possibly change the course of our collective trajectory because *it* is too big, and *we* are too small.

None of these precepts of the Power Over Paradigm are true. And none of them are supportive of a world of peace, equity, justice, and Thriving Life. However, they are the scaffolding upon which the institutions of our society are built. And, although we may not agree with some of these ideas consciously, many of us will discover that our ideas about the world and our place in it are often tied to versions of these lies that were woven into our minds as children. As we seek to counteract the indoctrination of this dominant paradigm, we have to become alert to all the ways in which these lies have taken root in our consciousness and how they affect the development of our children's worldview.

From the moment they're born, our children are learning about their world at a mind-boggling rate. They soak it all in. All the overt messages and all the cultural assumptions that hide within them. The direct experiences they have and the media, toys and education they're exposed to create the foundation of their worldview. They learn all about what it means to be human, who has what kind of power, what's possible and what's not, how to get what they want and what matters most. They're constantly watching, listening, mimicking, making sense of their world and picking up details that we often don't even notice.

In the first few years of life, toddlers create an elaborately detailed catalog of their world. The two-year-olds with whom I've worked can typically point out the difference between a digger, a cement truck and a dump truck (and the various other distinct pieces of construction equipment with which I'm unfamiliar.) They definitely know which dinosaur is the T-Rex and, if they've experienced a recent Halloween, they can point out the zombie, the ghost, the mummy and the witch. Their little minds memorize and categorize everything they've been exposed to. In the so-called "developed" world, what they are exposed to in these early years is often heavily influenced by an urban, industrial and commercialized perspective on the world.

By the time a child is three or four, they typically know how "cool" kids talk and walk. They know all about popularity and social power, what's socially acceptable and what isn't. They understand bullying and pick up on the social dynamics and attitudes that will get their needs met in the dominant paradigm. They're subconsciously trained to conform to certain standards and to envision themselves and their lives in specific ways.

One example of this (and its deleterious effects) is the way in which genderization is so *heavily* embedded into almost everything made for our kids, from toys to toothbrushes, and from TV shows to summer camps. Each one has a color, font or icon that signals whether it's meant for a girl or a boy. And *everyone* recognizes it, even the littlest kids. Trains, trucks, construction equipment, sports and dinosaurs are poured onto our boys when they're little. As they get older, they often become embroiled with battle mentality and military glorification through the video games that are target-marketed to them. Girls tend to be drawn into obsession with image and appearance by the excessive sparkly-rainbow-unicorn-and-princess-themed products and shows that hook them from their earliest ages. This obsession too often turns into a lifelong effort to be the prettiest girl in the room and a self-loathing that is almost universal among older girls and women. All this leaves little room for unique expression, individual thought or any personal experience that doesn't fit into the gender binary.

Our kids get the message about what the world is and who they can be in it. Loud and clear. As New Paradigm Parents, it's not enough to tell them they can "be anything" in a world that confines and constrains. It's not enough to tell them we have to "care for the Earth" in a lifestyle and society that treats the Earth like a lifeless resource, mined for our comfort. We have to *show* them what is true and what is possible by surrounding them with living examples and compelling expressions of the world we want them to live into.

Through these early years, everything they're exposed to is immediately absorbed and added to that catalog of the world and becomes embedded in their awareness of "how things are."

So how are things? And how do we want things to be?

If the world actually is a complex, living Being whose existence is in grave danger as a result of human behavior and we humans are a vital part of her Interbeingness,[2.2] then there are *way* more interesting and important things for our little ones to add to their mental catalog and worldview than construction vehicles, commercialized Halloween monsters and how to be "popular" in the schoolyard. Instead, we might want them to get to know the plants and animals that live all around them, how water moves around the planet and how to listen to each other with patience and love.

Beginning fresh with a brand-new human being gives us the chance to examine our own conditioning and consider which notions, ideas, assumptions, stories, and habits we need to give up in order to raise kids who have the ability to truly care for the world.

> *"Before you were born, while you roiled the insides of my belly, your father and I decided we were not 'bringing you into the world'...it just wasn't the right metaphor for how we wanted to hold you. That sounded like you were coming through parting clouds, descending from the naïve to the real. You were more real to us than a hovering ghost or a visiting messiah. So, we learned to say that you were coming out of the earth (not into it), that you were the domino effect of many parents – including animal and plant parents, and that you were a gift to us.*
> *You are wise, not a tabula rasa. You have the royalty of mountains, the determination of swooping hawks, the experience of bursting pollen, and the joy of opening flowers written into your bones. This is the reason we said, once you were born, once your jelly father held you in his hands, and once I breathed in your face, that we would follow you just as much as we wanted to instruct you. That we would listen to your questions not merely as things that you didn't know but as clues about what we also might need to unlearn. This has been our journey – to follow a child like the disciples of a rabbi follow hard behind the sandals of their master. And the questions you ask! Oh, how delightful! How surprising!"*
>
> – Ijeoma Precious Clement-Akomolafe [8.5]

Relearning the World

We're responsible for orienting our children to the world they were born into. But, as we reflect on our conditioning and deeply consider all that we don't know about the world and everything they'll experience in their lives that is beyond our ability to predict, we become students of the world all over again. This is our chance to rethink everything we thought we knew and relearn the world right beside our wide-eyed, curious, sweet little ones.

Instead of raising our kids to plug away at Business As Usual and succeed at the "Game of Life" in the old paradigm, we want to raise them to bring forward a whole new way of living. Our job is to raise children who can think critically and creatively, who understand and value equity, justice and Mutual Thriving, who are resilient and inspired to care for Life, and who are able to persevere through uncertainty. That's going to take a lot of learning, a lot of love and a lot of truth telling.

In each learning moment, we have the chance to observe, examine, contemplate, reflect honestly and be curious, alongside our children. The children in our lives are going to ask a gajillion questions. They'll ask about everything from how babies get made and how airplanes can fly to where plastic comes from and why our countries are at war. They're going to ask about every facet of life they encounter. These are our moments of opportunity.

When our children ask these questions, it's essential that we don't brush them off or give them the pre-programmed answers that may be in our heads. These moments are our opportunities to challenge ourselves to think about each question with our whole heart and mind and check it against what we've actually observed and experienced in our lives. Each answer to each question is a chance to be honest with ourselves and with our children.

As we "touch the box" through this honest inquiry, we'll notice that some of the things we were taught or assume about the world are simply not true. We can choose to pass along these untruths (perhaps because it's easier to "go with the flow") or we can choose to give our children honest answers about their world. Even if that means saying *"I don't know the answer to that question... Let's try to find out together."*

Most of the mainstream information, media perspective and educational curriculum our children are exposed to is incomplete, misleading and often even inaccurate about the way things actually are and have been. Our children are getting inundated with distorted perspectives and blatant lies on a moment-by-moment basis through books, shows, stories, commercials, news, and school lessons. Children are extremely sensitive to inauthenticity, so this barrage can degrade their sense of personal orientation and trust in their world, whether they are aware of it or not.

I believe this is one of the underlying causes of an eventual loss of self-esteem and disconnection from their own inner compass that often leads to disillusionment, depression, self-loathing, and apathy as many of our children grow into their teen years. As a parent, you have the opportunity to prevent or repair this disorientation by helping them anchor into an honest exploration of the world. You can gently expose these untruths and empower your children with real information in age-appropriate ways while encouraging them to always look beneath the surface of what they are being told.

When you don't have a clear answer for your child's question, you have a great opportunity to learn together. You can take some time with it and dig in deeper. Encourage your children to ask more questions and stay curious as they explore a concept with you. Stay close to the bone of what you find to be true. As you gain insights or understanding, try to be very honest and only say what you know or what you wonder. Together you might learn some fascinating things about our world.

If you have some answers, deliver them with humility. You don't know it all, and it's essential that your children realize that early in their lives. Do your best to make sure your answers are in language that they can understand at their current age. Be mindful not to use adult vocabulary and references that they won't get, while at the same time being careful not to baby-talk to them or oversimplify your explanation. Pay attention to see if they're picking up what you're putting down. Make sure you're connecting and that they're engaged. Be careful not to overdo it and launch into lecture mode! (My kid calls me out on that one every time.)

As they grow, and their ability to comprehend increases, children need to explore, learn, and relearn everything multiple times. Be prepared to revisit certain topics you thought you had already explored with them. Notice their growing capacity to understand more deeply each time. Give them room to grow and connect their new learning to their personal experiences, which are also expanding over time. This learning journey continues throughout their childhoods and lives, winding in a spiral around their developing minds.

When you find yourself explaining some aspect of nature or science or economy or religion or politics to a six-year-old in language that they can truly grasp you may discover that *you* are understanding it for the first time in any really meaningful way. Orienting a little one to the world in this way requires us to earnestly contemplate how things really are in our world and break complicated concepts down into their basic truths.

When I began writing this book, I lived in Portland, Oregon and was working full-time as a nanny. The city of Portland was built along the banks of the Willamette River, which runs from South to North right through the center of the city. That means thousands of people cross the river every day on one of the many bridges in cars, on bikes, on foot or on the commuter train.

As a newcomer to Portland and to urban life, I was struck by the interface between the river and this city. Heartbroken, really. I could feel the energy of this majestic, watery being flowing deep and wide beneath the bridges when I crossed over and it pained me to see her edges cemented in and crowded with industry, development, and pollution. I began a simple practice of greeting her with love, respect, and beauty at each crossing. So, whenever I crossed the river and was in the car by myself or with little ones or other adults with whom I felt comfortable, I would turn off the radio, pause the conversation and launch into a song in praise of the beautiful river-being that flowed beneath.

The two-year-old I cared for every day and his six-year-old sister (who was with us less often because of school) were familiar with this little ritual. One day, when we were driving in the car, the six-year-old asked, *"Jo, why do you sing to the river? Do you love the river?"*

What a brilliant question. What a beautiful opportunity.

I said, *"Yes, I do love the river. And I happen to notice all these people cross over her all day long, every day and they don't really seem to notice that she's even down there. I just like to say 'Hi' to her when we cross over and sing her something beautiful, so she doesn't get lonely, and she knows we didn't forget about her."*

That answer seemed to satisfy her and got her wheels turning with more questions.

"Do rivers understand our language?" was her next question.

I said, *"Oh, that's a really good question. Well, you know they have their own language. Have you heard it? The special sounds that river water makes when it moves?"*

She had.

"But they're also really good at understanding human languages, especially the really old languages. That's why I sing to her with those different words." (This was in reference to the Scottish Gaelic song I typically sang.) *"Humans and rivers have been friends with each other for a long, long time, so the rivers know those old human languages really well."*

On this particular day, we weren't actually crossing the river. We were heading south on I-5 and a thick fog was hanging in the air. The little girl said something like, *"Well, we're not crossing the river now so I guess we can't sing."*

Then I said, *"But is there any water around?"* and she lit up. She's very smart and likes using her quick little brain. She said, *"Yes! It's all around us!!"*

"That's right," I said, *"So, let's sing!"*

Then she and her little brother started into their versions of the Gaelic water song, playing with the melody and the sounds of the syllables and the conversation was over. Complete, just as it was.

As I examine the world and shake off the layers of indoctrination I've received into the modern, mechanized, secular economy that we call a society, one of the understandings I've come to is how utterly alive the world is. I've come to understand for myself that we are living parts of an enormous living Being. The rivers, fog, trees, plants, animals, weather, mountains and all the other beings that make up the biosphere are alive and worthy of our acknowledgement. This is true to me. A fact. I don't need to wonder about it. When a six-year-old asks me if the river is alive, I can say *"yes"* without hesitation. Is the river worthy of respect? Yes, absolutely! Is the river special? Beautiful? Important? Should we make sure the river is protected and safe and cared for in a good way? Undeniably.

When I can break down a concept to this level of understanding, it's easy to talk with a six-year-old about it. And it's really fun. It's an amazing feeling to get to talk openly with another human being about important things and learn about the world together.

Parental Intuition and Parental Sovereignty

You have an internal guidance system that is specifically designed for you and your children. It may be buried underneath layers of intellectual knowledge, self-doubt, ego, personal agenda, fear, conditioning and many other things swimming around inside of you. But it is there. And it *knows*.

As a New Paradigm Parent who is navigating new terrain and untangling yourself from the POP, it's important to make a practice of regularly digging down beneath all those layers to tune into that deep knowing so you can get familiar with it and use it to guide your parenting.

You may not have had to acquire any degrees or passed any exams to become a parent. But you, beyond any other person, government or corporate entity, are *uniquely qualified* to parent your own children (along with their other parent(s), of course). You are your children's parent for a reason. Your parental intuition will tell you exactly what you need to know for taking care of them and supporting them in the ways they need.

There's no instruction manual for parenthood. Many of us come into parenthood with very little experience with children and little to no clue what this whole parenting experience will entail. We can get bombarded with advice about how to raise our children. Our inboxes fill up with countless newsletters and blog posts pushing different parenting techniques and educational philosophies. Everyone we talk to seems to have an opinion on what we should do, or not do. Our own parents, relatives, doctors, the media and even strangers can try to force their ideas into our lives and drop horror stories on us about how our choices could threaten our children's lives, deprive them, or turn them into spoiled brats. Self-doubt and confusion often creep in and try to take hold.

As you venture through your parenting journey, you may even notice that certain forces will seek to undermine your parental sovereignty and your connection with your children. Since disconnection and isolation fuel consumerism and make people easier to manipulate, corporate interests often seek to sever the bond between parent and child to secure lifelong customers. Compulsory schooling and the factory work schedule are two of the ways the Industrial Growth Society strengthens loyalty and dependence on the state and industry rather than connection with self, family, and nature.

It's also common to see storylines in our popular media about some sort of parent/child disconnection or abandonment. Many of our classic children's stories begin with one or both parents having already died and the child needing to figure out how to make it on their own. Many modern stories and movies feature parents that are pointedly stupid or wrong. Portrayals of teenagers and their parents in the media are almost always negative and riddled with contention. Media messages and advertisements often reinforce the idea that children don't really need their parents and that their parents are just holding them back in some way from getting the things they desire. These stories perpetuate the Power Over agenda. Please don't let them throw you off or undermine you.

You are your children's parent! You and your children were perfectly made for each other. You have something special that no one else has access to and no book or blog could ever contain: *your own parental intuition and insight.* It's magical. It's made just for you and your child. It sometimes defies logic. When you feel it, you know.

As a New Paradigm Parent, part of your work is to tune into your own parental intuition and get really good at listening to and trusting it. Through this intuition, you'll be able to access the truth about how your children are really doing and what they truly need. As you develop and strengthen your relationship with this intuitive guidance, do your best to draw on it as you make parental decisions and care for your child.

Then, lovingly and fiercely protect yourself and your child from the onslaught of other people's opinions and corporate influence by resting confidently in this deep knowing. At times, you may need to defend your parental sovereignty and advocate for your children's best interest. It's part of the job. Your children need to see you stand up for them. They need to know that you've got their backs and that you're willing to make difficult choices or say uncomfortable things to protect and care for their wellbeing. This is one of the ways that you'll teach them by example how to do that for themselves as they grow into adulthood.

In this context, it's important to repeat that all the ideas and thoughts in this book are just here for you to consider, explore, try out, work with and assess for yourself. None of these ideas are intended to override your parental intuition or your parental sovereignty. May they simply support you in feeling empowered to make the best choices you can for your children from your own intuition about what they need.

PRACTICES FOR EMBRACING OUR ROLE AS NEW PARADIGM PARENTS

Embracing our roles as New Paradigm Parents takes practice. Whether you're a brand-new parent or your kids are older and you've been parenting for a while, you can always explore new ways of being as you and your children learn the world together. As you counteract your own indoctrination into the Power Over Paradigm you may discover the joys of lifelong learning and the magical ways our children can be our teachers, our students and our partners all at the same time. I've suggested these from among my favorite practices to give you a few ideas to support your discovery process. As always, please adapt them to your family's needs.

New Paradigm Parenting: Open Sentences for Co-Parents and Kids

Please refer to the instructions for Open Sentences in the practice section of Chapter 5: Grounding in Gratitude.

Open Sentences to use with your co-parents:

1. The examples and definitions of parenting that I was exposed to as a kid were…
2. Some of the new things I've learned about parenting since I was a child are…
3. One of the significant cultural shifts I hope to see in this coming generation is…

4. Beliefs, ideas and assumptions that I'm concerned my child(ren) will pick up from society are...
5. Some of the core beliefs I want my child(ren)'s worldview to be based on are...

Open Sentences to use with your kids:

1. Something important I've learned about the world is...
2. My favorite way to learn is by...
3. I can count on my parents to...
4. Something big that a lot of people believe but doesn't seem true to me is...
5. A big change that I want to see my generation make is...

Lessons from Mother Nature

Since our children are always learning, let's give them the opportunity to learn from the best teacher of all...Mother Nature. This is a quest to get their growing brains working on learning about important aspects of the natural world instead of cataloging every facet and feature of the industrialized, urban world.

Notice something in the natural world that particularly fascinates your child and geek out with them about it. Dive right in and explore it together, learning everything you can learn about it. It may be a certain animal or group of animals. It may be a natural phenomenon or weather pattern. It may be a body of water or land formation. Let their interests lead the way.

Then, meet those interests with new information and opportunities to connect and explore together. Spend time together in real life with this relative of the natural world. Gather books about it, search for information online, make art about it, play with the ideas around it. Make it fun. Do it with them. Use this learning experience as an opportunity to connect with each other and connect with the living world.

As you explore together, be sure to draw connections to all the relationships that this being or phenomenon is part of (hint: the natural world *is* a web of relationships so everything is connected to everything else). Then follow those connections to the next deep dive and keep learning together.

The amount of time that you spend on any one deep dive will depend on the topic, your child's age and their style of learning. You may spend an hour on a topic, or you may spend several months. But hopefully, the learning will be ongoing, as you follow one interest into another, exploring relationships and connections, discovering how nature works and why, being amazed by the interconnected magic of the living world and feeling your place within it.

Work That Reconnects Games for Kids (and parents too!)

Some of the classic Work That Reconnects practices outlined in *Coming Back to Life* by Joanna Macy and Molly Brown can be shared with your kids to explore and connect with the Thriving Life paradigm. The Systems Game and the Riddle of the Commons are both engaging games that help us understand dynamic living systems by playing them out together. The Council of All Beings is a ritual practice that involves artmaking and imagination, as participants embody different beings from the natural world and speak their concerns to one another. If you have a group of kids who are interested in playing with these ideas, these activities could be fun and enlightening. All three of these practices can both be found in Chapter 8 of *Coming Back to Life* by Joanna Macy and Molly Brown and in the Resource Library of the Work That Reconnects Network website: www.workthatreconnects.org

The Book of Unanswered Questions

One of the parents in my New Paradigm Parenting group shared a practice that she does with her son that I just loved and wanted to share with all of you. It's a great practice for raising kids in the information age and interrupting the impulse to get a quick and superficial answer with our handheld devices. For this family, it was also a way of making bedtime work more smoothly.

She shared that, each night at bedtime, her son would start asking questions. Some big and some small. Entertaining the questions in the moment was stretching out bedtime too long, so she came up with a new plan. She got a little journal to keep by the bedside to write down his questions. Instead of answering the questions in the moment, she would write them down with a commitment to revisit them the next day to explore their answers.

I love how this practice honors his inquisitiveness by making space for it, while also honoring bedtime. Instead of rushing through the answers or brushing off the questions to get him to bed at a certain time she captures the questions and makes time to come back to them later to explore them together.

She shared that this practice has also created an opportunity in their lives for the truly unanswered and unanswerable questions. This brings to my mind this passage from Rainer Maria Rilke that is a vital companion for lifelong learners:

> *"Be patient toward all that is unsolved in your heart and try to love the questions themselves, like locked rooms and like books that are now written in a very foreign tongue. Do not now seek the answers, which cannot be given you because you would not be able to live them. And the point is, to live everything. Live the questions now. Perhaps you will then gradually, without noticing it, live along some distant day into the answer."* [8.6]

9

CREATING CONDITIONS FOR KIDS TO THRIVE

> Do not ask your children
> to strive for extraordinary lives.
> Such striving may seem admirable,
> but it is the way of foolishness.
> Help them instead to find the wonder
> and the marvel of an ordinary life.
> Show them the joy of tasting
> tomatoes, apples and pears.
> Show them how to cry
> when pets and people die.
> Show them the infinite pleasure
> in the touch of a hand.
> And make the ordinary come alive for them.
> The extraordinary will take care of itself.
>
> – William Martin [9.1]

Cultivating a Nurturing Environment

Children respond to and grow from their environment like plants from soil. The physical and energetic conditions we create for them feed into every part of their being and guide their growth. As brand-new beings in the world, they look to the adults in their lives to set the tone and create the atmosphere for their experience. When they are very young, they'll accept and respond to whatever situation they find themselves in with no preconceived notions about what is "normal" or comparisons to any other possible situations.

When my baby was born and for the first three years of her life, she, her father and I lived in a canvas wall tent in the Rocky Mountains of Colorado. My mother was frantic about how *"a baby can't live in a tent!"* But our baby lived quite well in the tent. She had our loving arms, lots of breastmilk and a cozy family bed. She was happy as pie and had no idea that her life was any different than other babies. She was kept warm with a woodstove fire, drank the cleanest water, breathed the freshest air, enjoyed her papa's guitar music, and played on the land to her heart's content.

Babies and children have certain very important needs. They need our love and our arms. They need nourishment and safety. They need laughter and connection. They need to feel emotionally safe and energetically at ease. And they need to experience the grounded presence of loving adults. So long as these needs are met, they can thrive in a variety of situations, even without the extensive list of equipment and gadgets that are marketed to new parents and populate baby shower registries.

Young children are natural, cyclical beings and benefit greatly from rhythm and routine. They do really well when their days move in spirals that they can feel, anticipate and relax into. Their daily rhythm can emerge from their actual needs and be maintained and adapted, as needed, by the adults who care for them. This approach is quite different from imposing schedules and routines onto them because we think "they need structure."

Children need to eat meals and snacks every day. They need to move their little bodies, get their energy out and get outside. They need to have a nap (or maybe two). They need time for exploration and play, alone and with others. They also have certain things that they just love doing every day, like little rituals. As they grow, learn and change, these little rituals will organically emerge and then fade away as new ones are discovered.

Ideally, the adults who care for them will gather all this up and arrange it into a smoothly flowing rhythm that the child can ride through their day. A beautifully crafted daily rhythm gives children some sound anchor points of continuity and familiarity that they can count on each day. It provides a sense of groundedness and stability that helps them stay oriented in their lives.

This does not, at all, mean that every day needs to be exactly the same or that every moment needs to be planned out. There can be plenty of space for variation and spontaneity in each day while maintaining this familiar rhythmic flow. As you tune into the needs of your children and navigate each day with them, you may find that nap time "wants" to shift or that a new daily practice "wants" to be included.

You and your children may also find ways of responding to external conditions (like traveling, holidays, appointments, or other interruptions to the norm) while maintaining the quality of the daily rhythm. For example, even when you're away from home, you can set up a cozy place for naptime and move through your familiar naptime routines. This practice of responsive rhythm will cultivate a strong center of peace, resilience, and adaptability in your children.

Cultivating a nurturing environment for your little ones also includes the physical space you set up for them. Creating a simple, clear, beautiful, creative play and living space for them can make a huge difference in their wellbeing, their moods and the flow of the day. Ideally, their living space would be a kind of sanctuary or haven for them where they can really be themselves and relax, get goofy, explore and be a kid.

Instead of the traditional idea of "babyproofing" your adult living space to protect it from your kids, you can adjust your shared space so that it's more accessible and engaging for your children. You may still want to maintain portions of your living space for adult activities, but the space the kids are living, playing, eating and sleeping in should be comfortable, usable and inviting for them. Learning towers and step stools are great additions to kitchens when your children are young. Child-sized kitchen tools can help them contribute to family meals and feel more included. Climbing structures and playful furniture are great for living rooms and play spaces.

The physical space doesn't have to be elaborate in any way. In fact, rather than filling the space with all the stuff you can find, I encourage you to pay more attention to beauty, quality and usability. Clutter is one of the things that can be really disconcerting to children and leave them feeling disenfranchised. When there are too many toys and too many options, they often feel overwhelmed and get lost in the avalanche of stuff. Try to make sure there isn't *too much* and that each aspect of the space is meaningful, usable, beautiful and beneficial to your children's wellbeing at the specific age they are.

> "The way we nurture our children decides the template for all of their relationships. If we slow down and do the ordinary things like feeding, changing, brushing hair, setting limits, blowing noses, dressing, speaking...with great love, our children learn the art of peaceful partnerships – with great love."
>
> – *Pennie Brownlee* [9.2]

It's All About the Vibe

Babies and young children experience the world and process differently than adults. Instead of gathering and analyzing information with their rational brains, they are exploring and experiencing their world in a much more sensory way. In addition to the five physical senses – sight, hearing, smell, taste and touch – this includes more subtle perceptions of the energetic vibrations in their environment (a.k.a. vibes). Whether we're aware of it or not, our kids are always responding to the energy put out by their caregivers and the energetics in their environment. Calibrating your "vibe" is a more subtle aspect of parenting than attending to your children's physical needs, but it can make a world of difference to their ability to thrive and to the quality of connection experienced within our families.

Just as a horse may perceive and respond to the energetic state of its rider, babies can pick up on what's going on beneath the surface. Even when the horse's rider says all the right words and performs all the correct movements, if the rider is tense, nervous, scared or distracted, the horse will sense it and respond accordingly. Babies and little ones can sense all of that, as well. When their caregivers are not at ease or when their environment is overly stimulating, they will pick up on that and often respond to it by becoming tense and fussy.

Since your little ones will be responding to your energy, the most important thing you can do to make them feel at ease and safe is to regulate your own nervous system. Your energy – whether it's frantic and tense or relaxed and mellow – will create vibrations in your family space that affect your children on a subconscious level. No matter what their physical environment is, *your vibe* is the most critical aspect of that environment and the *main* thing that they'll be responding to. If they're spun out or grumpy or frequently whiny, it's important for you to check your vibe:

> *Are you spinning out about something? Ranting and raving about something that makes you angry? Distracted and panicking over a decision or some upcoming event? Amped up and frantic?*

If so, dial it back. Take a deep breath. Notice the impact you're having on your kids and bring yourself back to your center so you can create some space for your children to be at ease.

Like everything else about parenting, this is a balancing act. We want to create energetic space for our children's early development, but we also can't stop the clock and we don't want to shelter them entirely. It's important for us to have real feelings in front of our kids and to be honest and transparent with them in age-appropriate ways as they grow. Just notice the impacts and adjust your energy accordingly, so you can help them learn to regulate theirs.

In addition to learning from the way we model nervous system regulation, our children learn how to regulate their own emotional and energetic states through the process of co-regulation. Children develop the ability to soothe themselves by being effectively soothed by their caregivers. When they are upset or dysregulated, we can help them by first synching up with their energetic state and then gently bringing our energy to a state of calm and ease, while staying connected with them.

It's not just about staying calm all the time. And it's definitely not about being emotionally detached. Co-regulation is a responsive, dynamic dance in which the adult is in the lead. It begins with meeting the child where they are by acknowledging that they're upset and then rallying to respond with compassion. Then it proceeds in a fluid movement towards calm and ease, a little at a time, as you calm yourself and they, in turn, feel a bit calmer. It usually also involves rocking, singing, holding or gentle words as you communicate in a sensory way to the little body and nervous system that they are safe.

As a nanny, I was frequently able to take over the care of a whiny, defiant, grumpy kiddo (who was more than likely crying for mama) and within minutes of being together have them calm, happy and playful. When I was working as a temp nanny in Portland, I worked in a different house almost every day with kids who had never seen me before. During that time, I cared for over seventy children from the ages of two months to ten years old. Some of them *really* didn't want their parents to leave. They were all used to different styles of care and had different attitudes and ingrained behaviors, some of which were rather challenging. But within about fifteen minutes of mom or dad walking out the door, we inevitably found our groove and proceeded on to have excellent days.

I also happen to be highly successful in putting children and babies to sleep, even if they don't know me or are notoriously difficult to get to bed. In fact, some parents have called me a baby whisperer, as they shake their head in relieved disbelief.

My secret is not so much *what* I do or say, but rather *how* I do it and say it. It's all about the energy (or vibe) I carry when I'm relating with kids. My ability to stay centered, clear, grounded and present creates an energetic environment in which they find it easier to settle and relax. I think of this form of coregulation as a transferring of calm and safety from my energetic field to theirs. The way I recognize and respond to their needs respectfully, while sharing my energy field of *ease* with them, makes them feel safe, seen and held. This is an essential skill for New Paradigm Parenting that I've found to be just as effective with teenagers as it is with babies and toddlers.

Babies and children need a certain amount of energetic spaciousness to grow and develop healthfully. To thrive, they need to be able to be relaxed enough to be curious, to try things out, to follow their own natural rhythms, to listen to their bodies and to get lost in their own imaginations, free from distractions and external pressures. You can carve out a bit of that space for your children through choosing how you relate to them, deciding how you manage your own energy and emotions and adjusting the level of stimulation to which they are exposed.

Cultivating a low stress environment is especially important in the first two to three years of life as your little ones establish their neurological foundations, become aware of who they are and get their feet firmly planted on the Earth. As they grow into their preschool years and beyond, they can handle more and more stimulation. At each stage along the way, you can assess the energetic impacts of stimulation in their lives and make decisions about what feels helpful for your children. If, at any age, your children are showing signs of overwhelm, you can work with them to find age-appropriate ways to dial down the stressors in their environment, physically and energetically.

As adults, we tend to be unaware of how overstimulating our world can be for our children. Because of this, we might have to put some effort into figuring out what level of stimulation is appropriate for our kids so we can shift things in our lives enough to accommodate their need for calm. One of the first things we can do is to assess and mitigate the levels of chaos, fear and panic that leak into their awareness from the adult world of news, current events and all the things that might be worrying or upsetting us.

Calibrating our lives to support thriving kids may also include choosing to mellow out the fast pace of industrialized modern life with its hyper competition for everything from kindergarten spots to the "right" sneakers to the coolest friends. We may even want to minimize exposure to the zany enthusiasm of certain cartoon characters and the excited hype of advertisements. Kids get swept up in all of that very easily, and it can spin them away from their centers. Overexposure to this type of exaggerated stimulation can make it hard for them to stay in touch with their bodies and intuition and may even distort their natural development in ways we don't yet fully understand.

Fulfilling Evolutionary Expectations

When I was pregnant, I was given a copy of a book that completely changed the way I thought about caring for babies and children. In *The Continuum Concept,* Jean Liedloff [9.3] laid out a radically different understanding of what babies need than our conventional "modern" approach provides. Having lived with and among the Yequana people in the deep jungles of South America she was granted the opportunity to witness human beings living and raising children in their natural way outside of the Power Over Paradigm.

The concept around which the book is formed is that human babies have certain natural expectations that have developed over the long continuum of human evolution. We're evolutionarily designed to have these expectations and, when they are unfulfilled, we experience wounding or trauma that leads to negative outcomes throughout our lives. Evolutionary developments and changes are slow, complex and adaptive. They happen in a dynamic relationship between the development of a species and the changing environment over very long periods of time. Since the types of changes our society has experienced in the last few hundred years has drastically outpaced the natural timeline of human evolution, every new baby born continues to have these same evolutionary expectations, whether they are born in a hut in the jungle or a hospital in Manhattan.

These expectations are mostly oriented around the physical process of natural birth and receiving a natural welcoming into a loving, thriving family and community. According to Liedloff's observations, babies require constant physical contact, breastfeeding on cue and loving response to their needs. She talks extensively about the "in-arms" phase between birth and the beginning of crawling or creeping. Instead of putting our babies in cribs and car seats or carriers and strollers, Leidloff recommends that we carry or wear our babies as much as we can so they will feel the warmth, connection and movement of our bodies.

The teachings in that book profoundly impacted me and informed the way I cared for my child, especially in her early years. They also got my wheels turning on this concept of evolutionary expectations. While I'm caring for children, I find myself constantly checking in about how their current situation measures up in the context of their evolutionary expectations.

I imagine human beings have expectations to not only be received into a loving human family, but also to be embraced within the Family of Life beyond their human relatives. I imagine babies' ears are designed to hear the song of the river and that their eyes are meant to gaze upon the twinkling stars and the dancing fire. I imagine they are meant to feel the cool mountain air on their cheeks as they are bundled close to their parent's chest.

When they begin walking, I imagine they are meant to navigate uneven ground with their bare feet, unbound by stiff little sneakers. As they begin to learn about their world, I imagine they are meant to feel and smell the sources of their food, right there in their natural environment. I imagine that they expect to see people of all ages, working hard, creating beauty, and making Life live all around them and that they would naturally emulate those older people, learning the skills of life as they grow.

As you make choices about the type of environment, lifestyle and activities you set up for your children, I invite you to consider this concept. Tune into what you feel your children's evolutionary expectations are and see how you could help fulfill them.

> *"One generation full of deeply loving parents would change the brain of the next generation, and with that, the world."*
>
> – Charles Raison, M.D. [9.4]

Love, Safety and Belonging

Human babies are completely dependent on being nurtured, nourished and protected by the people with whom they belong. We wouldn't survive more than a day if we weren't cared for by the adults who receive us. This evolutionary, physical need extends through our psychology, as social beings, into a need to feel a sense of loving connection, acceptance and emotional safety within a family or group of people.

Optimally healthy brain development in babies and children requires the calmed nervous system created by abundant loving connection.[9.5] They need us to snuggle them and gaze into their eyes when they're babies. They need to be held and carried around and included in the hustle and bustle of the daily lives of the people that love them. They need to bond with trusted adults and siblings and to feel cherished.

In this pivotal time in the human experience, when so much has been damaged and so much is at stake, it is especially important for us, as parents, to create a loving and emotionally safe environment of belonging for our children. Those of us who didn't experience enough love, safety and belonging from our own parents and society when we were little will need to dig deep to give our children what we weren't given.

Fortunately, regardless of whether we received this love from our human parents and society, we have all been nourished and supported by the unfaltering and enduring love of Mother Earth and Father Sky. The radical generosity and fierce love of these more-than-human parents is the source of each breath, every bite of food, each sunrise and every season of growth. As New Paradigm Parents, we can align ourselves with this deep love to support us in becoming part of the generation of "deeply loving parents" that could change the way humans exist on Earth. This isn't about getting it perfect. This is about doing everything we can to open the floodgates of our heart connection for more high-quality love and empowering support to flow through us from the loving Earth and Sky to our children.

As human parents, rooted in this universal love, we have the blessed opportunity to fill our children's lives with deeply nourishing, loving presence and support. The quality of love we cultivate in our children's environment is the fertile ground from which they'll grow and blossom into their fullest expressions of brilliance. That's why it is essential that you make sure your children really know that you love them, thoroughly, deeply, authentically, for who they actually are, all the way through their beings, unconditionally, in the good times and in the hard times. Reinforce that love not just by the words you say but also by the way you show up for them. The way you really see them and are willing to get to know them through all their changes. The way you pay attention to what they have to say. The way you let them try and fail and learn and succeed and the way you root for them all along the way. The way you celebrate and cherish their weird, quirky precious uniqueness. The way you stand by them when all their chips are down.

Beyond unconditional love, it's also essential to cultivate a sense of belonging for our children. Belonging is one of the deepest and most universal human needs. It is directly connected to our evolutionary expectations and our ability to navigate the stressors and complexities of our lives. As social creatures, human beings are meant to be woven into a matrix of relationships to which they're mutually accountable and needed. When this need for belonging is fulfilled, it creates resilience, empowerment, and a profound sense of orientation.

Whether you're raising your children on your own as a single parent or as part of a large family or community, you can cultivate belonging for your children. If you have the blessing of extended family and community, make a practice of calling on and emphasizing these relationships throughout your children's lives. Even without a vibrant family or community, you can foster belonging in your children's lives by connecting them with valued mentors, participating in the care of your neighborhood, school or wider community and getting involved with activities that require building relationships and strengthening connection over time.

Regardless of the choices you make beyond your home, the foundation of belonging can start right there with the bond you create with your children, through mutual care, respect and accountability. Human development scholar, Pam Leo, says *"our effectiveness as parents is in direct proportion to the strength of the bond we have with our child."* [9.6] As you reflect on your own parenting practices and explore applying some of the ideas in this book you, I invite you to check them each against this concept. Pay attention to whether what you're doing increases or decreases your loving connection and bond with your children. Choose to nourish and strengthen that precious bond in every opportunity you get.

Your kids will change a lot. They'll go through a lot of stages and phases. They'll have lots of emotions and ups and downs and ins and outs, some of which you may not understand, from toddler tantrums to young adult life choices. Creating this loving bond and faithfully maintaining it through all the stages of your children's growth will be a foundational part of their overall wellness and development.

> "You do not have to be good.
> You do not have to walk on your knees
> for a hundred miles through the desert repenting.
> You only have to let the soft animal of your body
> love what it loves."
>
> – Mary Oliver [9.7]

Embodiment

In my early twenties I worked full-time at a large daycare center in Flagstaff, AZ. I was the lead teacher in the two-year-olds' room. We had sixteen two-year-olds on our roster! Most of them were there for forty or fifty hours per week. A huge part of my job was training these little ones to ignore and override their soft animal bodies. I had to feed them and bring them to the potty and put them down for nap on a very rigid schedule. For these little ones, I imagine this daycare experience was just the beginning of a long life of learning to ignore themselves in favor of conforming to our mechanized society. When I began to realize what an offense this was to their little beings, I couldn't participate any longer and I left that job, with a heavy place in my heart for all those little ones.

Unfortunately, the kids in that daycare are not the only ones who experience this. Most of us have been trained to override our natural physical cues to conform with society's expectations. I invite you to make space for your kids' sovereign, natural, physical experience and to help them feel a vibrant sense of belonging in their own body as much as possible. Instead of forcing them into prescribed schedules and ways of being, you can help them tune in to their physical needs and let their bodies lead the way.

Natural embodiment is one of the central threads in the consideration of evolutionary expectations.[9.8] Our children come into the world as undeniably embodied beings with wonderfully squishy, soft animal bodies, deeply in tune with their physical needs for nourishment, sleep, cuddles and movement. We can begin fostering their natural embodiment when they're babies by responding attentively to their physical needs, providing natural nourishment, loving arms, and engaging movement when they express themselves by squirming, vocalizing or perhaps giving you that certain look.

With methods like Elimination Communication,[9.9] we can teach them to pay attention to their body's signals for pee and poo even from birth if we have the time and energy to devote to this practice. Even if we don't begin in infancy, we can bring this awareness of embodiment into their potty-training process, helping them to tune into their own inner cues and encouraging their sovereignty and empowerment in responding to them without shame or constraint.

As they grow into crawlers and walkers, we can encourage their continued healthy embodiment by giving them the most natural conditions possible and by allowing them to be guided by their own bodies. We can make space for them to climb and run and move around in all the natural ways their bodies call them too. We can let them test their limits and stretch their abilities without being overly restrictive. We can let them go barefoot as much as possible and choose shoes that allow their feet to develop naturally and support their posture correctly.

We can even let them regulate the amount of food they eat and the amount and timing of their sleep. I know this part sounds a little radical. How could a child possibly know how much they should eat? Or when they should sleep? What kind of chaos could this cause? I've observed many parents putting a lot of energy into trying to control the amount and timing of their children's food and sleep. Often this battle becomes a central conflict between parents and their children. But little bodies know what they need. In partnership with adults who honor this awareness, healthy rhythms and reasonable parameters can be developed that work way more smoothly than the imposition of rigid expectations onto the ever-changing embodied beings in our care.

If children are hungry, they will eat. All you need to do is provide healthy food throughout the day at reasonable times. As your children learn how to tune into how much food they need to feel truly satisfied, it may mean that some days they eat more than other days. This allows for times of taking a lot of nutrients in to prepare for growth spurts and leaner times that allow for other forms of development, cleansing or, sometimes, fending off illnesses. I always like to ask kids, *"does your belly feel full?"* before moving on from meal or snack time. This encourages them to pause and feel the sensations in their body.

If children are tired, they will sleep. Your job is to create the conditions for them to drift into sleep naturally within the reasonable needs and schedule of the rest of the people in your family. The timing and amount of their sleep will fluctuate to some degree. Instead of requiring sleep at certain times you can establish quiet times during the day and a bedtime at night for them to rest, read or listen to gentle music until their natural sleep takes hold.

With each stage and phase, consider how you can support your children's natural embodiment by supporting them to find their own healthy relationship with eating, sleeping, hydrating, going potty, movement and exercise, play, cuddle time, alone time, wakeful rest and all their other bodily needs. By paying attention to their cues and using your adult foresight, experience and understanding of their needs you can formulate healthy rhythms and parameters that will work well for them while teaching them to follow their own internal cues. When their needs are met in this way, your days will be smoother, you'll learn together what it takes to be healthfully human and you'll teach your children to honor their precious animal bodies throughout their lives.

Protecting Children's Natural Health

Most children are born with a vibrant and robust natural health. It is a precious gift. As we raise them to contribute to Thriving Life, a big part of our responsibility is to protect that natal health against the onslaught of modern industrialized life. If our children are born with health challenges, this mission is even more important. Our commitment to protecting our children's natural health will often require us to go against the mainstream. At times we may be required to advocate for our children and stand up for their right to natural health against the many influences and forces that could degrade and damage it.

But the most important way we can protect their lifelong health is to provide them with a strong foundation in the early months and years of their lives. The environment, foods and activities they experience as babies, toddlers and young kids are literally the building blocks for their bodies and brains. On a physical level, this time is our precious opportunity to nourish our children with the best quality materials and resources for the development of their muscles, bones, metabolisms, endocrine systems, neural pathways and everything else that goes into the beings they are becoming.

On a psychological level, this is our opportunity to establish rhythms and habits for natural self-care that will be deeply embedded into their awareness for the rest of their lives. The food they eat as children will strongly influence their adult food patterns. They'll carry a subconscious connection with the flavors, sensations, and comfort foods of their early years. These patterns are intricately woven into their biochemical expectations, emotions, sense of fulfillment, and cultural needs.

Any adult who has tried to alter their diet (for health or weight loss, for example) can attest to the power of these lifelong patterns. When it comes to food choices, there is something at play that is much stronger than simple, rational decision making. Many adults who try to change their diets often even experience symptoms of addiction and withdrawal as they go through the painful process of disengaging from unhealthy patterns they may have developed in childhood. As parents, we can offer our children the healthiest possible food habits and patterns as a gift to the adult they will become; a gift that honors the miracle of their natural health.

Health can seem complicated and confusing in these times, especially with all the different perspectives, advice and marketing that bombard us. But most children will thrive with simple natural care and nourishment. When it comes to staying healthy, nature generally knows best. In making decisions for your children's lifestyle, the best rule of thumb is to keep it all as natural as possible with minimal intervention so nature can guide the way. If it's possible for you to start from conception and carry this practice on through birth and throughout their childhoods, that's wonderful. If you're already well into your parenting journey, you can use this guidance to gradually shift your family practices for food, lifestyle, exercise and health care to become more and more natural, as you're able.

Along this natural health journey, it's helpful to become knowledgeable and resourced in natural health care practices. If possible, finding a holistic pediatrician or natural health practitioner to work with can be a great support. As you develop your awareness and skills in natural health empowerment, you'll become an informed patient and advocate for your children. Through this process, you'll learn how to engage conventional medicine critically and use its valuable and sometimes life-saving skills and techniques in strategic ways that support your family's overall natural health, rather than allowing it to run the show.

To care for and protect our kids' health we have to be aware of and alert to the ways in which their health may be threatened, even by seemingly normal parts of mainstream life. Toxins in food and toys, or sprayed on grass, or in certain pharmaceuticals can have significant deleterious effects on our children's brain development, reproductive health, mental health and other aspects of their long-term health. As their guardians and advocates, it's up to us to do our research and be as informed as possible about the choices we're making on their behalf.

Modern mainstream society promotes the illusion that all these influences are inevitable and mostly benign. We're made to believe that we don't really have a choice about most of these things and that it's silly to worry about them or to concern ourselves with trying to know too much about what our children are being exposed to. As good citizens and consumers, we're meant to remain naive about the causes and effects of Business As Usual, even when we can clearly trace the link between our society's most common health issues and the commonly used toxins that cause them. Breaking free of this imposed denial is an important aspect of our paradigm shift to a Thriving Life Paradigm. Being empowered around your children's health and modeling that empowerment for them can go a long way to support their wellbeing in a world that is not designed to care for their best interest.

Diving into this topic can quickly become overwhelming so I encourage you to pace yourself and make the changes that you're able to make without panicking about the ones you may not be able to make. As you work to reduce toxic exposure for your children, it's important to create natural support in their lives by bringing in more whole foods nourishment and using natural herbal remedies to tend to your children's baseline health, build their immune systems and support their vitality.

Our children will learn the most about caring for their personal health by the way we care for *our* personal health. It's our actions, not our words, that leave indelible impressions on our kids. This can be a huge commitment and even a terrifying obstacle for many parents. As we commit to caring for our children's health and modeling healthy behavior for them, we may have to confront ingrained patterns, traumas and wounds that we've been carrying for decades. Again, be gentle with yourself and try to welcome this as an opportunity to deepen your own healing. Often our kids can be the inspiration we need to align our own selves with Thriving Life.

When it comes to nourishment, for example, this practice extends beyond the food we choose to feed them and into *how we eat*. Are we rushing? Feeling guilty? Overeating? Undereating? Are we grateful for our food? Relaxed when we're eating? Enjoying the food? Chewing it well? These subtle aspects of diet will be passed from parent to child, so they are worth considering. Celebration, enjoyment and a sense of ease around food are all important parts of a healthy diet.

As our children are learning about holistic natural health and self-care, it's also important for us to model authentic appreciation for our bodies. We want to teach them *and show them* that it's special to be in a body. We want them to feel that their body is perfect, beautiful and wonderful exactly the way it is. We want them to have a sense of the sanctity of their own bodies and learn how to care for them as the precious gifts they are. While they're kiddos, we help them learn how to do this by making healthy choices, establishing healthy patterns and teaching them the skills they'll need to care for themselves. At the same time, we're modeling for them how to carry on that commitment to self-care throughout their lives by being adults who prioritize our own wellness.

As I mentioned before, health can be complicated and we can't control everything, so it's important not to freak out about all this. I encourage you to make the best conscious, informed choices you're able to about the things that you can choose and to release attachment and anxiety about the things you don't have control over. This is especially important as our kids get older. If they've been eating well at home and cultivating a taste for nourishing foods throughout their early childhood, they'll be able to handle extraneous influences and random junk food in their teen years without taking them on as their own pattern. Most children stray from their family diet during their teenage and young adult years and then return to it to some extent as they settle into adulthood. Continuing to support their natural health in the ways we can, and to model adult wellness are the best things we can do for them as we gradually loosen the reins so they can make their own choices.

PRACTICES FOR CREATING CONDITIONS FOR KIDS TO THRIVE

Creating conditions for kids to thrive within a society that is not designed for thriving requires a delicate balance in our households and in our relationships. It means making conscious choices when we're able to and letting go of attachment or tension when the choices we want to make are not available to us. These practices can help you reflect on the conditions you are creating for your kids and offer some powerful ideas to play with while you support your children to thrive! Please adapt them as needed to meet your family's needs.

Creating Conditions for Kids to Thrive: Open Sentences for Co-Parents and Kids

Please refer to the instructions for Open Sentences in the practice section of Chapter 5: Grounding in Gratitude.

Open Sentences to use with your co-parents:

1. In this phase of growth, the daily/weekly rhythm that seems to work best for our kids is...
2. I notice the sense of connection I feel with our kids increase when... (decrease when...)
3. Some of the ways that we are modeling healthy living in our household are...
4. Some ways we could improve our family's natural health are...
5. We could increase the sense of love, safety and belonging our children experience by...

Open Sentences to use with your kids:

1. The parts of the day (or week) I most look forward to are...
2. I know I've had a good night's sleep when...
3. Some of the ways Mama Earth and Papa Sky take care of me are...
4. Some of the people who love me a lot and are really looking out for me are...
5. My body feels healthy and strong when...

Family Rhythm

Designing and experimenting with family rhythms is like dancing. It begins by noticing the natural tendencies and needs of the various members of your family. It then moves into a dynamic and ongoing responsiveness to those needs, creating patterns, like dance steps, that guide the movement of your family in ways its members can count on without feeling restrained. These daily and weekly rhythms will adapt and shift as your children grow, and as different needs arise. In this practice, you'll be reflecting on your family rhythm and the ways you could fine-tune it to be smoother and more nourishing for all members of the family, while also coming further into alignment with the Thriving Life Paradigm.

Your family rhythm will include the things you are doing and the things you are *not doing.* Just like in dance and music, stillness (or silence) is an essential aspect of healthy rhythm. Make sure there is adequate nourishing space designed into your family rhythm, including regular screen-free time, open hang out time, solo time, together time, nature time, etc.

Begin by writing down the members of your household and listing their perceived needs beside their names (for example: twice a day naptime for the toddler, exercise for mama three times per week, date night for parents every other week, etc.) Once this list is written, take a moment to notice and circle any of the needs that you notice are not being met well in your current routines.

Then write out a rough outline of your current daily/weekly routines and start thinking through ways that you could adjust and fine-tune them to create a more responsive rhythm that meets more of the needs with more grace. For example: complete lunch by 1:30pm so toddler can get their second nap in before it gets too late in the day, trade off dinner prep with partner to make time for exercising, ask grandma to schedule a special visit with the baby every other week so we can have a date night, etc.

Some questions for reflection:

1. What systems and practices could be worked in to make your daily/weekly rhythm more efficient and less stressful?
2. How can you anticipate various needs of the members of your household and meet them in a way that prioritizes mutual thriving?
3. What little daily or weekly rituals would bring more connection, joy and beauty into your family flow?

Walk Like a Duck

This is a simple movement game that you can play with kids to free up your bodies and explore the ways they can move. Rip up little pieces of paper and write the name of a different type of animal on each piece (for example: duck, elephant, horse, whale, etc.). Depending on the age of the kids, they could help with this part. Take turns randomly selecting a piece of paper from the collection and mimicking the way the animal moves. The person who selects the animal can start the movement, taking a moment to really get into it, and then the rest of the group can join in. Spend some time moving like a herd or a flock and really feel into the different ways our bodies can move and how it feels inside. Have fun. Get silly. Try different movements. For an extra credit bonus challenge, play this game with a group of pre-teens or teens.

Eating Rainbows

You could embrace this practice not only to improve your family's diet, but also as a learning adventure you can share with your kids. You could adapt it in a variety of ways to help you focus on increasing the whole foods in your family's diet. Get curious and adventurous as you and your children learn about natural foods, try incorporating new foods into your meals and maybe even try growing some food together. Here's one version to play with:

Introduce the idea that whole foods come directly from the Earth and are extra good for our bodies. They have all the nutrients that our bodies need to grow strong and healthy, especially when we eat a wide variety of them. Tell them how the different colors of the natural foods mean they carry different special nutrients to help our bodies, so it's a good idea to eat a rainbow of natural foods each week. (Be sure to make it very clear that this only counts for natural whole foods, not processed and dyed foods. Depending on the age of your children and their interest level, this could lead into a bigger exploration of why food companies dye foods and the effects of food colorings on our health.)

Put a poster up on the wall with a blank rainbow drawn onto it (just the arcs, without the color). Get some seed catalogs with pictures of colorful vegetables. Then start adding in different colorful vegetables into your meals. Each time you eat something new, your children can look through the catalogs to find a colorful picture of the food and cut it out. Then they can paste it up onto the rainbow. As you eat more and more colorful foods, the rainbow will fill in and become more and more beautiful.

You can take this opportunity to learn about the natural food cycle and how the nutrients in these natural foods are actually just stored up sunshine and loving nourishment from the soil. You can explore the properties of each food to discover which vitamins and minerals it carries and the ways that it supports our health. Take note of which foods you and your children really like and which ones you're not so fond of. Just because it's natural and healthy doesn't mean that you have to like it. If you didn't like a particular food, you may want to experiment and explore different ways of preparing it to see if you can come up with a more enjoyable meal.

The key to this whole practice is to stay open and curious as you and your children expand your horizons and improve your diet in natural ways that support joy, health and vitality.

10

IT TAKES A VILLAGE

One of the most universally known, recognized, and repeated parenting proverbs is said to have emerged from the community-based cultures of the African continent:

"It takes a village to raise a child."

Often attributed to the Igbo and Yoruba people, this proverb is one version of many similar sayings shared among African cultures that speak to the power and importance of raising children in community.[10.1] Among cultures around the world that have not been entirely assimilated into Power Over Paradigm society, care for children is often distributed across a complex matrix of intergenerational relationships and extended family. Grandparents and other elders usually play a significant role in caring for and mentoring young ones.

In his book *The Healing Wisdom of Africa,* Malidoma Somé[10.2] shares about how the Dagara people of West Africa traditionally welcome newborn babies and care for children as a whole community. He says, *"Throughout children's life in the village there is a strong message that they belong to a community of people who value them almost beyond anything else. It starts when grandparents participate in the birthing and are the first to* hold the newborn." He goes on to describe the special bond that develops between the very young and the very old, highlighting special rituals and cultural practices that encourage this bond. He notes that this relationship is not only with a child's biological grandparents but is woven broadly throughout the many families of the village.

In his description of a traditional birth ritual that he attended in his village he says a group of elder women were tending to the mother during labor while chanting to the soon-to-be-born baby. Their chants alternated between a litany of the names of ancestors and messages of encouragement for the baby. One of these messages was, *"You have come to a crossroads. The light you see in front of you is the light of the village that awaits you."*

In cultures such as this, the community holds the wellbeing of each child in their loving embrace from conception through birth and into childhood. As children grow in this environment, I imagine they feel a strong sense of belonging and responsibility to their community.

Loss of Community in the Industrialized World

Unfortunately, to most modern people, this form of community sounds more like a fairy tale than anything real. Intact, land-based, multi-generational community has been one of the biggest casualties of the Power Over Paradigm and the Industrial Growth Society. As industrial extractive capitalism and colonization has ravaged the world, it has replaced connection, mutual reliance and continuity with obsessive individualism, competition and short-term profit, leaving us increasingly isolated with each generation.

Even in the last few generations of industrialized society, there has been a drastic decline in the intergenerational, extended family and community support in caring for children. It has become more and more common for young adults to head out and start a life for themselves somewhere far from their childhood homes and families. By the time many of us become parents, it's not uncommon for us to live a great distance from our children's grandparents, aunties, uncles and cousins. With this increase in mobility and the growing instability in jobs and real estate, there has also been a breakdown in the sense of community once experienced in our towns and neighborhoods. And, in the early 2020s, as the Coronavirus pandemic took the world in its grip, many families lost the sense of connection and socialization that they had created for themselves and their kids through school, extra-curricular activities and friends.

Many of us feel a deep sense of loss and longing as we become parents and put forward our best efforts to raise our children without the support of extended family and community. Not only do we find it physically and emotionally taxing to try to be *everything* for our kids, but we often have a nagging feeling inside that raising kids like this just isn't right.

As social creatures, human beings are designed to rely on real-life, long-term, interactive relationships with other human beings *(and the more-than-human world)*. For healthy growth and development, we actually *need* to be in relationships that require us to build trust with one another over time, learn from each other, and rely on each other in countless big and small ways. From securing an adequate food supply to experiencing a sense of meaning in our lives, individual humans have never been able to go it alone. The community-based experience of being "in it together" with our people is a necessary part of the human design.

One of the places that this social intimacy and interdependence is most important is in raising children. Children need this complex web of relationships right from the very beginning of their lives so they can learn about their world and their place within it. They need to get to know and learn from many different mature adults and elders to develop into mature adults and to understand the options on the path before them. They also need to connect with, have fun with and struggle with other children of many ages to discover their sense of self and find their way forward within their peer group. And they need the joy, sense of purpose and compassion that comes from caring for and mentoring those who are younger than themselves.

Parents need all these relationships to be in place too! This notion that one or two parents, working full-time jobs and making ends meet within the Industrial Growth Society, should be able to raise their kids all on their own is ludicrous. We can't do it all, and we shouldn't have to try. We're meant to be held within a vibrant, interconnected community of people of all ages who deeply care about us and our kids.

When I was getting ready to become a mom, I longed for community and sought it out to the best of my ability. My daughter's father and I drove across the United States multiple times looking for a community of people within which we could raise our children with the care and continuity we craved. The prospects were bleak. But after about three years of searching and praying, we were incredibly fortunate to be guided to a small town with many other young parents, kiddos and elders. We felt drawn in and welcome immediately.

This town wasn't an intentional community, and it didn't function as an intact, holistic, traditional community. It was just a town full of a bunch of wayward deserters and outcasts from the Industrial Growth Society. We shared many common aspirations for *something different* than the status quo. We also carried a fair amount of baggage and wounds from our time *out there* in the world of Business As Usual. Over the years, we struggled to manifest our visions and maintain healthy relationships with each other (sometimes unsuccessfully).

While my once starry-eyed hopes of community didn't come to fruition exactly as I had dreamed, the other parents in the community and I managed to weave some kind of thread of continuity for our children by investing ourselves in these relationships and trying our best to stick with them over many years. Our children grew up feeling held, loved, cared for, understood and watched over by many "aunties" and "uncles" and adopted grandparents. They grew up caring for their little "cousins" and being part of a continuum of life that was bigger than any of our individual households. Even in this much-less-than-perfect scenario, it has been amazing to see and experience the benefits of raising children within a web of long-term intergenerational relationships.

For me, one of the fun reflections of this is what my child wanted for her 16th birthday party after a year of being away from this small town: *a big multigenerational potluck.* She wanted to hold babies, talk with old people, and feel held and witnessed within an extended network of people who had known her and paid attention to her growth since she was inside my belly. That's what she missed and longed for after a year in the city. That's one of the ways I can tell our efforts had a positive effect on her.

Working With What We've Got

It's easy to feel discouraged and frustrated when we look around and see that our lives are lacking the rich community experience we long for. But regardless of our circumstances, we're not raising our children in a vacuum. There *are* other people in your children's lives and, depending on the choices you make as they grow up and the energy you put into cultivating these relationships, they could grow into some version of long-term continuity and support.

Every child is shaped by multiple influences as they're growing. In the Industrial Growth Society, they often come from impersonal media, corporate or institutional sources, rather than long-term personal relationships. You won't have control over many of the influences in your children's lives but as a parent, you can make a conscious effort to gather some real, live human beings around you and your children and to foster relationships with them over time. As your children grow, you can intentionally build relationships with the parents of their friends, your neighbors, or other families who share your family's interests or philosophies, as well as those who carry different perspectives and philosophies. You can also look for ways to align your children with high quality mentors and teachers who nourish their interests.

In a society that values short-term gain and transactional relationships, it is a truly counter-cultural endeavor to cultivate authentic long-term relationships with the people in our children's lives, whether they are neighbors, teachers, nannies, etc. But that is one of the things that makes it so beautiful and meaningful! Here in the middle of all this loss and emptiness, we can create beauty and plant seeds for the Thriving Life Paradigm by stretching beyond the transaction and building connection with the people in our lives. As we do this throughout our children's young lives, we teach them to do it as well. As they grow, we may find that they too continue looking for ways to connect, build resilience and gather community around them, within whatever circumstances they find themselves.

For elementary and middle school, my daughter attended a very small charter school in our very small town. She and all the other students called their teachers by their first names and got to know them on a personal level as we would see them around town and participate in social events with them outside school. In addition to this, I was actively involved in the school and made an extra effort to connect with each of the teachers personally to get to know them. I would check in with them regularly, listen to their challenges, share in their joys and express my gratitude to them often. I saw them and respected them as very active influences in my child's life, and I valued and cared for them as such. In turn, my child grew to love and appreciate her teachers as real human beings with depth and character.

When she transferred to a conventional high school that was 15 times the size of her original K-12 school, she took this sense of connection and valuing her teachers with her. In our new city, I wasn't involved in the high school community at all. She began the school year all on her own, navigating the new situation and cultural expectations of large-scale institutionalized education with her own inner compass. When I attended the parent conference night about two months into her first school year, she had already developed meaningful connections with her teachers and was truly excited to introduce me to them. In this short amount of time, she had become friends with many of her teachers and developed a rich quality of mutual appreciation with them. Over the course of the next three years, she continued to cultivate these connections and build on that mutual respect. Each time I had an opportunity to see her interact with her teachers, I was moved by the way she carried her appreciation of community with her and by her capacity to create it in some way everywhere she goes.

As you assess your own situation, begin to consider how you can gather support around yourself and your children. Think about how you can strengthen relationships with the other parents in your local community and with the teachers and mentors in your children's lives. Think about how you can make space in your life to learn more about them and about the ways that you can support them and build trust with them over the long term. Notice the people that your children connect with on some level and stretch into forming relationships with them, even if you feel shy or wouldn't necessarily be friends with them if it weren't for your children.

Community is about relationships and mutual reliance over the long-term. Even though very few of us have inherited a fully functional, intact community culture, we can begin to piece it together slowly over time by nurturing these relationships and allowing our children to experience their benefits.

Finding Your Place in Your Children's Care Team

As a parent, you have an extraordinary amount of influence over your kids. It's important to be aware of your impact and to work to avoid the unhealthy patterns that could result from it. From a third-party perspective, as a daycare provider, nanny and teacher, I have been amazed to witness how a child is so dramatically affected by the presence of their parents. A child's personality can appear to turn on a dime when one of their parents enters a room. In many cases, they immediately fall into playing out patterns established in that relationship and lose sight of their own agency and groundedness. I also notice that parents don't usually realize they have this effect on their children. The parent/child bond is precious and special. If it's cared for with awareness, it can be a source of great wellness in a child. However, if the parent doesn't make space for other adults in their children's lives, dysfunction and codependency can develop.

Even if you're the primary parent, you are only a part of your children's care team. It's important to encourage bonding with other adults and to allow trusted adults to support your children in ways that you can't. Let your children develop special connections with mentors, teachers, aunties, uncles and grandparents. It is a liberating and beautiful experience to let go of the notion that you have got to be everything for your child.

If you're relatively new to working with and caring for children, I encourage you to seek out and learn from people who have more experience than you. No one besides you knows exactly what *you* need to know to parent your children. But professionals that have focused their careers on facilitating learning and encouraging childhood development can offer perspectives, experiences and skills to benefit you and your child.

A big part of contributing to your children's care team is consciously uplifting the other adults in your kids' life. Even you don't feel drawn to being close friends with some of them, I encourage you to make the effort to learn about the other adults who love and support your children. Try to understand what they do for the children, what perspectives they bring forward, and what their challenges and strengths are. Look for ways to support them. Find ways to cooperate with and learn from them.

When adults are working together respectfully on behalf of a child, the child gets the message that they are loved and valued. This doesn't mean that the adults have to agree about everything or be completely on the same page. It certainly doesn't mean that the adults do everything the same way. It *does* mean that we make space for the other adults in our children's lives and are mindful not to let jealousy, pettiness, sabotage or any other expressions of ego interfere with what is best for the child. When differences can be held with respect, they become the strength in the situation, providing a child with multiple examples and possibilities of mature adulthood.

Personally, I've found it to be a great joy to see the special spark that is kindled between my daughter and the other adults in her life. I'm delighted to know that she has an entourage! Besides me, she has her dad, her stepmom, her stepdad, her stepdad's ex-wife, two biological aunties and countless community aunties, an adult cousin who loves her dearly, loving grandparents (from every biological and step side), and a whole community of parents, elders and teachers who have supported her through her childhood. And beyond all these wonderful people, there are my own three best friends from childhood. They live all the way across the country, but my daughter has seen them at least once a year throughout her whole life and they each love her fiercely.

I love that each one of these people brings their own unique perspectives and skills to her life. I love stepping back and witnessing these relationships unfold over the years. I love that she knows that there are people in just about every corner of the United States (and beyond) who love her and are paying attention to her milestones as she grows.

Centering Your Child's Wellbeing as You Co-Parent

All this making-space-for-other-adults is especially important when it comes to working with your children's other parent(s). In the case of divorce, philosophical disagreements, or estrangement, this can be particularly difficult. In these cases, it's *even more* important to consciously put the child's wellbeing at the center. The mutual love that these disparate adults have for this child has the potential to push each of the adults to learn, grow and mature beyond their own fear-based self-interest, into adults capable of tending to the healthy growth of the children in their lives and cooperating across their differences.

Whether you're together as a couple or not, you're not going to agree with your co-parent(s) about everything. You're going to have your different ideas about parenting and your different styles. You'll have different strengths and gifts to bring to parenting. You'll also have different hang ups, short-comings, traumas and triggers.

To center your children's wellbeing, you'll need to see beyond these differences and learn to work across them. It's important to distinguish what's necessary for your child to be safe and well from your preferences, personal feelings and parenting styles. This can be tricky. You may be really convinced that your way is the "right" way. You may be making very intentional choices in your approach to parenting that you believe are serving your children's wellbeing. For example, you may think the methods and ideas in this book are the best way to support your children's wellbeing. And I agree with you; that's why I wrote them down. But I also know that expecting the other adults in your children's life to fully agree with you, or imposing your ideas on them in a way that causes a breakdown of trust within those relationships, is not in your children's best interest.

In the case of conflict with the other parent(s) it is *absolutely essential* not to disparage them in front of your children. When children are young, their identity and their sense of safety is entangled with the identity and wellbeing of their parents. When parents are at odds with each other, fighting and tearing each other down, it can feel like an internal battle for a child. It can feel as if two parts of themselves are in conflict. When one parent spews off insults about the other parent, children can often take those assaults personally, as if they themselves were being attacked or assuming that there is something wrong with them personally. Beyond that, when those other parents are doing well, they'll be much more able to support your children's wellbeing. So, hold them in a good light, look for ways to make it possible for them to thrive and support them to the best of your ability.

When the children are reasonably safe, the main focus of co-parenting should be on cultivating mutually respectful relationships that uplift and support the wellbeing and autonomy of each parent. If you have an emotionally safe relationship with your co-parents in which each of you feels respected, you can talk about and explore parenting concepts and choices. If that foundation is not there, it's usually more important to foster it through respecting differences than it is to try to force any specific parenting issue. Over time, that respect will generally go further in giving you a foundation to tend to bigger things.

Over many of the years of my daughter's childhood, her father and I lived in the same small town. We had very different styles of parenting and different lifestyle choices. We had a weekly schedule in which she was with her dad for some days and with me for others. Sometimes, we would run into each other at a school event or a party or some other social gathering and she would get momentarily confused about whose rules she was following. Occasionally she would ask me for permission for something (to eat cake or something like that) and if it was her dad's day I would defer to her dad's rules and redirect her to check in with him.

This was challenging at times because I have really strong opinions about parenting and what choices best serve my child's wellbeing in regard to styles of communication, emotional fluency, dietary choices, media and consumerism and more. But I knew that her dad's autonomy and worth was also a big factor in her wellbeing, so I made a conscious decision to uphold it.

This choice and direction came from some very strong spiritual guidance I received while we were going through our divorce when our child was three years old. Her dad was struggling with alcoholism and out of work. We were deeply in debt. I had no money and no prospects for work but had to take care of our child on my own for a while. One of the options in front of me was to go the route of filing for full custody and demanding child support. I was hurt and angry and there was a small part of me that wanted to do that. Many people in my life were telling me that I should.

But when I tuned into what was best for her, I received strong intuitive guidance not to choose that path. I knew that her dad was struggling and that he wouldn't be able to pay child support at that point in his life. I knew that if I chose that path, I'd be setting him up for failure and a downward spiral that would degrade his sense of self-worth and ultimately rob my child of having a solid, empowered father. She needed him to be strong. He is, after all, half of her.

This guidance showed me that her self-worth was intricately bound with his worth and that for her to thrive, I had to hold him in loving compassion and high regard. Although it was challenging at times, this understanding gave me the patience and courage to cultivate a close friendship with him in the years after our divorce. Fortunately, he received similar guidance and was able to meet me there in the midst of that hard work.

Part of this choice had to do with my awareness of his birth family trauma and how a similar situation had played out when his parents had divorced when *he* was three. I made a conscious choice not to follow that same path and repeat the pattern all over again. I hoped that it would give him the freedom he needed to grow into the dad our child needed. Fortunately, it did indeed.

It's important to note that in this scenario, her dad loved her with all his heart and was not in any way dangerous or harmful to her. If your children are in danger and experiencing mental or physical abuse, it is essential that you draw a firm line to protect them. It is not always possible to co-parent effectively. Sometimes, the other parent is mentally unstable or abusive. You need to determine if this is the case and if so, to draw a strong boundary, sometimes by limiting parental access and privileges through a court order. However, this type of action should be reserved for serious situations in which your children's safety is at risk, not differences in lifestyles and parenting choices or hard times that are within reason.

It can be hard to know where that line is. This is where your personal work and self-reflection is the key. If you are experiencing trauma related to this relationship, it may skew your perception in one way or another.

You may be overreacting to differences that are actually within reason because they trigger old wounds. These differences may make you feel powerless and anxious. They may trigger feelings about your own self-worth. You may just be feeling angry and sad that things didn't work out the way you wanted them to. In these cases, you need to do the work of separating out your own adult feelings so you can see your children's situation more clearly. Are they ok? Are they safe in the other parent's care? Your work is to see the whole picture and trust that the value of them developing their own relationship with their other parent outweighs the areas in which that parent may not match your ideal. Then, you can focus your energy and attention on *your* parenting and do your best to meet your children's needs by being the most present, attentive and loving parent you can be.

Trauma can work the other way too. If you are having a trauma response regarding your children's other parent, you might underestimate the degree of danger your children are in. This is common in cases of abuse. If you have been a victim of physical or emotional abuse, you may be operating with some conditioning that excuses or allows abusive behavior. In some cases, this can cause you fail to see how bad or risky a situation really is. Trauma can also cause you to feel paralyzed and unable to do anything about a dangerous circumstance.

If it is unclear to you where this line should be drawn and whether your children are *actually* in danger with their other parents, please seek support and perspective from a trusted counselor, friend, or family member who is emotionally stable and mature.

Gathering Support Around Your Parenting

Your children are not the only ones who need the support of a community. You need it too! This parenting thing is hard work, and you deserve to feel held and supported as you traverse it.

Over the years, I've found great solace in my relationships with other parents. I've sought out and cherished connections with parents who have kids older than mine. In these friendships, I've been able to observe their relationships with their kids and talk with them about the challenges, crossroads and insights they've experienced. It has been an enormous relief to be able to call someone with years more experience than me when I find myself in a moment of panic or confusion.

I've also sought out and built relationships with parents who have kids the same age as mine and younger and share some of my parental leanings, styles and intentions. We don't all parent in exactly the same way and there are many differences in the choices and approaches we've taken over the years. But it has been a profound blessing to navigate this uncharted terrain of conscious parenting alongside others who are also trying their best and are able to reflect on the process and experience of raising children consciously.

As you venture into New Paradigm Parenting (and any other aspects of conscious parenting that call to you) I encourage you to try to intentionally gather a community of other parents around you who are also cultivating the skills of conscious parenting. When we're surrounded by the status quo, this paradigm-shifting work can often feel like shoveling against the tide. To ease that stress and lessen our fatigue, it's important to be in relationship with others who are also dedicated to this work so we can feel connected to the shifting tide of parents who are seeking a new way for themselves and their children.

As you engage with the content and practices in this book, I hope you feel inspired to reach out to other parents to form study groups, practice groups, playgroups and discussion groups that support your New Paradigm Parenting practice. My hope is that you're inspired to gather a small group of parents around you and start building a deep quality of trusting, connected, conscious support among yourselves. Ideally, this group would include your actual partners in parenting, your co-parents and the parents who are already in your children's lives. The process of gathering this group may also help you discover new connections that you would only make because of your shared interest in raising children for Thriving Life.

Whether the relationships are old or new, I hope they nourish you deeply over the long-haul of your parenting experience and that you feel supported and cared for in the precious work you are doing to care for this next generation.

PRACTICES FOR IT TAKES A VILLAGE

Cultivating community around our parenting experience and in our children's lives can be challenging, to put it gently. These practices can help you understand and relate to the concepts shared in this chapter and provide some ideas for you to experiment with in your own life. Please adapt them, as needed, to meet your family's needs.

It Takes a Village: Open Sentences for Co-Parents and Kids

Please refer to the instructions for Open Sentences in the practice section of Chapter 5: Grounding in Gratitude.

Open Sentences to use with your co-parents:

1. When I tune into the community of relations gathered around me and my kids, I notice and feel...
2. Even though our community connection may not be perfect, some things I really appreciate about the level of community and connection we do experience are...
3. The ways in which I feel disappointment, loss and longing in relation to our community connections are...
4. Some ways I could improve my relationship and ability to co-parent with my children's other parent(s) are...
5. Some ways I could strengthen the sense of belonging within the community connections our family already has are...

Open Sentences to use with your kids:

1. Some of my favorite adults and other kids in my life are...
2. Besides my parents, some of the adults I know I can count on to help me out are...
3. A cool thing I learned from an older kid was...
4. One of the times I helped out a younger kid was...
5. When I help other people, I feel...

Mentoring Across the Ages

This practice is an invitation to seek out and cultivate intergenerational mentoring relationships for your kids (and yourself). Mentors are not just teachers. They're people we get to know over time and with whom we build relationships based on learning and care. Engaging in being mentored or mentoring other people is a rich experience that deepens our sense of community and belonging.

Begin by finding out what your kids want to learn. Then, seek out adults with those specific skills, talents or expertise. Invite them to begin a mentorship or apprenticeship with your child. Be sure to honor their time and attention in a way that feels meaningful to them (possibly monetary compensation or trade). If it feels like a good fit, do your best to support and nurture this relationship over an extended period. Relationships that span many years and phases of growth are most beneficial.

When looking for mentors, seek out people with perspectives and backgrounds that differ from the adults in your family. This gives your children the invaluable opportunity to develop meaningful relationships across difference and to see the world through a wider lens than you are able to offer.

Simultaneously, find out what kind of mentoring your kids could provide to others and connect them. You could also start mentoring another person or find your own mentor and share about that experience with your kids. This practice is all about intentionally building mentorship and apprenticing relationships into your lives in all the ways you can.

Pitching in Together

Service is an excellent path towards community. When we're in service, we get connected. When you pitch in together with others, you usually meet people quickly, learn more about what's going on in our world and start to feel the sense of belonging that comes with being part of something. As you experience the rewards of service, it may become a more regular part of your life. As your children are raised with this practice as a norm, they will learn to see the world through a web of belonging and naturally seek out opportunities to help. You can start with little, short-term projects and build as you go.

What does your local community, neighborhood, congregation or town need? What programs or initiatives are already in place that could use some volunteer support? How can you and your kids get involved with helping out? Is there a community garden to be part of? Or a cooperative of some kind? If you're going to an event, see if you and your kids can volunteer.

The relationships you form with others as you're working towards a common goal or tending to something you all care about may form into meaningful, long-lasting friendships that deepen the sense of community in your life.

11

PARTNERING WITH OUR KIDS

"You cannot raise any child without the input of that child. You cannot be the best teacher or guide for that young learner if you are deciding for them instead of with them. You and I must see partnering with young people as personal leadership work, social justice work, not just educational activism. This is bigger than that. This is about power, about reimagining it by taking it out of the context of power-over and applying it to our deliberate efforts to raise and be people who know how to share our power and how to not stand in the way of someone else's power."

– Akilah S. Richards [11.1]

The opportunity to live in deep partnership with our children is an outrageous blessing we are offered when they come into our lives. But it is not guaranteed. It requires a conscious choice to supplant and transcend mainstream assumptions about the relationship between adults and children. It requires the daily, ongoing practice of learning together how to navigate our lives with mutual respect and collaboration.

As I've worked to stretch into this partnership with the children in my life, I've often wondered if we have some sort of work to do together in a context much bigger than our mundane lives. I've wondered if we *choose* each other on some cosmic level. And if we come into each other's lives with just the right combination of qualities to help each other heal and grow. I've imagined the possibility that, prior to birth, children can clearly see the circumstances of their pending human experience from a much wider perspective. They can see their parents, their physical and social locations, their struggles and their joys, the socio-political circumstances of their lives and everything else. They understand what it would mean to enter all of that, and they knowingly choose to step into it with courageous hearts, intentionally choosing to partner with their parents on some level, because their souls have work to do together.

Many traditional, intact cultures – such as the Dagara people of West Africa[11.2] and the Tz'utujil Mayan people[11.3] – believe that children come into their lives with purpose and with specific work to do. A common cross-cultural understanding is that the process of human birth causes or requires forgetting what we knew before we were born. For this reason, many of these communities practice specific technologies, rituals and ceremonies to help their people remember or reorient to their purpose after their birth and throughout their young lives. This way of welcoming a child into their lives is the beginning of a deep partnership. It recognizes that they do not come to us as blank slates or blobs of clay for us to mold with our intentions and desires. They come to us with work to do, and by the force of their own intentions, which will combine with ours into something new, as we learn to work together.

Those of us conditioned into modern society, without the support of a truly intact culture, may not have access to these technologies. And yet, by opening our hearts to this possibility and regarding our children as partners who have come here with a specific mission, we may be led into some level of remembrance and a reawakening of our complementary purposes in life.

Whether this cosmic perspective resonates with you or not, it's clear that parents and children are truly in this life *together*. We're here with each other and for each other and will have to navigate the circumstances of our lives *together* over the course of many decades. If we're willing, we'll see that we're here to learn from each other in many ways. Nourishing our connection as allies, collaborators and co-learners can create an unbreakable lifelong bond and empower us to respond to the crises we face on Earth in ways we never could on our own.

Understanding Power Dynamics

When we're committed to partnering with our kids, it's important for us to recognize and understand the power dynamics in our relationships. In general, our society conditions us to see adults as authority figures and children as their subordinates. This is a symptom of the "might makes right" mentality of the Power Over Paradigm that only recognizes certain types of power such as size, strength, money and influence. It's also a result of the top-down hierarchy of the POP, which has most of us scrambling up the pyramid to claim our position. According to this worldview, power is not an inherent quality that flows through all living beings. It is something outside ourselves that must be obtained and defended. Every scrap of power needs to be struggled and sweated for, and could be lost at any time, so we can never stop struggling and sweating for it. The POP is a zero-sum game: one person's power and wellbeing comes at the expense of someone else's power and wellbeing.

In our current society, adults are recognized as full citizens with political and economic agency while children are generally viewed as "works in progress" on their way to earning their right to be full citizens with the powers of adulthood.

As adults, parents have considerably more voice and choice than our kids over the major factors that affect our lives and their lives. We create the energetic and physical conditions into which they're born. We generally choose where we live, decide how most of our time is spent and set the household rules. We're also bigger and stronger and have access to money, information and adult choices. We know how things work in the physical world and are generally much more capable than children when it comes to getting things done and taking care of ourselves.

These are all significant forms of parental power. These forms of power don't make us better than our kids. They don't even make us more powerful than them! These are simply specific forms of power that need to be understood and wielded consciously in respectful partnership, along with the forms of power our children have and the power that is generated through our partnership with them.

Children's forms of power tend to be unrecognized or unappreciated in the eyes of the Power Over Paradigm. These special forms of power also happen to be essential to our collective ability to grow into the Thriving Life Paradigm. The simple act of recognizing and honoring these other forms of power can chip away at the calcifications of our POP conditioning and show us new ways of seeing and being in the world.

Babies and young ones are imbued with a magical connection to the Source of all Life that carries potent lessons for humankind. Their raw, authentic expression of life can shake us loose from the Business As Usual trance, reignite our curiosity and orient us more deeply to beauty and mutual wellness. Their unconditioned needs can guide us in shedding our own conditioning and reconnecting to the ways in which humans are meant to live with the Earth. As we allow ourselves to be guided by these authentic needs, we're often presented with opportunities for healing on many levels, unlocking trauma and releasing layers of oppression that have been blocking the flow of natural power in our lineages for many generations. There is also great inherent strength and power in the openness, curiosity, playfulness and innocence of children. Their resilience, endurance and drive to learn, grow and develop are remarkably powerful.

As we align our awareness with the Thriving Life Paradigm, we also discover that power is not really something that any of us "have" on our own. It is a dynamic force that arises through connection and relationship. It is an unfolding of possibilities, agencies and outcomes that manifest through partnership and collaboration. As we weave this awareness into our parenting practices, it can become a dance that includes all the forms of power that we've explored here and creates an empowering partnership for both parents and children.

To tend to this power dynamic responsibly, it's important that we have done and *are doing* our own emotional and spiritual work so we can be grounded and present enough to care for our children, protect them, advocate for them and guide them in respectful ways. This personal work helps us become centered and secure enough in our own self-worth to also learn *from* them, be guided *by* them, and to be humble and vulnerable with them. It may take a lot of work to decondition and retrain ourselves to experience power in this new way. But don't worry, our kids help us learn as we practice living life in partnership with them.

Humbling Ourselves to Cultivate Connection

Being in true partnership with your children means realizing that your parenting experience is not about *you*. It's not about the fulfillment of your life goals or your image. It's not about your pleasure, entertainment, satisfaction, disappointment, or expectations. It's about your care for the tender soul that has entered this challenging, beautiful, confusing world through you. It's about your shared mission to be of service in some way. It's about helping each other out as you each learn and grow.

Parenting well requires a lot of humility and a lot of self-reflection. This can be extremely challenging because it goes against the grain of our societal conditioning. We have generally been trained to either defend ourselves and protect our ego at all costs or else to doubt and hate ourselves. Most commonly, we vacillate between the two, depending on circumstance. Authentic humility is not self-deprecation or self-hatred. It can only happen when we truly love ourselves and understand our precious (but small) place in the expansive interconnected web of existence. Authentic humility allows us to observe ourselves with compassion and to reflect on our experiences and choices.

This compassionate self-reflection is invaluable for New Paradigm Parenting. As a parent in these tumultuous times, you'll have to make countless choices. Some of them will be *impossible* choices. You'll have to compromise in ways you could never have imagined. You'll have to think fast and make quick decisions. You'll react. You'll get triggered. You'll make mistakes. A lot of mistakes. You'll cause harm. If you are unable to honestly reflect on these experiences and you choose, instead, to live in arrogant defense and/or shame in relation to them, you won't learn and you won't be able to authentically partner with your kids.

Without learning, you won't be able to grow and change your behavior. The children in your life will feel this and, in a very real way, they will feel abandoned by it, because they are counting on you to be present on the journey with them. They are counting on you to be "the adult in the room" and to provide an example of how to be. Children are highly skilled detectors of bullshit and hypocrisy. If unaddressed, this lack of humility and self-reflection is bound to drive a wedge between you and the precious children in your life.

One way of circumnavigating our tendencies toward egoic defense or shame is to become a student of adult/child relationships. Since it's often easier to see patterns and behaviors play out from a third-party perspective, you can begin by paying attention to the relationships and interactions between children and their parents, teachers and other adults. Study the dynamics, choices and outcomes. Observe how things go. Notice when the interactions create a power struggle or a sense of disconnection or withdrawal. Look for examples of interactions that move the adult and child toward greater connection and mutual empowerment. This increased connection is the main indicator on the path of partnership. As we commit to a partnering path with our kids, we always want to be building trust and working towards more connection and greater sense of belonging.

When you're observing adult/child interactions, you can ask questions like: *How do these interactions play out for the child? Do they foster healthy behavior and wellness or do they perpetuate dysfunctional patterns? Do they stimulate creativity and passion, or do they stifle them? Do they increase the child's sense of trust and support or do they push the child toward isolation?*

Notice if and when the kids start to "tune out" the adults or withdraw energetically (hint: this happens frequently in typical adult/child interactions). Notice when they appear energized and engaged and free to express themselves. Look for examples of some of the things we explore in this chapter and notice how they go. Make connections. Notice patterns. See for yourself. Then turn your attention to your own relationships with the children in your life and apply what you've learned to make choices that create more openness, connection and empowerment within your relationship with them.

It's important to be aware that a good parent/child partnership can be established at any point in your children's life, even if you didn't start early and even if you feel that your current relationship is far from a true partnership. At any time, you can choose to consciously orient yourself toward partnership with your child and invite them to meet you there. To establish partnership with older children requires even deeper authenticity and humility. The basic message that needs to come across is, *"I see you. I'm here. You're here. We're in this together. Let's do what we can to work it out together."* That message should be followed by *a lot* of listening and a generous willingness to receive feedback from your children.

Whether you begin in early childhood or later, intentional partnership needs to be nurtured ongoingly as children grow. They learn the true meaning of partnership when they feel that you have their back, over and over. They feel it when you listen to them and try to understand, instead of reacting. It is strengthened when you show up for them authentically, human to human. They feel empowered by it when you help them clarify and execute their own plans and dreams, instead of imposing yours onto them. They know that you are in partnership with them when you thank them for waking you up in the middle of the night because they needed your help, instead of getting mad at them for disturbing you. So much changes for kids as they grow from babies to young adults. To know that you're truly there for them and *with* them, they need to feel your presence and support every step of the way.

Power and Will

In partnership with your children, it's essential to recognize that you each have will and you each have power. You and your child are each sovereign beings and, as such, you're each endowed with your own distinct identity and volition. Having a strong-willed kid is often thought of as a negative thing in our Power Over Paradigm. Since the power over structure requires that someone is always in the dominant position in each of our relationships, having a willful kid is seen as a setup for endless power struggles. And yet, beyond the POP, free will is a natural and precious human attribute that can be honored and celebrated in our children. Since it's not necessary to determine who has *more* power, it's perfectly acceptable for everyone to stand in their own power and work together toward common goals. Instead of following POP convention to crush their tenacious spirits and bring them into line with the status quo, we can seek to foster the development and maturity of this natural personal power and encourage them to maintain it throughout their lives.

Parenting a child in this way is a dynamic dance. It keeps us on our toes and requires us to pay attention, challenge our preconceived notions, let go, be flexible and stand our ground lovingly and respectfully, when necessary. To provide for and protect your children, you do need to wield a certain amount of parental power and will. Often, you know more about situations they may find themselves in, have more physical skills and have more experience and perspective. In some cases, you may have to put your foot down or be firm in your guidance on a certain issue. But, even in these moments, there is no need to become authoritarian or to deny the will and power of the younger, sovereign human being.

Sometimes, your children may know more than you about a situation in which they find themselves. Or they may know what *they* need to know from an intuitive or spiritual source that you might not understand. Or they may need to learn for themselves by trying. You can't know *for* them. Their bodies and spirits need to guide them. They need to learn to listen to their internal messages and to trust themselves. No amount of parental authority can override their internal truth, whether spiritual or physical.

For example, you can't *make* a little kid fall asleep if they aren't tired enough. You could get into a power struggle with them about it, for sure. Many have. Many do. But, if their bodies aren't ready to sleep, they won't be able to. Instead of engaging in the nightly bedtime battle, you can work together to craft a solution that works for everyone. You can also set and lovingly hold clear boundaries about rest and let your children know that they need to be quiet and calm in bed during certain hours so they (and others in the house) can get the rest they need.

The skillful use of parental power and a few magical adult abilities can be applied to situations like this. When we realize that setting the energetic tone in the house is one of our powers, we can consciously center ourselves and focus the energies and activities in the house to meet the desired outcome. In this bedtime-with-littles scenario, we can anticipate pre-bedtime needs and help our children prepare their bodies and minds for bed. We can communicate clear expectations and establish healthy boundaries around bedtime and then *follow through consistently* for multiple nights in a row, so they understand how it works (See more about this in the Boundaries and Limits section of Chapter 12). We can then use our enchanting adult powers to coax the kids into sleep with just the right combination of environment and song without entertaining their attempts to engage you in a battle.

All this can be done without *breaking* their will and without battle or domination.

Children need to feel that they have agency as a contributing member of a team or partnership. When they feel valued and respected in this way, they'll be much easier to work with and much more willing to cooperate with you (and the other members of the family) to work together towards common goals. Even a child as young as one or two is capable of understanding and cooperating at this level if they feel empowered and respected.

There's never a *good* reason to get into a power struggle with your kids. If you find yourself fighting and arguing with your kids, asking them to do something repeatedly, having to nag and nag while they ignore you and finally winding up yelling at them just to get their attention, you can be pretty sure that you've been snagged by the Power Over Paradigm trap. When kids try to fight with us, talk back and ignore us, they're revealing symptoms of disempowerment and disconnection within our relationship. They're showing us that they don't feel like they're in a partnership and they don't feel respected.

The way out of this trap is to stop and connect. First, check in with yourself to see if what you're asking them is necessary and important. If it is, slow down and connect with them, if possible. If it's not possible in the moment because of safety or timing, let them know that it has to be this way right now but that you will circle back and talk with them about it when you can. Then… make sure you keep your word!

When you talk with them, make sure you are on their eye level in a comfortable way. Check in with them about the situation at hand. You can express your needs and listen to their needs. Respectfully ask them to work with you to find a mutually agreeable path forward. Let them know their contribution is important. If they have concerns, objections or issues with what you're asking, listen to them and take them into account. If any adjustments can be made to the plan so it works out for all involved, make those adjustments. Successes in partnership like this go a long way to building trust and connection within your relationship with your children.

Slowing down enough to have these conversations and work together with your child as two equally valuable sovereign beings is *deeply* healing. It dismantles the old power-over structure and creates a completely new template for power dynamics in your growing child's mind and experience. It also can bring to light your own hang-ups and give you a safe and clear way of letting them go. I know it can be scary to be honest like this, but you're safe. Your child loves you and wants to be close with you. If you are real with them and practice this form of authentic humility and respectful, responsive parenting, they will cherish you even more deeply.

Including kids in decision making in age-appropriate ways builds on this partnership as they grow. This can include checking in with them on what kind of experiences they want to have, what they want to learn, what they'd like to eat for dinner and how they may want to spend a free day or vacation. Let them know that you value them and realize that they have preferences and desires of their own. Be clear and transparent about what you're able to do and how the decisions you make together need to accommodate your needs and the needs of other family members, as well. Include them in their life in empowering, reasonable ways.

That being said, I've noticed a somewhat problematic trend in parenting around giving children *choices*. This must have been encouraged in a popular child rearing book or blog, and it has really taken hold among this generation of parents. I'm all for giving children choices but it's *extremely* important to make sure those choices are both meaningful and possible. Before offering a choice to your child, be absolutely positive that you can happily and comfortably follow through with any of the options you present. I've seen a lot of well-meaning parents who seem to have missed the point of choices or get themselves into tricky situations by presenting the choices in a way that doesn't really work. If you know something needs to happen, it cannot be presented as a choice to your child. If the toddler needs to get a new diaper on before naptime, it's not a choice. The choice can be whether they want to come to you right away on their own or if you're going to pick them up and bring them to the diaper changing spot.

You don't have to give your kids a choice about *everything*. It can be overwhelming for kids to have excessive choices and can create unnecessary chaos in their lives. It's unnatural to have as many choices about superficial things as we tend to have in the developed world. When children are little, it's important for us to keep their environment and their choices relatively simple and manageable for them. Too many choices can keep kids focused on unnecessarily shallow things, like whether they want the blue bowl or the purple bowl. Kids often pitch fits about this sort of thing when they are not grounded in true connection and empowerment. If kids don't feel a sense of authentic empowerment, they may use these choice making opportunities to try to wield power in a dysfunctional way. Instead of the endless barrage of choices, it is better to set up their environment in a way that allows them to have agency and power within a manageable context.

My daughter taught me a big lesson on this topic when she was four years old. I was a single mom, and she was going to her first preschool. Every weekday morning, we had to wake up and get dressed and hustle to get out the door on time. The unique being that she is includes these qualities: she has *never* been a morning person, she is extremely strong willed, and she has been obsessed with the art of fashion and style since before she could walk. Choosing her outfit for the day turned into a daily power struggle that was driving me crazy. We were living in Massachusetts at the time, and it was a bitter cold winter. Inevitably, she would choose one of the summer dresses hanging in her closet and refuse to wear long sleeves or leggings along with it because that wouldn't be stylish. I would argue with her that it was too cold for her chosen outfit, and we would go back and forth in our little mother-daughter battle.

Then it dawned on me. It was really important to her that she was able to pick out her own outfit, and it was really important to me that she was dressed warmly enough for the weather and that we got out of the house on time. So, I used my magical parental powers to clean out her closet and drawers and tuck away the frilly dresses and summer options for another time. I set up the conditions so all the choices available to her were appropriate for the season. Then I let her know that as long as she got out of bed by a certain time, she could choose her own outfit every day without any interference from me. She could dress as wildly as she wanted and express her unique sense of beauty and flare confidently. But if she stayed in bed too long, I would get to choose her clothes. This put the power and agency in her hands, motivated her to take action and completely eliminated any need for the daily power struggle.

Another important part of the work of facilitating our children's developing empowerment and sense of sovereignty within the parental partnership and family team is to keep kids informed about and involved with what's going on in their lives and what they can expect. This can also include talking with them and getting their input about the plan for the day, the weekend, the summer, etc. It helps them feel grounded and in control in their own lives and reduces the chaos they experience. Imagine, for a moment, how chaotic it would feel to be whisked around from here to there, picked up and relocated, have food shoved in your mouth and told to sleep without having a clue about what's happening or what's coming next.

Our kids are extremely conscious and aware, even from their birth. Just because they lack the ability to walk and talk doesn't mean they don't understand or need to know what's going on. Even babies respond very well to being kept informed. Narrating the events of the day out loud to our babies encourages their cognitive development and helps them orient to their world in important ways.

I've practiced this with my child since she was a baby (and continue to this day) and with all the other kids I've cared for. It works very well to create a smooth adult/child experience. In my various childcare roles, I always let the kids know the plan for the day, whether there are any changes to our regular routine, and whether they're going anywhere or have anything special to look forward to. When the two-year-old I cared for was upset or distressed, I could calm him right down by telling him what we're doing now and what was coming next. It shook him loose of his panic and planted him squarely in his present moment with an idea of what to look forward to, when he could expect to see his mom again and what steps we'd take through our day. He understood that we have to do certain things first in order to get to the next things. All of a sudden, he had a handle on his day, and he was centered in his own power.

Supporting the development of skills that will help our kids feel competent at each stage of their growth is also a great way to support their empowerment. When my child was little, before she could read, she realized, as we bopped around in town, in stores, on roads, etc. that I seemed to mysteriously know things that she didn't know. She noticed that there were signs all over the place with words on them and, since I could read, I knew what they said. She wanted to be in the loop and know what was going on in the world around her, so she started asking about the signs and I started helping her learn to read, one sign at a time. Gaining that skill was a huge boon to her empowerment at that stage in her life.

As kids grow, we've got to recognize their increased capacities and let them explore their personal power in increasingly meaningful ways. As they learn how to manage and regulate themselves, you can release certain parameters you had to hold in place for them when they were younger. At some point along the way (maybe sooner than later) they'll be able to decide how much and what kind of food they're going to eat, when they're going to bed, what they'll do with their free time, how they'll make and manage their money, and what interests and life path they'll pursue. If you support the development of their capacities along the way, they'll be prepared to make these decisions in a deeply empowered way.

Building Trust

Your kids need to trust you if you are going to have a high-quality partnership. True partnership is a choice for both the adult *and* for the child. That choice must be rooted in trust. Many parents think that children automatically and unconditionally trust their parents, but that's not true at all. Children may start out with a certain amount of trust for their parents by default, but if it's not cultivated and maintained throughout their childhood, it can be lost altogether. Your children's trust is not guaranteed, and it should not be taken for granted. It needs to be built and maintained throughout their childhood.

Building trust is not about appeasing your child or constantly making them feel comfortable by giving them everything they want. Quite the contrary, it's about being consistent and reliable and standing in integrity with what you understand is in your children's and family's best interest, even when it's uncomfortable and even when it goes against what your children want in that moment. We can't force, coerce, trick, bribe, "win over" or otherwise manipulate kids into trusting us. We have to build and maintain trust with them by *being trustworthy*. This is an ongoing daily practice that takes time and attention and requires a great degree of consistency. Children learn to trust us when we do what we say we're going to do, *whether it's what they say they want or not.*

As a nanny, building this trust with babies and toddlers is easy-peazy compared to building it with five to ten-year-olds. Older kids are circumspect. Most of them don't open up to just anyone right away. They are waiting to see how things will go. This careful skepticism can make adults *really* uncomfortable. Often, they want to rush past this phase by winning the children over in some way. They give presents or take them out to do something special or always say *"yes"* and give them what they want. I witness adults doing this with children all the time. And I've been pressured to do this by well-meaning parents who want to expedite the bonding process between their kids and their new nanny.

But I know that kids see right through this game and will respond accordingly. The result of this approach won't be a high-quality partnership grounded in trust. Instead, it will be a sort of ongoing transaction that both the adult and the child get trapped in. So, I avoid it as much as I can and take the slow, sometimes uncomfortable, road of being real with kids. I let them take their time and keep their distance at first. I show up lovingly and consistently, with presence. I do what I say. Every time. And, as they see that I'm someone they can really count on, our partnership develops. The rewards of this slow, consistent trust building are *so phenomenal*. An authentic hug. A real sense of safety. A genuine appreciation and regard for one another. A willingness to be vulnerable with each other and to work things out so everybody's needs get met. It's what I live for!

Sadly, even though parents generally get to start out with their little ones as babies, I see parents who are stuck in this transactional trap all the time. That is because their kids don't *fully* trust them. They love their parents, of course, but they don't trust them. When parents are distracted and inconsistent, children lose faith in them on some level. If the foundation of trust isn't strong in our relationships with our kids, the situation only gets worse as the years go on. Children figure out how to get their needs met through manipulation and withholding, and often grow into teenagers who can't be trusted by their parents. Meanwhile, parents exhaust themselves trying to constantly stay on their kids' good side by *making things fun,* instead of being real with them. Real fun happens naturally when parents and children are real with each other because they can be at ease, and they know they're in it together.

Building trust happens one moment at a time, as we show our children that we are trustworthy by doing what we say we're going to do and following through with consistency. It includes communicating with your children about things that affect them directly and managing their expectations in a reasonable way. If they're looking forward to something or counting on something that you said was going to happen and then it doesn't happen (especially with no explanation), that degrades their sense of trust in you.

I nannied full time for a family with four children for about a year. The mom didn't work at all but was highly distracted by her personal life and adult preoccupations. She was also really overwhelmed by having four children. The kids didn't get very much one-on-one time with her. One of the most exciting things in their little worlds was to get to go to the grocery store alone with their mom. When she would tell me the plan for the day in the morning, it would occasionally include a grocery trip with one of the kids. The chosen kid would look forward to it with all their heart *all day!* Unfortunately, she would often get wrapped up doing other things and postpone, cancel at the last minute, or even forget entirely what she had promised. To her, it was just going to pick up some chicken for dinner. To her child, it was heartbreak.

This doesn't mean that you have to be able to predict the future or have every day meticulously planned out. Children aren't fragile and we don't have to get obsessive about controlling their reality to prevent them from ever getting disappointed. We just have to keep them informed respectfully, and to try to understand their perspective. Notice what really matters to your kids and tend to those things with love and care. Carry the promises and plans you make with your children with as much value as you would a business colleague or revered mentor. If the plan needs to change, be sure to communicate with them respectfully, as if their feelings really matter, because they do.

It's essential to do what you say you're going to do, even if it's not something they want you to do. If you threaten some form of consequence or set a limit and then you fail to follow through with it, that also degrades their trust and respect in you. This might seem counterintuitive. You might think they'd be relieved (and maybe on some level they are) but remember that children are learning in every moment. They're learning what kind of person you are. They're learning whether they can count on you. They're learning whether what you say matters. So, *make no empty promises and no empty threats.* Really, it's better to make no *threats* at all. Just be straight with your kids. Let them know what needs to happen if they want a particular thing, and then stand by what you said.

Kids are learning from your actions way more than they're learning from your words. For example, if you say that they need to get their shoes on right now because it's time to walk out the door and go to school, but then you get distracted and start doing something else while they're sitting around waiting for you, the next time you say, *"It's time to go!"* they'll understandably be less inclined to take your words seriously. If you do that same thing day after day, they will learn from your actions that it's not *actually* time to leave until you have *your* shoes on and are walking out the door. They will learn that what you say doesn't matter.

When you become aware of this, you can begin the practice of only asking your children to do something when it's *really* time for them to do it and when you are *really* available to follow through with them. Practicing this consistently and establishing this level of trust and accountability with them when they are young is very helpful as they get older and you have less direct influence and involvement in their daily life. When they know they can count on your word, then your word itself carries much more weight and they'll feel accountable to your agreements even when they're out and about in the world without you.

Presence, Respect and Compassion

If we're paying attention with respect and compassion, our kids will give us all the information we need about how to take care of them properly. The feedback they give us through the states of their physical, emotional and mental wellness is way more valuable than anything we could read in a book or blog. As we get to know them and bring our attentive presence to our relationship with them, we'll understand exactly what to do for them.

Something I notice to a staggering degree at the playgrounds, parks and museums of Portland (and everywhere, really) is how disconnected and distant many parents appear to be from their children. Due to the state of our collective mental and emotional health, this isn't at all surprising. But it breaks my heart when I hear children trying to get their parents' attention and being completely ignored or brushed off. It's like the kids and parents are on two different sides of a thick glass wall. The parents are lost in their own thoughts or absorbed by their adult preoccupations and the kids are banging on the glass, trying to secure the loving bond they need to survive.

It appears that many of these parents don't truly see their children as human beings of equal worth. I have often witnessed parents answer phone calls and walk away from their children without saying anything *while* the child is in the middle of telling them something. Nearly every time I go into a store, there is a child whining and screaming in a shopping cart while the parent calmly browses through the clothing rack like she's the only person in the store who can't hear the commotion. And, of course, we have all experienced a child saying, *"Watch me, mom!"* twenty thousand times before their mother turns her head. This type of parental absence creates a vast loneliness inside our children that they will seek to fill (usually in unhealthy ways) for the rest of their lives.

I know, firsthand, how demanding caring for children can be and I understand why parents slip into this lack of presence. It's what we're set up for by the dysfunctional society that raised us. And it feels like the easiest way to cope with the seemingly endless demands for attention. The irony of it, though, is that when a child feels your authentic presence, they don't have the need to bang on the glass all the time. When you respond with presence at the first request, you can create a connection with your child that fills them up and they become much more independent and less needy.

> *"Speak to your children as if they are the wisest, kindest, most beautiful and magical humans on earth, for what they believe is what they will become."*
>
> – Brooke Hampton [11.4]

Your children are amazing! Truly. Remember, they emerged into this life with a complete soul, a rich personality and a mission that is deeply worthy of your respect. You have a lot to learn together, and they have a lot of development to do along the way, but they are not incomplete or inferior to you in any way. They have equal worth and, if you pay close enough attention, you may see that their intelligence and capacity wildly outshine yours. They are carrying messages and memories that we adults have long since forgotten. They are growing, changing, learning and figuring things out at a rate that you will never again achieve in your adult life. They are accomplishing outrageous successes daily. They are more than worthy of your respect.

In the Thriving Life Paradigm, respect is a two-way channel. It is mutual, reciprocal, regenerative and unconditional. Sadly, the popular dictionaries of our times define respect using examples straight from the Power Over Paradigm. These definitions give some insight into the hurdles we're facing as we seek to break the cycle of authoritarian parenting with its *"because I said so"* mentality.

From the Oxford Learners Online Dictionary, I found these two definitions:

1. a strong feeling of approval of somebody/something because of their good qualities or achievements. *"I have the utmost respect for her and her work."*
2. polite behavior towards or care for somebody/something that you think is important. *"He has a lack of respect for authority."*

In the first definition we're led to believe that respect has to be earned and that it is conditional upon your achievements and abilities. This puts into perspective the general lack of respect typically shown to children, who haven't had the time or opportunity to develop or prove their abilities and accomplishments. The second definition uses an example that shines a spotlight on our general understanding of respect as a one-way thing that flows from subordinates to superiors, revealing the unconscious hierarchical bias built into us by the Power Over Paradigm.

When I found the word respect in the Merriam-Webster online dictionary it had much more of the quality we are looking to cultivate in our relationships with our children.

1. to consider worthy of high regard
2. to refrain from interfering with

Holding our children in high regard and refraining from interfering with their sovereign paths is a great summation of the type of respect we can practice in our parenting. Children need us to hold them in high regard unconditionally, even (and perhaps especially) when they're struggling or not behaving the way we want them to. When we hold our children in high regard, we're more able to work with them to move through challenges instead of getting frustrated with them and disparaging them when they don't meet our expectations.

Practicing respect for our children also involves refraining from interfering with them and letting them have their own learning experiences. When they're in process with something, try not to interrupt them if you can help it. Let them follow their discoveries through in their own time. That can take a lot of patience for adults. Sometimes this means letting go of our attachment to getting things done quickly or steering the situation towards a specific outcome. It can also mean letting go of our impulse or desire to show off our own skills in a certain area. We have to let them struggle sometimes. We have to trust them.

Respecting our kids means listening to them and honoring their personal experiences, their challenges and their accomplishments in the context of the stage of life they are in. Each stage of growth has its own obstacles and challenges. These are *very* real to the children who are experiencing them.

When a baby fusses, if we're only looking through our adult perspective, we might not perceive the incredibly hard work they're doing to adjust to their embodied experience, develop a digestive system and cut teeth, all without the ability to communicate their needs and pains. Since you've matured beyond preteen social drama, it could be hard to remember how very real the pain of being teased and embarrassed in front of your friends can be. Or now that you manage a whole household, hold down a job and juggle all your other adult responsibilities, you might not think it's all that impressive that your child finally cleaned their room. But when your child comes to you with their pain or with their accomplishments, remember to take into account where *they* are in their process.

As we make respecting our kids a conscious discipline, we can strive to practice kindness and decency in each of our interactions. Remember, you are raising a future adult. Treat them the way you hope they will treat everyone they meet throughout their lives. If you notice them acting disrespectfully towards you or their siblings, take a moment to honestly reflect on how you talk to them. Could they have picked up that tone from you? You may notice unconscious habits that you can start to shift. Or you may notice that they are repeating behavior that they see on TV, with their other parent(s) or with their friends. This is an opportunity to let them know how much you value your relationship with them and how important it is to be kind and supportive of each other. You can clearly express to them the way you want to be treated and then you can reinforce that request by actively treating them with the same level of respect until the behavior shifts.

When children do something helpful or fulfill a request you made, say *"Thank you!"* They are working hard in their little ways, and they benefit greatly from your appreciation. Even if they tried to help but they made a mess along the way, you can thank them for their effort. I think *"Thank you"* is one of the most common phrases I use when caring for little ones. *"Thank you for listening." "Thank you for helping." "Thank you for cooperating."* This kind of appreciation and positive feedback helps them feel a sense of personal value and know that their efforts are worth the trouble. *"Thank you"* was also a common phrase I used with my teenage daughter as I acknowledged her cooperation and the choices that she would make to care for our relationship. *"Thank you for cooking tonight." "Thank you for sharing with me so openly." "Thank you for asking for my help."*

As I've mentioned before, over the course of your parenting experience, you will make a lot of mistakes. You will be wrong from time to time, and you'll cause some harm. I don't think there is any way around that. Apologize to your children when you are wrong. Admit your mistakes openly and seek to make amends. Respecting your children in this way and modeling this emotional maturity will help them stay centered in their own worth and wellbeing and will show them that we are all growing and learning all the time. It will help them carry respect and compassion for themselves and others throughout the rest of their lives. And it will deepen their respect for you and their sense of being in partnership with you.

Another important way to respect our children is to be honest with them. Make sure your praise is always authentic, honest and reasonably attached to merit. Kids know when you're being fake. Be enthusiastic, encouraging *and* honest. Don't tell them they did a great job if they didn't. Don't shower them with empty praise. Give them honest, loving feedback and help them develop an accurate gauge for self-reflection. Respect their ability to grow and learn. They don't need to be coddled by false compliments.

Your children each have their own unique, viable life paths. They have their own karma and destiny. They came to Earth right now for specific reasons. As they grow, your children need you to see them for who they are and to respect their sovereign right to pursue their callings, without judgment or rebuke. In the Power Over Paradigm, parents often feel some sort of ownership over their kids and some need to control who they become. But your children's relationship with their Divine Purpose is much bigger than their relationship with you. If you don't respect that relationship and who they are because of it, it will poison your connection with them. Your children don't need you to tell them who to be. They need you to see and respect them for who they are.

Each child also has their own unique bundle of qualities. You might recognize them as aspects of their physical constitution, dosha, temperament, aptitudes, cognitive processing style or astrology. Their bundle might be very different from your own and you might not fully understand it. But these characteristics are what makes your child the particular person they are. If you have more than one child, you'll quickly realize that their pregnancies, their births and their personalities are noticeably distinct. Just because you "figured it out" with one child doesn't mean you have the formula for the second. There is no formula.

With this in mind, be careful not to focus too heavily on comparisons or competitions with friends, siblings or even between multiples. Each child is unique, and they have the right to be themselves without having to measure up to anyone else. Get to know your child ongoingly by paying attention to them with an open, curious mind and a compassionate heart. Notice them. What works for them and what doesn't. Be willing to continue to get to know them as they grow and change. Don't keep them bound to any artificial identity you may have constructed for them at a particular stage along the way. They are unique, unfolding, growing beings. You may want to venture into astrology or Ayurveda or some other methods of understanding their individual makeup. Since your children's qualities and needs will differ from yours, these tools can provide helpful insights. However, be careful not to use them to limit your child in any way. It is unlikely that any single method or model can tell the whole story of who your child is and will be.

Your child's experience is their own. Pay attention with deep respect and love in your heart so that you can support them in what *they* need to feel grounded, safe, loved and validated as they grow, no matter what. They may be working something out for their own growth and healing, for your lineage, or for humanity as a whole. They may simply be expressing a unique facet of the Divine that only they can express. It's not your place as a parent to approve or disapprove. It's your place to love and support.

Gender Identity and Sexual Orientation

An area of particular importance for practicing this level of authentic presence, respect and compassion as we raise and support our kids is in regard to gender identity and sexual orientation. One of the main precepts of the Power Over Paradigm is a binary mentality. Within the POP perspective, everything in the world is defined in a static and unchanging way as either "this" or "that." Black or white. Male or female. It *is* or it is *not*. But the world is not static and binary. It's a dynamic, living, changing diversity of expressions.

Diversity in gender expression, identity and sexual orientation have always existed. For thousands of years, in cultures not ruled by the POP, non-binary people have been (and still are) fully respected members of their communities. In many cultures, non-binary people are particularly cherished for the unique perspectives and insights they carry and often hold venerated positions in society. Through colonization, this gender diversity has been systematically and violently repressed to enforce the binary mentality that the dominator society relies on for its rigid structure and hierarchy.

As the grip of the POP is beginning to loosen, gender diversity is now breaking out of its repressed position within our society and this binary mentality is falling apart. With the advancement of representation of the Queer Community and LGBTQIA+ people in politics, media and other mainstream institutions in certain countries, more people are coming to understand that many diverse expressions of gender exist, both between and beyond the two previously acceptable options. This increased gender awareness and appreciation is one of the many ways we're learning that life and reality are quite a lot more fluid, complex, beautiful, rich and diverse than we've been led to believe under the reign of the POP.

It's important to note that there are still many miles to go in this process and, even as advancement is happening in understanding, recognition and rights for Queer people, we are also seeing many forms of backlash by the Power Over Paradigm as frightening anti-trans and anti-gay laws are being pushed through legislation and violence against members of the Queer Community continues.

As New Paradigm Parents, it's important for us to let go of conforming to or upholding the old binary standards of this dying paradigm. As your children develop their own sense of who they are in the world, their gender expression and identity will be an aspect of their discovery. This is definitely an area where you can't know *for* them. They have to know for themselves (or be in the question for themselves). Their gender expression has nothing to do with you. It's not about your image. It's not about whether you think life will be hard for them if they don't conform. It's not about any ideologies you or your family or your community have previously held. It's not even about whether you understand. It is about the way they experience their own lives and their place in the world. It is not your job to approve or disapprove of their expression. All you need to do is to love them for exactly who they are in each moment.

Self-described gender nonconforming and gender creative kid, C.J., had this advice for parents in a blog post entitled *Gender is Over*,[11.5] that he wrote at age 13:

> "My advice to parents who have a kid like me is they should let their kid be who they were born to be. It's okay. There's nothing wrong with your child. You need to learn to accept it, because you aren't going to be able to change it. And, if you try to change it, you're just making your child upset. You're probably making yourself upset, too. And your child might grow up to not love themselves. Everyone should love themselves."

Centering your child's wellbeing and supporting their authentic self-expression in our excessively gender-based society can be very challenging. The overwhelming emphasis on gender almost eclipses all other aspects of their young lives. Right from the beginning of pregnancy, every expectant parent is faced with the question of whether they want to discover the sex of their baby via sonogram. "Gender" reveal parties have become widely popular. The first thing that most people ask about our babies when they're born is whether it's a boy or a girl. It can feel like there are two well-worn, deeply rutted tracks laid out for our children as soon as they are born, without much room for anything else.

Beyond being a main focus of attention, gender is also a primary and pervasive source of societal conditioning. As the baby gifts pour in and choices around clothing and toys begin to arise, gender norms and expectations are reinforced over and over throughout our children's young lives. Messages about what a "boy should do" and "how a girl should be" come at them from every direction, usually associating boys with action and girls with presentation. Marketing designed to target children often makes gender the central theme, whether they're selling TV shows, bikes, snacks or lunch boxes. Our kids may also experience pressure from extended family, classmates and teachers to conform to gender norms. They may suffer extreme ridicule when they don't.

Alok Vaid-Menon, author of *Beyond the Gender Binary*,[11.6] poignantly describes their experience of being a gender non-conforming child and the pressure they experienced:

> "I learned about gender through shame. In so many ways, they became inseparable for me. As I grew older, people told me to stop being so feminine and grow up. Gender non-conformity is seen as something immature, something to grow out of to become adults. Overnight, so many of the things that I loved not only became associated with femininity but with shame. Because I was a 'boy' I was no longer allowed to want to be a dancer or a fashion designer. Because I was a 'boy,' I had to stop. Stop dancing. Stop being myself."

We can't change or control all the external influences to which our children will be exposed, but we can create a loving, open and responsive home for our children, in which they can be the unique and amazing individuals they are, without expectations of conforming to a specific gender classification. Part of your New Paradigm Parenting practice may already be to be mindful of the ways in which the old POP mentality infiltrates your child's young life through the indoctrinating influences of books, media, toys, and more. As you reflect on these choices, consider the ways in which gender is represented in the books and media they're exposed to and how gender-based pressure enters their life.

Strive to deemphasize the gender norms and expectations in your household by creating a more gender-neutral and authentically supportive environment. As your children grow up, make sure they know, through both your words *and* your actions, that they are safe to be fully themselves, regardless of whether their expression lines up with conventional gender norms and assumptions about who they should be based on their assigned sex at birth. This may involve actively advocating for them in situations beyond the home, as well as encouraging them to be confident in advocating for themselves.

When it comes to sexuality, don't assume that your children are straight or will have a heteronormative love life. Even though you may think it's cute, refrain from coupling them up with their little friends of the opposite sex or projecting stories into the future about how they'll fulfill certain conventional milestones in life that reinforce heterosexual norms. When they begin to date or express romantic feelings for others, stay open and supportive. Recognize that they are having a unique and entirely new moment of discovery. Listen to them and honor them for exactly who they are without comparisons or judgment. Focus your attention more on whether they are having a good time and whether they feel safe, respected, seen, loved and supported by their partners, rather than whether or not their relationship falls into a category that is considered socially acceptable.

My child has taught me a great deal about the nuances and complexity of gender identity and expression during our journey together. In retrospect, I realize that I entered into parenthood with a limited awareness of the depth of this aspect of reality. I was a progressive, liberal, bisexual, independent, empowered woman who shunned female beauty standards, social norms and the limitations generally imposed on females in our society. I understood that sexual orientation and expression existed on a spectrum, and I was totally comfortable with that, but I still saw gender exclusively through a binary lens.

My child is AFAB (Assigned Female at Birth). Without ever questioning this declaration, I considered her to be a girl and raised her as a girl. I always encouraged and allowed her to explore what she was interested in and express herself fully, without judgment. But it never occurred to me to question whether she was a girl.

When she was little, I was generally disturbed by the gender-based influences that kept creeping into our lives through the toys, shows, clothes, and other items she was given or drawn to. She had a penchant for nail polish and high heels that I could never quite relate to. She gravitated to Barbie, American Girl Dolls and Polly Pockets. She also loved building things and taking them apart, climbing trees and being tough. I tried to limit exposure to the overtly and commercially "girly" things but ultimately, I had to let go. When I asked her recently about my attempt to limit gendered toys and media in her youth she said, *"children should be given the opportunity to explore all of the options, regardless of gender, so they can embrace their passions above gender stereotypes, and above our protests against them."*

She always had her own unique way of being in the world and, as she got older, it became increasingly clear to her that she wasn't in alignment with the status quo trajectory. She felt uncomfortable in her body. When her friends would change in front of each other and talk openly about sex, it became clear to her that there was something different about her experience. Without the words for these thoughts and feelings, she felt alone and confused. When we moved to Portland, OR she was exposed to a variety of gender identities and new language to express the experiences she'd been having. The social isolation caused by Covid during her first year at college gave her the opportunity for deep self-reflection. She/they was able to unmask and find a more authentic self-expression in gender fluidity.

They became clear that they are *not* a girl. Some parts of them are still feminine, but they realized that they exist and live outside the singular experience of womanhood tied to the female sex. As their journey of self-discovery continues, they/he is experiencing himself as more and more masculine, coming out as trans masc and claiming that identity as his own. He continues to reflect and ground into his gender identity while allowing it to be fluid, like all things in life are fluid. He aims to be deeply authentic in who he is, courageous in his expression and embracing of all that has made him and continues to nourish his life.

His message to the parents who will be reading this book is:

"Growing up in an unconventional environment gave me an interesting relationship with gender and sexuality. There was a lot of talk of the sacred feminine and the sacred masculine, but sometimes the men wore skirts and the women didn't shave their legs. In small ways, my community was in protest of the gender binary and dominant heteronormative culture outside our little bubble. I always felt very strong in my womanhood and clear that my role in life was to show up as an independent, fierce and intelligent woman.

When covid hit, I spent nine months alone in my dorm. It was the first time I was really on my own and had room to breathe. It was the first time I didn't have to perform for anybody. With the curtains closed, I had time to reflect on who I actually was at my core. Waves of subconscious realizations from my life flooded in. Being 12 or so in the bath and attempting to push my developing chest to the side and see it flat again. Struggling to relate to my body and the girls who just seemed so comfortable in themselves. Trying so hard and failing to perform womanhood in the way I thought it was 'supposed' to look.

I think it took me longer to realize that I was trans because everybody in my hometown knew me and who I was as an individual. When I moved to Portland or when I met new people, they would see my long hair and my boobs and make assumptions about my character. They would see me as a woman before they saw me as a person or as myself. It was frustrating being put in the box of woman when it was not accurate. I didn't know I felt different than 'woman' until I had other people tell and show me what it meant. I think some part of me still feels identified with my definition of the word woman, but this version of woman I have encountered in their assumptions based on a body I did not choose, is not me.

As of this moment, I go by the name Blue. I use he/they pronouns and identify as trans masc. When my mom started writing this book I identified as genderfluid and was using all pronouns. I have no shame about my fluctuating and fluid gender expression. I am comfortable with my mom using 'she' and 'daughter' for me throughout this book because that part of me won't just disappear. The little girl I was is still with me. It doesn't feel right to say that I am my parents' son because our dynamic was built on the foundation of my girlhood. Just know that the words 'she' and 'daughter' do not encompass all of who I am now. I have no idea how my gender and identity will develop as I continue to grow, but I feel safe and accepted and loved, and I know I will be thriving no matter what pronouns I use.

Gender, sex, sexuality, and expression are more complex than could ever be condensed into a few pages. The binary is a myth and a dysfunctional one at that. The most important thing is to remember that understanding is not your primary goal as a parent. Love is. When your child comes to you, and tells you who they are, wrap them in a hug and tell them how grateful you are that you get to love even more of them. Be there and fight for them because the world is angry and afraid. They are strong, but they shouldn't have to be, and your fear won't help them. Be patient with yourself and when you say the wrong thing, accept it, learn from it and don't take it too personally. Just love them."

Along the way on this journey, I'm so deeply grateful that my child has been open with me, sharing his learning and self-reflection as it's happening, being patient with me as I learn and helping me adjust to the changes in a graceful way. Rooted in trust, humility, presence, respect and compassion, this aspect of our relationship has been a profound experience of partnership that continues to teach us and enrich our lives as we grow and learn together.

> *"Trauma is a wound. How I think about it is that if I wounded you, if I cut your flesh, the healing would involve scar tissue forming. If the wound was great enough, you'd get a big scar, and it would be without nerve endings so you wouldn't feel, and it would be much less flexible than your normal tissue. Trauma is when there is a loss of feeling and there is a reduced flexibility in responding to the world. Trauma is a psychic wound that hardens you psychologically that then interferes with your ability to grow and develop."*
>
> – Dr. Gabor Maté [11.7]

Intergenerational Trauma and Lineage Work

Being born into a society that is based on power, domination and disconnection has embedded trauma deeply into all our lineages. The brutal history of conquest and colonization that has created the conditions in which we find ourselves today has affected all our families and ancestors in various ways. The violence of the Power Over Paradigm is so acutely at odds with our natural human needs that both those who perpetrate the violence and those who are the victims of it suffer deep wounding and internalize trauma. That trauma is then passed down from generation to generation and exacerbated as wounded people raise children whose needs are, in turn, neglected or violated.

When our basic human needs for safety, belonging and meaning are interrupted, either through violence or negligence, we are wounded. When the wound is not adequately addressed, we carry it into our lives as trauma. Like a scar, trauma effects our ability to be flexible and responsive. It interferes with our capacity to feel safe, to be fully present and to bond intimately with our loved ones. All this can adversely affect our family life and, if left unaddressed, can be passed down from generation to generation in a complicated, tangled knot that binds us to the pain of the past and prevents us (and our children) from responding to the world healthfully. Raising children with the level of partnership we've been exploring here allows us to work together with our children to untangle this knot and even heal some of the wounds carried through the generations of our lineage in the form of trauma.

Trauma in parents and other adults is the root cause of many (if not all) harmful and abusive behaviors that traumatize children. As they say, *hurt people hurt people.* Likewise, hurt parents hurt kids. Whether we are carrying high intensity personal trauma, intergenerational trauma or the more muted trauma of being raised in our wounded society, part of our work as New Paradigm Parents is to interrupt the passage of trauma along our lineage by how we raise our kids. In seeking to minimize the trauma our children take on through their childhoods, our first step is to recognize that we are the link between generations and that substantial healing of deep wounds can happen when we engage in the healing process.

As you raise your children, each stage or threshold they pass through will bring you right back to the parallel moment in your own life or in the story of your family lineage. You may find yourself flooded with emotions or feeling the urge to react in a certain way when your child is in a similar situation or reaches the age you were when you experienced a personal trauma. You may notice your child subconsciously embodying certain struggles that are woven throughout the generations of your family. Or you may find that becoming the age your parents or grandparents were when they experienced a particular hardship brings up some heavy feelings and reactions for you or your partner.

If you can steady yourself in the awareness that each of these moments is an opportunity for healing, you can transcend the fear and panic of the trigger and can then respond, instead of reacting. In each of these moments, you're given the opportunity to relive the experience and tend to the unmet needs of your inner child (or the unmet needs of the inner children of your ancestors), both by doing your own personal healing work and by taking care of your children in the ways that you weren't cared for as a child. Depending on the severity of the traumas you're working with, you may want to seek out professional support to guide you through deep healing work as you traverse these thresholds.

We have all inherited trauma and experienced personal wounding, and we are all passing it down to our kids. We can't completely prevent this. No matter how "perfectly" we parent, there will be some passing down of trauma. This healing work is not about perfection or purity. It's about awareness and our willingness to take responsibility for our healing while giving our children as much support and resourcing as possible to tend to theirs. It is lineage work and legacy work that extends well beyond our individual lifetimes.

This healing process involves shaking ourselves awake right in the middle of the nightmare of disconnection that the Power Over Paradigm perpetuates and trying our best to see clearly. It is about reclaiming our personal will and sovereignty, living our lives with greater dignity and self-love and behaving like the sacred beings we are. Our children will benefit greatly from every little bit we can possibly grow in this direction.

Healing won't erase what is. It won't absolve or remove the long history of harm from which we descend. Healing is not about bypassing the harm that has been done and putting a pretty spin on it all by pretending that it's "all good" now. The healing I'm talking about is metabolizing the grief, pain, confusion and fear that's been handed to us. Transmuting it. Composting it and then planting seeds of new possibilities into the soil it becomes to nourish our children and their children. The more we do this type of work before and during our children's lives, the more possibilities they will have in their lives and the less of their precious lifeforce energy they'll have to spend battling the same old battles as previous generations. They'll be emancipated from whatever part of the work you've been able to do, and they'll have that much more strength to do whatever part of the work is left for them to do.

Through this process, they'll also learn from your example. They'll come to understand that life is about learning and healing, taking good care of Life, working hard to keep Life living and making things better and more beautiful for the ones yet to be. Having learned from your example, they'll be able to journey even deeper into the healing process for your lineage.

Rooted in Deep Time,[11.8] we are radically interconnected with and interdependent upon all those who came before us and all those who will come after. I've come to understand that the healing work each of us does permeates through our entire lineage, back through generations of ancestors and down through generations of future beings. And since time isn't *actually* linear, we're really all here together, facing these wounds and these opportunities to heal. As the ones who are alive in this moment, learning and growing together, you and your children have the greatest access to that healing work.

Two of my favorite teachers and speakers, Woman Stands Shining (Pat McCabe)[11.09] and her daughter, Lyla June Johnston,[11.10] are excellent examples of this in the way they live. They both have deep wisdom to share on this topic. They are Diné women (incorrectly known as Navajo) and have both worked hard in their lifetimes to heal the wounds inflicted upon their people and passed down to them through their family lineage. They both speak of *"ending the genocide"* of their people by refusing to forget their ancestors and the beauty from which they come. By consciously choosing to live with dignity, as *"holy earth surface walkers,"* the way their people have for thousands of years, they are bringing healing to the wounds inflicted on them and their people by the Power Over Paradigm.

They both counsel those of all lineages to remember our ancestors, to feed them and keep them alive with our attention and prayers. Whenever the assault on our lineage began, whether it was 500 years ago or 5,000 years ago, we can end it here by reaching all the way back through the long story of our family lines to remember those ones who carried the original instructions for our people.

I recently heard Woman Stands Shining talking about trauma in an interview for an online summit. She said that in her healing process, she had this realization: *"I am not willing to be farmed for my trauma any longer."* She spoke about how the systems of the Power Over Paradigm use our trauma to keep us hooked into their lies and vulnerable to their predation. When we are bound up in the fear, shame and disconnection caused by trauma, we can no longer see clearly or make truly sovereign, empowered decisions for ourselves and our families. This entanglement with trauma allows the systems of the POP to feed off our power to strengthen their own.

Here, within our parenting experience, is the place we can take a stand and say, *"I will not be farmed for my trauma any longer."* We can do this for the sake of our lineage and for the sake of our kids and their possible future. If they are going to have a future, the abuse must end somewhere. Let it end with us, through this healing.

PRACTICES FOR PARTNERING WITH OUR KIDS

Partnering with our children is a learning journey that evolves throughout their childhood as their capacities increase and we stay committed to getting to know them each step of the way. These practices are here to help you explore how the concepts shared in this chapter can be worked with in your household in a playful and empowering way. Please experiment with them and adapt them, as needed, to meet your family's needs.

Partnering with Our Kids: Open Sentences for Co-Parents and Kids

Please refer to the instructions for Open Sentences in the practice section of Chapter 5: Grounding in Gratitude.

Open Sentences to use with your co-parents:

1. Some of the joys and blessings I experience in partnering with my children are…
2. Some of the challenges and frustrations I experience in partnering with my children are…
3. The purpose I feel my children and I share in this lifetime is…
4. A time when my children and I felt a strong sense of mutual empowerment was…
5. Intergenerational patterns I notice playing out in my parenting and my children's lives are…

Open Sentences to use with your kids:

1. The things I most want to learn and experience this year are...
2. Some of the things I feel are most important in life are...
3. I really feel like part of the family team when...
4. Some of the decisions I want to be part of are...
5. I feel respected by the adults in my life when...

Magical Awesome Me

This is a creative way to help your children celebrate their uniqueness and learn how to advocate for themselves. It's best to start the project part of this practice in a moment of relative ease and joy so you can come back to it as a resource when a challenge arises.

Please note that you'll need to have a significant amount of emotional safety and trust in your relationship with your child for this practice to work well. If they don't feel emotionally safe or the practice feels forced or inauthentic, they may push back. This is why it's best to start the project part of the practice when they're feeling at ease.

Get a really big piece of paper and some markers (the more colors the better). Lay the paper out on the floor or hang it on a wall. Then have your child lay down on the paper or stand up against it so you can draw an outline of their whole body. They can strike a fun pose if they're inspired to or stretch out or just stand normally. Then the two of you can spend some time together adorning the outline with some of the many qualities, attributes, particularities and quirks that make your kid the amazing person that they are. You can color and draw and write words to represent their special traits. Remember to tap into a wide range of areas from physical attributes to emotional qualities to their interests and the ways they help others or create joy and beauty with their lives. You can also include the relationships they have with family and community and their connection to the Earth and their orientation within the wider Family of Life (maybe they have roots or an animal or element they feel especially connected with is in the background or on their shoulder).

Get creative and have fun. Stay tuned in with their energy and level of interest and be mindful not to get carried away or turn it into something that feels forced at any point. You can put on some music that you both like, maybe have some snacks on hand and just play around with it for a while. They may even want to do one for you at some point, which could be great too.

Once your art session feels complete, you can hang up the image somewhere they'll see it on a regular basis. You can add to it, periodically, as either of you thinks of new things or have additional art sessions to add to it together. When challenges and self-doubt arise, it may serve as a helpful reminder to your child of just how great they really are.

When your child is having a particularly difficult time, you can look to the drawing together and use it to guide a conversation that helps them connect with their strength and self-worth. If they're getting teased or pressured about something, this could be an opportunity to explore the subject of the teasing or pressure to reframe it as a quality they can celebrate and to connect with the many other amazing parts of themself. This practice can also help them learn how to stand up for themselves and walk with confidence in the world, even in the face of obstacles and ridicule.

An essential aspect of this practice and the conversations that you may have while doing it is that *everyone* is awesome in their own unique ways and that all our unique awesomenesses work together to make the world a beautiful place. Be sure to acknowledge that this awesomeness comes from many things, some seen and some unseen, including our relationships and connection with Life.

Feeding the Family Tree

Create a family tree with your children that goes back as many generations as you can with the genealogical information that you're able to find. If you have pictures of ancestors or stories about them, you can include these in this creation. Talk with your children about each of the ancestors on the tree, sharing where they lived, how they're related to the family and any interesting things you know about them.

Be honest about the great qualities of these ancestors and the crappy ones. If some of your ancestors were unwell or did terrible things, be honest about that and talk about how people do those things when they're hurt or disconnected in some way. Talk about how this lifetime is a chance for you and your kids to do the little parts you're able to do to feed the family tree and help it become as healthy as it can be. Talk about what actions you both may take or how you'll choose to live that would nourish or restore wellness for your lineage.

You may choose to create a space in your home to hang up the family tree where it will be visible. You may even add a family altar that includes photographs and items from your ancestors. If you choose, you could start a tradition of literally feeding your ancestors throughout the year by making offerings of the things they loved and/or the things they need to be well. The simplest and perhaps most effective offering is a small cup of water, refreshed daily.

Whether on your own or with your children, the time of making offerings is a good opportunity to think about your family lineage, to feel gratitude for all the blessings and love that were passed on through the generations, to grieve and feel the pain of all the harm and struggle that were passed on through the generations, and to offer yourself in service to wellness on behalf of your ancestors and the ones yet to be.

12

GUIDING GROWTH

"...raising capable adults doesn't start at age sixteen when they can't do anything for themselves, it starts at age three when they need you to back off and let them make a tsunami in your dish room."

– Brooke Hampton [12.1]

Between the moment of their birth and the time they move out of your house, your children are going to grow and learn an immeasurable amount. They will be learning in each moment they're alive and their learning will have its own spiraling, organic shape. Growth and development happen in their own timing and in their own way for each child. It doesn't need to be forced or fretted over. It's not our job to teach them everything they'll learn or to micromanage their growth experience. Our job is to practice empowering ways to guide our children through their natural stages of growth while fostering their self-worth, capacity and confidence.

The Learning Zone

For growth and learning to happen, children (like all people) have to regularly venture out of their comfort zone and into their learning zone. Learning doesn't occur when we're sheltered from discomfort and everything comes easily to us. It doesn't happen when we're playing it safe and taking no risks. As much as we might feel compelled to nurture and protect our children, one of our most important jobs in guiding and supporting the growth of our children is to back off and let them sweat it out sometimes. When children overcome challenges and move through fears, they enter the territory of learning. When they accomplish something in this learning zone, they build new capacities and grow in confidence and competence.

As our children get older, their learning zone will shift and change with each new stage of their development. Part of our work is to get good at sensing the seasons of their growth and to adjust our approach accordingly. Without pushing the river, we can notice what kind of conditions our kids need to stretch into their learning zone while staying reasonably safe and not being pushed into panic. Different ages have very different levels of ability. For example, you might be able to ask an eleven-year-old to take the public bus to meet you somewhere downtown. But thrusting that on a four-year-old could be dangerously beyond their capabilities.

However, most parents do the opposite and wildly underestimate what their kids can do. Many parents tend to cling nostalgically to their children's babyhood, wishing they could stay little, cute and innocent. This isn't good for our kids. They need us to see them at the top edge of their capacity and let them stretch into it. They need us to let go and get out of the way as much as possible. From the moment of conception onward, letting go and allowing growth to happen is what parenting is all about. Our children need us to recognize their new skills and understandings and to hold a vision of their grown selves as preciously as most parents clutch the memory of their sweet little sleeping cherubs.

It's important that we don't do any more than necessary for them while they're in a learning experience. We can show them how to do something and guide them as they practice. We can help them out when they ask, but only as much as they need. We can let them know they can do it and give them the information that they need to accomplish the task at hand. But even if it's messy or they get frustrated or we could do it faster, we've got to hang back and let them work it out. This is as true for helping them figure out how to eat with a spoon and tie their own shoes as it is for helping them learn how to drive and take care of their own medical appointments and taxes. We've got to help them build their muscles, strengthen their capacities and feel the real reward of accomplishment.

When we guide our children in this way, it helps them stay centered in their power. One small example of this style of guidance is how I responded to the two-year-old I cared for when he was climbing the rope net at one of our favorite playgrounds. He was an excellent climber and could get a good way up the net confidently. When he got nervous, though, he would look at me, reach out a hand and say, *"Jo, help,"* risking his center of gravity and hoping that I'd hold his hand to make it easier. But if I held his hand, it wouldn't have been easier. It would have become awkward and unbalanced. Instead, I would tell him, *"I'll spot you, but you've got to hold onto the ropes."* This reoriented him to his own center and his own agency. I was there and he was safe. I would never have let him fall to the ground, but I also would not do it for him or give him the illusion that he was doing it when he really wasn't. I would give him suggestions of where to place a foot or a hand when he was unsure and he would carry on, getting stronger and developing his climbing skills by learning to do it himself.

What you do and how you are with your children when they are very little is intricately connected to how things will go for them in their teen years and throughout their lives. It really is all connected, and those little moments are so important, even the ones they will be too young to consciously remember.

From their very early years, we should be letting them know that they are important participants and contributors to their world by giving them meaningful and challenging work to do at every age. I love Brooke Hampton's blog post, called *Lazy Parents Raise Better Kids*,[12.1] referenced in the quote above. She articulates what I have also come to understand about how to help our kids learn to be capable, functional people. They need to be needed and they need to be challenged. It's unrealistic and even a little cruel to do everything for our children and make their lives extremely easy and then expect them to suddenly get a job and be responsible when they're teenagers or young adults.

I love to cook, and my daughter was always in the kitchen with me when she was little. When she was a baby, I would wear her in a wrap. When she was a toddler, she would stand up on a stool or sit on the counter. I included her in the cooking process by giving her tasks that she could manage. At two years old, she would take vegetable scraps to the compost for me and crack eggs. We would take turns stirring and she would bring me things from the other end of the counter. These were all things that I could have easily done by myself, more quickly and with less shells in the batter. But if I had tried to rush through the cooking quickly with my adult agenda, she would have been bored and disconnected and she wouldn't have learned anything. Including her in the cooking process deepened our connection, grew her skills and made her feel good about herself.

By three or four years old she knew how to make French toast all by herself. She learned how to flip her own fried eggs and make pancakes shortly after that. By about nine years old she could make Pasta Fagioli, one of our ancestral Italian family dinners, which carried an even more meaningful sense of continuity and accomplishment. All through her high school years, she made the family dinner twice a week on a rotating schedule with myself and my husband. I don't think any of her other friends were capable of doing that. In fact, I know that several of them had no idea how to cook a meal. By starting young and building on skills incrementally as our children grow, we encourage a growth mindset in them, foster confidence and prepare them for their adult lives.

Empowering Kids to Help

As we support and guide our children's growth, we can also instill important values that will help them grow into adults who can care for the world, like teaching them how to clean up after themselves. Our world is in a horrible mess largely because of adults who fail to clean up after themselves or take responsibility for the trash and pollution they and their corporations pump into our environment. Noticing our impact on the world around us and consciously choosing to make each place better and healthier than we found it is a value that we can instill in our children from the beginning.

When our kids show interest and enthusiasm in something, it's important for us to meet them in those moments and build on their interest intentionally. Teaching our children to put their toys away before moving on to the next activity is a great example of this. In addition to helping keep the home tidy, this practice helps them pace themselves and feel more grounded. When parents of older children would see the toddler I cared for joyfully picking up his toys, they would often comment cynically about how their kids used to like to clean up at that age too, but now they have to nag them.

Toddlers have a natural enthusiasm for throwing all the blocks back in the box, but if we don't make time for toddler-style cleanup and practice it with them consistently and joyfully, they'll lose interest as they get older. If we push them away or make it unfun or treat it like a chore, then they'll look for ways to avoid it. Teaching this skill requires *us* to slow down and take a moment to help them transition mindfully from one thing to the next instead of letting them just tear through the space leaving a trail of toys in their wake.

If your four-year-old wants to wash the dishes, let them! Start them out with dishes they can handle at that age and then increase their dishwashing responsibilities as they get older. Let them feel their accomplishments and cultivate their enthusiasm. One little guy I cared for always wanted to help make his sister's bed, so we would pull up the comforter and fold it over together. His side usually turned out a little askew. Sometimes I might adjust it a bit, but mostly I would let it be. And then he would enthusiastically place her decorative pillows, each time in a different placement. It was not exactly the way I would do it as an adult, but it was excellent, and it was his own accomplishment. I would leave it the way he set it up. We would celebrate it and he felt a sense of pride.

When I had folded towels to bring down to the kitchen, he would ask to help me carry them. I'd give him two or three hand towels and carry the rest myself. He would walk carefully and make sure they stayed folded the whole time and then place them gently in the drawer. I didn't *need* his help to do these chores, but he needed to feel helpful. So, part of my job was allowing as many opportunities for his helpfulness as possible.

It's also important to let children *earn* their accomplishments so they can build a sense of genuine self-worth. Instead of handing everything to them (even if we can) it helps them more in the long run if they have to put effort into it. When my child told me that she was ready to get her driver's license, I told her I was happy to help her out and then let her know what she would have to do to make it happen. To step into this very adult responsibility, she was going to have to do some very adult work. I told her that driving was a privilege and an expense and that if she wanted to drive, she was going to have to get a job so she could pay for her own portion of the car insurance and her own gas money. I also told her she was going to have to take a Driver's Education course, to make sure she was ready and to reduce her insurance cost. At first, this took the wind out of her sails a little bit. These requirements seemed to take some of the fun out of her big ideas of getting her license quickly.

But, as she moved through the process over the next six months, she grew in confidence and maturity. She stuck it out through the long, boring Driver's Education classes, got all her driving hours in and became an exceptionally responsible, competent driver. By the time she was ready to get her license, I felt as comfortable in her passenger seat as I feel being driven by any other adult. And I could see that she felt confident behind the wheel. She also found a good part time job and that allowed her to pay her monthly bills and start *saving money!* This responsibility created a whole new level of maturity and sovereignty for her. I helped her as much as she needed me to, but *not more* than she needed, so she knows that she accomplished that goal.

Our children also need to see themselves along a continuum of growth and learning. We can help them with this by surrounding them with examples of development and mastery in the areas they're interested in so they can look forward to accomplishments that they haven't yet achieved. When I was a little girl, I was enthralled with ballet. I took classes at a local dance academy that had classes for all ages of children and even adults. I remember how I used to watch the teenage girls and aspired to be like them. It motivated me to strive toward their level of mastery.

I also took piano lessons all through my childhood. Every time my piano teacher gave me a new song to learn she would play it for me first so I could hear what it was supposed to sound like. She was a brilliant pianist and made the songs sound so beautiful. Sometimes, they would look impossible, especially as I got older and they became more complicated. I would be intimidated and wonder how I would ever learn how to play such a hard song. Then, she would teach me one section at a time, and I would practice – and practice! – until it came together as the fancy song she had played for me. Learning how to learn and how to work hard is a gift that every child should receive.

Boundaries and Limits

Many of the parents I work with have a hard time setting and holding firm boundaries in a grounded and loving way. I often hear from parents that try to be easy going, sweet parents but find themselves losing their temper and snapping at their kids in particular moments of overwhelm and frustration. They feel terribly guilty for taking their anger out on their kids but just can't figure out how to keep things from getting out of control in certain moments. They question their approach to discipline and reflect on the discipline of their own upbringing to try to come up with answers.

Since most of our examples of discipline come from Power Over scenarios, many well-meaning modern parents have developed a sort of phobia around boundaries and limits. I've noticed that parents tend to be afraid of being too authoritarian with their kids. They want their children to have fun and feel *free*. They want them to express themselves fully and feel that there's no limit to what they can accomplish, experience and create. In an effort to create this sense of freedom for their children, many parents avoid setting meaningful boundaries or struggle to hold them firmly and consistently. But an absence of intentional, healthy boundaries often leads to overwhelming or unsafe situations that ultimately force us to slip into unplanned moments of reactive authoritarian parenting – the very thing we were trying to avoid in the first place!

As we find ourselves at the limit of possible human consumption and pollution within our finite and interconnected biosphere, it's time to reckon with boundaries and embrace them as an essential part of our reality. In nature, everything has limits. Boundless growth, eternal life and endless pleasure are fantasies and lies propagated by the Power Over Paradigm as part of its campaign to keep us striving and disconnected. Much of the destruction caused by the POP is fueled by the idea that it's possible – and even desirable – to escape the limitations of our human bodies and the laws of nature.

But limitations and boundaries are beautiful and essential aspects of the Living World. They are the thresholds between "us" and everything to which we are connected. They define our interactions with and responsibilities to our world and all our relations. When seen through the lens of mutual thriving, they come into focus as the vital links that weave us into blessed Interbeing[2.2] while giving us our unique forms, identities and structures. The natural boundaries of living and dying, of giving and receiving, of inhaling and exhaling are the containers that support the natural order of mutual thriving.

The interconnected and mutually supportive relationships in our households can be modeled after this natural order. By assessing the mutual and individual needs of the people in your family, you can arrive at healthy boundaries that meet those needs. Like many of the typical household rules of the Power Over Paradigm, these boundaries may have to do with behavior, communication, time, sleep, space, responsibilities, personal belongings and other common family things. But these boundaries are not arbitrary rules based on external norms or predetermined values. They are responses to the actual, current needs and capacities of the members of your family.

Children need boundaries and structure to feel safe and to understand who they are in relation to the world. As we work to raise children who can function within a Life Sustaining Society, they need to understand that they belong to a world with parameters. Fortunately, kids intuitively know this, and they constantly look to us to clue them in on what those parameters are. Little ones often try things out and look at us to see our reaction. Teenagers often take risks to test boundaries and see for themselves what kind of a person they are growing into. Kids of all ages question, push and test to discover where the edges are and what (or whom) they can count on. When we meet them there mindfully and lovingly, they learn that they can count on us.

Boundaries are not just rules to be imposed on kids. They're lines. They are the edges of the containers that hold and nurture them at their different stages of growth. Because of this, they need to be both firm and flexible so they can hold our children well, and also adjust, as needed, to accommodate change and growth.

Within that flexibility, one of the most important parental technologies for creating and maintaining healthy boundaries is consistency! Consistency builds trust and helps kids understand what to expect. If a boundary has been communicated, it's essential to stand by it. So, it's important to deeply consider the boundaries you set to make sure they're reasonable, not unnecessarily confining and that you're capable of upholding them consistently. It does much more harm than good to communicate a boundary and then fail to uphold it.

If cleaning up after yourself is an agreement in your household, then it's important to hold them to that as a gateway for their next experience. If they say, *"Can I go out and play in the sprinkler, Mom?"* You can lovingly and joyfully say, *"Once you clean up that board game, you sure can! Have fun!"* When we're on top of accountability in this way, we can avoid power struggles and punishments. They know what the expectation is, and they know what they have to do to get what they want. Their fulfillment is in their own hands.

Expressing our expectations clearly and addressing the needs involved in a situation ahead of time helps hold a boundary. Give kids a heads up and prepare them for what to expect. For example, if you know you need to leave the playground by a certain time, you can let your child know that before they start playing. You can also tell them that you'll give them a five-minute warning before you leave so they can finish their game, say goodbye to friends and prepare for the transition. If you need your teenager to be home by a certain time, you can talk with them about that ahead of time so they can arrange their plans accordingly and have fun with their friends until then without feeling interrupted or confined.

You'll know if the boundaries you're using are working or not by the effects they have on your relationship. Check in on a regular basis to assess whether the boundaries you're setting are creating more connection and empowerment or not. If everyone in the situation is feeling empowered, supported, and connected, then they're working well. If not, you may need to investigate and strategize on how to adjust them.

For example, if you're feeling constantly stressed out because the house is always messy and you're the only one cleaning up, a boundary needs to be adjusted. If your child has frequent meltdowns at bedtime (or another transition moment), a boundary needs to be adjusted. If you're worrying excessively about your teenager's safety, some boundaries may need to be adjusted. If your children are closed off and withdrawn from you, some boundaries may need to be adjusted.

Kids should be involved in the creation and adjustment of the boundaries and agreements that involve them. Since the goal is to meet the needs of all family members, their involvement is essential. Your kids will have their own boundaries and needs. They will express them more and more as they get older. It's important to respect the boundaries they express all along the way to build connection and trust. This will help them feel safer and more seen. It will also help them understand and respect the boundaries that we express.

If your kid has a reasonable objection about a boundary that you've expressed, it's important to listen to the objection and try to work with it in a way that respectfully meets the needs and safety of everyone involved. In this case, encourage your kids to work with you in strategizing and creating healthy boundaries that support unmet needs. When they're involved in determining the boundaries, they'll be more invested in them and more likely to abide by them.

Questions to ask (and answers to listen to): *What isn't working for you about this situation? What do you want? What do you need? How can we work together to meet all the needs at hand?*

When you engage them in this process, be sure to confidently advocate for your own needs, the needs of the other people involved, needs for safety and other concerns to avoid a "teenagers rule the roost" situation. At the same time, challenge yourself to be authentically flexible. If they're making a reasonable request or the boundary could be adjusted to fulfill their needs without compromising safety, then see if you can stretch into it. If you can and do adjust, this could be a great solution that generates connection, respect and increased agency and autonomy for your growing kiddo.

When you're reflecting on your own needs and concerns, check in with yourself to make sure they're based on your child's and family's actual wellbeing. Sometimes our concerns stem from our projected fears, our need to be in control or to be right, our image or ego, our outdated ideas of how things "should be", our impatience, our insecurities, or something else. If you find that the boundary you've been trying to hold was motivated by something of this nature, then admit to that transparently and refocus your awareness on what is really in the child's and family's best interest.

When a boundary must be upheld against pushback, we can stay centered and grounded in love, without getting harsh and authoritarian. Even in the most emotionally charged moments, it's possible to say *"no"* lovingly and without any punitive vitriol. Your *"no"* doesn't have to be a punishment, a judgment or a harsh denial of their joy. If you are truly partnering with your children, you can empathize with what they want while, at times, seeing from your adult perspective that it is not the best choice in the moment (or maybe that it's not even possible.)

Pay attention to the energy and tone that comes with your *"no."* Do your work to stay grounded and centered in love as you make your decision and communicate the boundary. We have such a long, deeply ingrained history of dysfunctional power over dynamics and authoritarian punishment that we may unwittingly slip into the role of tyrant when we find ourselves with the need to say *"no."* But you don't have to go there. That's an old story. The story you are growing into now is a loving story of mutual thriving. You are communicating this boundary as an act of care for your children, so be sure that comes across in your body language, your tone and your energy.

It may be hard to believe, but a high quality *"no"* can often make a kid much happier than saying *"yes"* to them. They may say they *want* you to say *"yes,"* and they may whine and plead and try to manipulate you and even get mad and call you yucky names while they are in the torrent of their desire. But when you say *"no"* in a meaningful way, they are often relieved. They are suddenly released from their agony. They are no longer striving and straining. They know that whatever it is they wanted to happen is not going to happen, so they can let it go. In that time, they may even be able to see that you cared about them enough to deeply consider what they were asking and to give them the more difficult answer, which was actually in their best interest. And, on some level, they will feel grateful. (However, don't expect a thank you card or a medal just yet!)

This definitely doesn't mean you should say *"no"* all the time. In fact, the need for high quality *"no's"* should be pretty few and far between if you have cultivated a respectful partnership with your children and have clear, mutually developed family agreements. When checking in with yourself to assess the quality of your *"no"* you always want to make sure that it doesn't stem from a triggered reaction, an authoritarian projection or a fearful desire to control your children. A high quality *"no"* is authentically based on what is best for your child. It trusts their ability to handle their own unique life path, take risks and learn from experience.

Only say *"no"* when you mean it. When it matters. And then make sure your *"no"* really means *"no."* Don't teach them that if they just keep pushing and whining and begging that they'll get you to cave in. That pattern sets up both children and adults for a lifetime of disempowerment and dysfunction. If we want our kids to trust us and to respond to us, we have to teach them that the words that come out of our mouths mean something. And if we want our children to function well in society and minimize the harm they inflict on others, we have to teach them that when someone says *"no,"* that's the answer.

That being said, it's actually important to practice saying *"yes"* as much as you can without jeopardizing your kids' safety, letting them harm others or putting yourself out unnecessarily. It doesn't do any good to overdo it on boundaries and limitations. That makes them feel untrusted and overly controlled and often causes them to break the rules behind our backs and sneak around. Instead, practice letting them take reasonable risks and trying things out on their own. You have nothing to prove by controlling them.

There are some good lessons about this in the story I told earlier about my daughter wanting to choose her own school clothes when she was four. It was important that she was dressed warm enough for winter weather, but it wasn't good for our relationship to have me telling her *"no"* every morning. Rearranging her clothing supply so she only had access to winter clothes was a way of setting a boundary while allowing her the creative freedom to choose her own outfits. It wasn't important that I won a battle every morning and proved myself to be dominant. And it wasn't important whether I liked the outfit she chose. It was just important that she was warm enough and that we were building trust, connection and partnership in our relationship.

Another example of boundary setting comes from her teen years. It was Halloween night. We had moved from a *very* rural community in Colorado to the city of Portland, Oregon just two months before, at the beginning of the school year. She and her brand-new friend (who was also a new kid) were hanging out at our house because they didn't know anyone else yet and hadn't heard of any parties or events. They were kind of bored and disappointed and really wanted to have some fun so they asked if they could go out walking around downtown. It was late (around 10:30pm) on Halloween night. Trick-or-treating would be long over. They were two beautiful 15-year-old sophomores with no experience in the city and nothing to do but wander around. That sounded like a set up for disaster to me. Knowing how crazy things can get on Halloween night and how very real the threat of sexual predation is for teenage girls, I couldn't get behind them going out to aimlessly wander. I explained my concerns to them and, even though they were disappointed and pushed back a little, they understood and appreciated that I was looking out for them.

This lesson in boundaries and limitations helped my daughter put into perspective what was safe and what was not safe. It taught her the value of self-preservation, limits and awareness of the situations she chooses. Over the course of her sophomore year, she gained experience in navigating the city in various situations that were reasonably safe and became much more capable of assessing risks and handling them herself. By the end of that school year, I felt totally comfortable letting her and that same friend go out to concerts downtown. They had great fun and knew how to stay safe.

Sometimes the boundaries we set come from our gut-based parental intuition. They might not have clearly defined reasons we can explain to our children. If the boundary you're setting is truly coming from intuition, you can let them know that. But you shouldn't pull that card all the time and slip into the modes of *"because I said so"* and *"don't question my authority."* If they trust you and they know you're really looking out for them and you're not just trying to control them, they'll appreciate your intuition, even when it doesn't tell them what they want to hear.

This is true for toddlers and little kids as well, even though you may not go into as full a discussion with them. If you know it's time for them to eat or that there's been too much TV or that they'll do better if they go home for nap instead of staying to play all afternoon, you have to clearly set that boundary and follow through with it effectively. They may resist you at first, but if you're grounded and making the decision based on what they truly need, they'll adjust quickly and feel relieved and at ease that you are the parent and you have a handle on the situation.

It can be extremely challenging to hold healthy boundaries when we're not resourced or when we're stretched beyond our capacity. When we feel overwhelmed, it's like the floodgates have opened and all the lines get washed away. This time of global crisis involves the breakdown of many of the support systems we've relied on in the past. It is hard to avoid overwhelm. The terrain seems to be constantly shifting, and the pressures to be constantly increasing.

For these reasons, we often have to make very conscious choices to resource ourselves and to minimize the stress and overwhelm in our lives. When we're more resourced and centered, we're less reactive and can more lovingly and confidently set healthy boundaries. We will also be more resilient and more able to bear the uncomfortable moments when our kids push back against the boundaries we've set.

Holding healthy boundaries as a parent requires us to cultivate our own personal boundaries and (dare I say) our personal discipline. Making healthy choices, knowing our limits, setting ourselves up for wellness, choosing when to eat and sleep, saying *"no"* to extra work, and tending to self-care, homecare and mental health needs are all important foundations for setting health boundaries for our kids.

Exercising personal discipline and self-awareness regarding our own emotions and personal baggage is also essential to setting healthy boundaries for our kids. If we notice that something our kids are doing triggers big emotions in us, it may be that they are stirring up emotional baggage that we are carrying from our lineage or our own childhood. Rather than react emotionally and set boundaries in a way that is dysregulated, it's important to have the discipline to process our emotions and unpack them in our own adult space (on our own or with friends, a support group or a counselor). Taking charge of our emotional healing helps us learn to identify and create appropriate and meaningful boundaries that are based in love and respect and that are relevant to this particular moment and child.

Sometimes, to uphold a boundary, we have to be willing to be in inconvenient and uncomfortable situations. We may need to leave a party or the park earlier than we planned. We may need to have a hard conversation with one of our kids when we've got loads of work to do and we're tired. We may need to do or say something in a public setting that is unpopular. The more resourced we are, the more capable we'll be to meet these uncomfortable moments with strength.

One time, when I was at a playground with a little one I was caring for, I witnessed an unfortunate incident involving another caregiver who was not well resourced. Before she arrived, my little one and I were the only ones there, having a sweet and mellow time climbing, sliding and swinging. Then this young grandmother and two little kids arrived to start playing. She seemed stressed out and overextended. In the first few moments they were there, the two-year-old girl was climbing up the slide while her five-year-old brother was at the top of the slide, hanging from the horizontal bar that kids use to launch themselves. As she approached the top, he lifted his feet off the platform and kicked her squarely in the face. His grandmother yelled at him to stop doing that while he continued to kick her intentionally and forcefully *at least four more times!*

The grandmother yelled and yelled and told him that if he didn't stop that and come down to her, they would have to leave right away. He didn't stop until he was good and ready. And he didn't come down to his grandmother. He ran away from her as she yelled at him. And they didn't go home right away. They stayed and played like nothing had really happened. The grandmother put the little girl in a swing and the boy kept his distance from them, doing his own thing, until he was pretty sure he'd face no consequences.

I witnessed the whole scene with a pit in my stomach, wondering what happens to a little boy who learns that he can kick his little sister in the face with no consequences when he becomes a man. I wondered what happens to his sister and the other women in his life. I'd love to tell you that this was an anomaly. I'd love to say that I've never witnessed anything like that before. That I've never had that pit in my stomach before. But sadly, I have witnessed many boys growing up without clear, healthy boundaries and it gives me great concern. Actually, it gives me torment and heartbreak to consider what such behavior means for the men they will become and the women they will affect.

Consent is an essential boundary for our children to learn as they are growing up. When caring for multiple children or guiding a child in an interaction with new people (or new plants and animals) we can teach them to pay attention to the needs of the other beings and respect their sovereignty and consent. When I've got a bunch of kiddos playing with each other, I always remind them that each kid gets to make their own choices about what they want to do or not do. If they don't want to play a certain game or be touched by another kid, it's okay to say *"no."* And it's important to take *"no"* for an answer.

In situations like this, I pay special attention to the body language and interactions between the kids and help them understand each other when there is difficulty. I teach kids to ask permission and wait for the answer even (or especially) if the other kid is younger. I don't stand by and allow grabbing toys from hands or pushing. I always intervene in moments like that, and help kids navigate their dynamics and their communication so everyone feels is safe and respected. If necessary, I help them work together to find something that works for everyone, even if that means some kids are doing different things or sitting out if they want to. Instead of forcing sharing or playing together, I reinforce choice.

Many kids don't learn to respect consent and many kids suffer from that lack of consent awareness in their peers. My heart breaks when I hear the teenage girls I know talking about the abuse and harassment they receive from their male peers in person and online. Sometimes girls excuse this behavior away saying that they're not *bad people*, they just never learned how to take *"no"* for an answer. While this may be exactly true, it terrifies me. Our growing-up little girls shouldn't need to fight off (or to be scared of) our growing-up little boys. That's on us, as parents. We need to teach them early and consistently throughout their lives that *"no"* is a perfectly reasonable and acceptable answer.

I realize and acknowledge that abuse can be perpetrated by members of any gender. It's not always boys and men causing the harm, and it's not always girls and women being harmed. It's important that we teach *all* our children how to take *"no"* for an answer, how to respect consent, and how to love and respect themselves enough to prevent themselves from becoming harmful. I also recognize that there are some very strong tendencies and patterns in our patriarchal Power Over Paradigm that can turn little boys into harmful men without us even realizing it. Within this societal landscape, we have to be *very* mindful of this while we are raising male identifying children.

Often, in order to hold healthy boundaries for our kids and ourselves, we have to go against the grain of Business As Usual. That can cause a lot of tension. Throughout their lives, our kids will experience the influences of peer pressure and marketing. We also are constantly under certain forms of social pressure to conform and go along with mainstream lifestyle choices that may be in direct opposition to what we feel to be healthy. This is a major aspect of being a New Paradigm Parent. It can be really challenging. It may at times require a lot of resilience and stamina to stay true to your values and stand by your families' wellbeing, even when it's not a popular path. This can get particularly challenging during teenage years. Staying honest, loving and connected as you stand strong in your values and hold healthy boundaries will ultimately model for your kids how they can do the same in the face of peer and societal pressure.

> *"Beneath every behavior is a feeling. And beneath every feeling is a need. And when we meet that need rather than focus on the behavior, we begin to deal with the cause, not the symptom."*
>
> – Ashleigh Warner [12.2]

Managing Behavior

In every situation, children are simply responding to their environment and trying to get their needs met. There really are no "problem children." There are just children who are having a problem getting their needs met in a way that is acceptable to the adults in their life. The responsibility falls to the adults to assess the situation and discover what feelings and needs are instigating the so-called "problem behavior."

Often, children aren't able to express their needs with words, so you have to decipher the needs between the lines of their behavior. If the needs are not obvious to you at first, you may need to reflect on the situation. Consider the bigger issues at hand, the loss of empowerment the child may be experiencing, the patterns of abuse (sometimes quite subtle) that are at play, the ways in which the child's evolutionary expectations[9.8] have been interrupted, etc. If you are too close to the situation to see it clearly, it can be very helpful to get support from someone experienced with working with children in this way.

My first big lesson in this understanding came when I was working at a daycare in Flagstaff, AZ in my early twenties. I had sixteen two-year-olds in my care, and one of them was a biter! Every time I turned around, she was biting another kid and causing a huge commotion. I had no idea what to do. I was at my wits end and was so mad at her. I thought she was just a *really bad kid*.

Fortunately, I had a chance to meet with the director of the daycare and she taught me something that completely turned the situation around for this little girl and has significantly impacted my work with children ever since. She told me that this little girl was doing what she had to do to get her needs met. She told me that this little girl's parents didn't speak English at home and that she likely didn't have the language to express what she needed in this all-English setting. She said that biting was her form of communication.

After that conversation, I started to observe this little girl and her interactions with the other toddlers with a fresh perspective. I noticed that every time she tried to bite someone, it was because they had stolen a toy from her or pushed her out of the way or did something that violated her boundaries. Quickly, I started being able to anticipate these situations and intervene in just the right moment to help her stand up for herself without biting. Through these interventions, I taught her tools and words that she could use to hold her ground with her peers all by herself.

All children struggle with expressing their needs. Their needs often exceed their verbal ability and emotional maturity, even when the language spoken at home is the same as the one spoken at school. Paying attention to see what is happening before and during some sort of "bad behavior" will help us understand what needs a child may be trying to fulfill. Then, we can intervene with simple tools that they can use to get their needs met in a way that works out for them and the other people involved. This is one way that we can not only prevent "bad behavior" but also empower them from the beginning to employ their personal agency.

I've found baby sign language to be extremely helpful in this regard. Babies and toddlers have a lot of needs, desires and awarenesses brewing inside their little minds long before they're able to say words and form sentences verbally. When we teach them to communicate with their hands, they are empowered to express their needs in a way that works for them. They can easily ask for milk, or food, or water without whining. They can participate in respectful partnership and dialogue with their adults by saying *"please"* and *"thank you"* and *"more"* and *"all done"* with their hands. It puts the power of communication literally *in their hands* and can prevent a massive volume of temper tantrums, if used well.

I also like to teach the little ones I work with to ask for help very early on. Babies and toddlers often get frustrated when they try to do something and it doesn't work out. They tend to cry, whine or act out when they're frustrated. I let them know that they can always ask for help, whether it's with sign language or a simple verbal, *"help, please!"* When a child asks for my help in this way, I make sure to respond right away so they get the affirmation that this approach works. If I see them struggling with something, I ask them if they would like some help. Their choice to ask for and receive help allows them to stay centered in their power while learning how to communicate their needs in a respectful and functional way. This practice and the trust that it builds between children and adults only get more important as children get older, and their needs become more complex.

Needs and wants are not the same. Meeting our children's needs doesn't mean becoming a servant to fulfilling every request they throw our way. On the contrary, helping them meet their needs for sovereignty and empowerment will fulfill them infinitely more deeply than any amount of wishes you could grant them. To understand their needs, we have to look beyond their requests. They may say they want to watch a TV show but really, they need to be comforted, grounded or engaged. Maybe they're acting out, being rude, ignoring you or picking on their sibling. It's up to us to find out what feelings are beneath these behaviors and what needs are beneath those feelings.

When children are freaking out or whining, even if they're asking for help while they're doing it, I ask them to calm down and use their "regular" voice. I don't like to say "big kid voice" or "nice voice" because this isn't about chastising them or shaming them into behaving the way I want them to. It's about helping them orient to their center and their own power. They have a voice they use to ask you for things when they're centered in their personal empowerment. When they're at ease. When they're not desperate. Help them anchor into that place and speak from there. It's important for them to practice this. It will serve them for the rest of their lives. This approach can work with whiny tweens and teenagers too. They want to feel power. Teaching this skill helps them learn how to access their power and act with agency in their lives.

If you feel you've been plagued with a whiner, this practice delivers some very exciting and potentially hard to believe news for you. Children don't *have to* whine. Whining is not an inevitable part of childhood and its disappearance from your life is *entirely* in your hands. Whining is not about the kids at all. It's about the adults and their vibe. Usually, it's about the adults' general lack of presence, distance, ambivalence, desperation, confusion and/or overwhelm. These states communicate to children that there is no grounded adult in the room. Whining happens when children panic because they have a need or desire that they can't fulfill without the help of a grounded adult. When that need is not acknowledged and responded to, they start to freak out and the whining begins. They feel abandoned and disempowered, so they start grasping and flailing about to capture some version of power.

"Either we spend time meeting children's emotional needs by filling their cup with love or we spend time dealing with the behaviors caused from their unmet needs. Either way we spend the time."

– Pam Leo [9.6]

When my baby was 6 weeks old, she, her father and I moved into a house with another family we were friends with for a couple of months while the two dads were working on a remodeling project together. The other family had four children between the ages of one and eight. So, my baby was suddenly the youngest of five, and I had the blessing of some high-quality mama mentoring with my dear friend who had *a lot* of mothering experience. I learned many lessons during that time, but one particularly stands out. It seems so simple in retrospect, but at the time it was a big one for me, and I know that it's something that other parents struggle with, as well.

There was a lot of activity in the house with five kids eight years old and under. But, on top of all that, I wanted to do some canning. I was used to achieving and accomplishing a lot. I tended to have a "get 'er done" kind of mentality that was just about focusing and pushing to get through a project until it was done. In the middle of my canning project, my baby started to fuss because she needed to nurse. As I was trying to stay focused on my project and ignore her fussing until I got to a good stopping point, the tension in the room heightened. I was stressed and anxious. My baby was getting more agitated. I was feeling exasperated, as the sound of her cry raised my blood pressure, and I fumbled through my work.

My friend, wise woman that she was, said, *"Jo, just pause and take care of her needs."* She taught me that taking a short moment out of my "important business" to fill my baby up, not only with milk but also with my presence, would set her up to be satisfied and chill so I could then get back to work and finish it up well. Revolutionary!

Many parents feel overwhelmed by their children's neediness. They wind up spending a lot of time and energy pushing their kids away because they feel like they'll never get anything else done if they don't just power through and stay focused on their adult business. When parents are able to pause periodically to fill up their kids with their presence or help them meet their needs, the kids are generally satisfied, and the parents are able to get back into their groove. Kids who receive high quality presence like this from their parents wind up being pretty independent and quickly need us less and less. It's like getting filled up with really good, satisfying, healthy food as opposed to pigging out on junk food that always leaves you craving and hungry.

When it comes to managing challenging behavior or arguments between siblings and friends, we can help children learn and establish mutually respectful ways of interacting based on the Thriving Life Paradigm qualities we explored in Chapter 7. The intention for this help is not to avoid conflict, bottle up feelings or behave in an "acceptable" manner. The intention is to guide our children towards respectful, creative and authentic collaboration for mutual thriving. Considering specific moments of challenge with your children through the lens of these qualities can help you reflect on what you really want to teach them and how you could go about it.

For example, I help kids understand how to mutually address the needs of everyone involved by teaching them that sharing is really awesome, but that it's not mandatory. I also teach them that if someone is uncomfortable or scared by something someone else is doing, whatever's bothering them should be stopped. When there's a conflict or a disagreement, I help them try to figure out and understand what each kid needs and how those needs can be met by working together.

Once your children have a decent foundation in these practices, it's good to let them work things out amongst themselves as often as possible. It's better to let them try to sort things out on their own than to swoop in and intervene every time. But occasional, conscious support can be really helpful. You can eavesdrop to see how they're doing. Notice what happens and whether they're coming up with good solutions on their own or getting stuck in dysfunction. If you notice unhealthy power dynamics playing out, you can step in to gently redirect them towards solutions for mutual thriving when necessary. Sometimes it takes guidance and creative problem solving with adult support to figure out functional agreements that work for the situation.

Natural Consequences

Even with the best New Paradigm Parenting practices deeply cultivated in your relationship with your children, there will be moments when their behavior "crosses the line"; when they do something intentionally naughty, lie to you, ignore the boundaries you've established together or fail to do something important. In these moments, you may think you need to punish them to make them learn their lesson.

This form of punitive justice is the lifeblood of the Power Over Paradigm. The fear of punishment from those who hold more power than they do is what generally drives people to comply with the POP. As we raise children who can think and function beyond this destructive paradigm, we have to help them "learn their lessons" in ways that empower them to behave more responsibly, rather than scaring them into compliance.

Natural consequences are the best way for children to learn from their choices. These are the consequences that naturally arise from their actions and are in direct proportion to their behavior. This approach is different from the typical forms of punishment in a punitive system that generally are designed to make a child feel confined and controlled, like grounding them or taking away their phone or some other unrelated privilege. When we use natural consequences, we stay in our power as loving adults, and they get to stay in their power as learning children. It's not about making them suffer. It's about helping them learn.

Examples of natural consequences could be:

- You were rude to your friend and now they don't want to play with you.
- You didn't bring your favorite shoes in from the yard before it rained and now they're too wet to wear.
- You didn't get your homework done in time so you can't go out to the movies tonight.
- You broke something you shouldn't have been playing with and you have to work to repair it or pay for its repair.

In some situations, we have to simulate natural consequences because either the actual natural consequence would be too harsh or because the consequence doesn't unfold in a completely natural way. In the case of a consequence that would be too harsh, like getting hit by a car if they run into the street, you can startle them by grabbing them quickly and stopping them where they are. In a case where the consequence may not unfold in a completely natural way, like they actually *could* keep dirtying new dishes, you can firmly hold the boundary that they have to wash all the dishes they have in their room before they use another dish. When simulating a consequence, be sure that it is directly related to and in proportion to the behavior. Also, make sure that they understand that it is a consequence of their choice and an opportunity to learn.

When behavioral situations get more complex, especially as children get older, it can be helpful to use the tools and principles of Restorative Justice[12.3] and Restorative Practices.[12.4] By focusing on repair, rather than punishment, these practices deepen connections and empower children (and everyone involved) to take action on behalf of collective wellbeing. This type of Thriving Life approach is, and has been, commonplace in non-POP communities for countless generations.

In his book *The Healing Wisdom of Africa,* Malidoma Somé[10.2] illuminates the essential difference between punitive discipline and a restorative approach by saying:

> *"Accountability in the form of punishment is debilitating; it encourages concealment, secrecy, and even distortion of reality. It is no wonder that people who are threatened with shaming punishment will try to conceal their deed. Such an urge, to indigenous people, would be legitimate, for it would show a desire to protect the self from annihilation. Accountability defined as a deepening of relationship, by contrast, becomes a productive example in service to the greater whole. For example, when someone causes hurt in someone else, correction rather than punishment is in order; the wrongdoer makes things right by deepening the relationship with the person hurt, maintaining it for the rest of one's life."*

Restorative practices focus on repairing harm. When a child causes some form of harm, a restorative approach can help them understand the scope of the harm they caused and can empower them to make amends, restore trust and fix whatever was broken. In this approach, the person who caused the harm meets with the person(s) who were harmed and, through a facilitated process, hears their story and understands the impact of the incident.

Instead of seeking a punishment, all parties work together to figure out the best way to repair the damage done (physically and/or emotionally). The person who caused the harm then carries out the agreed upon restorative action. This practice is another way of helping our children stand firmly in their own power as they learn that they not only have the power to *cause* damage but also the power to *repair* the damage done and to *prevent* similar situations in the future. See the practices at the end of this chapter for a detailed explanation of how to use Restorative Practices in your household.

> *"What we are teaches the child far more than what we say, so we must be what we want our children to become."*
>
> – Joseph Chilton Pearce [12.5]

Lead by Example

The main occupation of young people is imitating the older people they see in their lives. It's particularly obvious (and cute) when toddlers wear their parents' shoes or pretend to drive the car or copy the adult phrases they hear. But it extends all the way through childhood and into all the not-so-cute areas, as well. Children are designed to model themselves after their adults, so it's up to us to *be* what we want our children to learn.

Hopefully the old phrase *"do as I say, not as I do"* will never seriously run across your lips or even through your mind. That's not how it works. Children will always mimic you and rarely listen to you if your words aren't backed up by actions. We can't control or mold our children. We can only inspire them by how we live.

When they're very little, they will naturally want to emulate you. If a child feels inspired by your example, if it is uplifting, empowering and healthy, they may continue to want to emulate you on some level as they get older. If a child feels wounded by your example, they may be more inclined to rebel. In either case (and sometimes much to their chagrin) they will wind up replicating many of your qualities, habits and patterns. If you're honest with yourself, you can probably see many ways that you are like your own parents. You can probably see examples of this in the people you're close with, as well; your spouse, close friends etc. We *do* learn by example. We *do* repeat patterns, habits and qualities.

Having this awareness can help you to be mindful and intentional about the example you're setting for the children in your life. You can engage this awareness by periodically reflecting on your own behavior to see if it aligns with how you want your children to behave, and then make adjustments, as needed. Ask yourself: *How do I talk to my kids? Do I have a kind tone or a harsh tone? Do I interrupt them? Snap at them? Command them? Do I grab things from their hands? Do I move them or make big changes to their experience without communicating with them?* Most adults do these things frequently without realizing it, and then expect their children to ask politely for things, not to grab, not to whine and so on, just because that's what they were told to do.

The book *Redirecting Children's Behavior* by Kathryn J. Kvols[12.6] and the parenting courses that go along with it provide excellent resources for putting this awareness into practice. I hate to spoil it for you if you plan to read it, but I've got to tell you the thing I love best about it. Not only are the recommendations it provides extremely effective, but it is all about redirecting *adults'* behavior. The author perfectly reorients parents into understanding that *we* are the ones who set the tone and create the environment to which our children are responding. It shows us how all children's behavior is an expression of that response. This significant shift in perspective diffuses power struggles between parents and children by re-empowering everyone in the situation and teaching us how to cultivate meaningful partnerships with our kids.

Although it's incredibly helpful to begin our parenting experience with this awareness, it's *never* too late to bring it into our relationships with our children. Even if things have gotten out of hand in your household (maybe the kids are rude to each other, nobody's cleaning up after themselves, kids talk back to the parents, etc.) at any point in time, you can choose to set a different tone. The most important thing to remember, though, is that you have to start with yourself. Any issue we have with a child needs to be addressed by looking at our own behaviors first. This doesn't mean that kids never do anything "wrong" and parents are always at "fault." It means that kids are always responding to their situation. Their behavior reflects their situation, over which you, as their adult, have a lot of influence. Even if you don't see them very often, you can create a powerfully positive influence for them if you are willing to be very intentional about the quality of presence you hold in relation to them and the environment you create for them when they're with you.

PRACTICES FOR GUIDING GROWTH

As your children grow, they'll be looking to you for support and guidance. Each step along the way will offer you the opportunity to consider your approach to this guidance through the lens of the Thriving Life Paradigm. Co-creating healthy boundaries and holding them lovingly, stretching together into your learning zones and being mindful of which lessons are being emphasized along the way are all parts of this journey. These practices are here to help you explore how the concepts shared in this chapter can be worked with in your household in a playful and empowering way. Please experiment with them and adapt them, as needed, to meet your family's needs.

Guiding Growth: Open Sentences for Co-Parents and Kids

Please refer to the instructions for Open Sentences in the practice section of Chapter 5: Grounding in Gratitude.

Open Sentences to use with your co-parents:

1. Some of the ways we could encourage more meaningful contributions from the kids in this coming year are…
2. The types of moments and situations when I find myself reverting to punitive styles of discipline are…
3. The ways in which I feel our family agreements are working (or not working) are…
4. Some ways I could support our kids in getting their needs met are…
5. Some ways I could be a better example for our kids are…

Open Sentences to use with your kids:

1. When I'm in my learning zone I feel...
2. Some of the responsibilities and freedoms I feel like I'm ready for in this next year are...
3. The family agreements that really seem to be working (or not working) are...
4. When I go against one of our family agreements, I feel like the adults in my life should...
5. The adults in my life show me good examples of behaving by...

Family Agreements

Many families have household rules, spoken or unspoken, with consequences for breaking them. Some families have chore charts and behavior charts with methods for tracking how the kids are doing. For the most part, these systems are created and monitored by parents to maintain parental sanity and an orderly household. Sometimes the kids are included in the process, but without a deeply rooted practice of partnering with our children, these attempts for inclusion can fall flat. If you've got a chore chart or set of household rules that often gets ignored, it may be that your kids don't really feel connected to them or feel that they serve them in a meaningful way.

As New Paradigm Parents, it's important to acknowledge that our families are complex, dynamic teams of people working together daily. Each family member (of every age) has needs and each family member (of every age) has gifts to offer to fulfill those needs and help make things run smoothly for everyone. So it makes sense that we would communicate those needs with each other and make agreements with each other about how we're going to help each other meet those needs, right?

When your kids are very little, you and the other adult(s) in the family may take the lead on thinking through and developing agreements. But, even then, be sure to honestly consider your children's needs, preferences and capacities to help in the equation. As your children get a little older (perhaps 3 or 4) you can start including them in the process of co-creating agreements in areas that are most relevant to them. This doesn't have to be a big sit-down thing. It could be as simple as deciding what roles everyone has in setting up for dinner and cleaning up afterwards so dinner can be a fun and joyful experience for everyone. As they get older, the process of co-creating agreements will evolve and they will have more and more to contribute.

The practice of co-creating family agreements should always be rooted in cultivating an authentic sense of connection and belonging. The goal isn't to create boundaries and limits to control behavior. The goal is to continually get better at working together to make everything flow as smoothly as possible.

As kids grow up and family dynamics change, agreements will need to be revisited and adjusted. Your family may be called to revisit and adjust their agreements by a breach of a former agreement or a new threshold behavior that hasn't been addressed yet (like a middle schooler staying out with friends after school and not communicating with parents). Sometimes a new phase of growth (like a teen getting a driver's license) will be the impetus to revisit or enhance agreements. A major life change (like a parent getting a different job or the family moving to a new place) could be cause for updating agreements to meet the needs of the new situation. Even if everything is going along smoothly, with no big changes, I recommend checking in with your agreements about once a year, perhaps at a time that feels like the beginning of a new cycle (the beginning of the calendar year, school year or growing season, for example). This will give you all a chance to tune into whether the agreements have been working well and to look ahead to the next yearly cycle to see if you anticipate any new needs arising.

Ask questions like: *What do we each need in order for our shared daily life to go well? What do we each need to feel happy, safe and empowered?* Then listen to each other actively and collaborate openly on how to pitch in to make this happen. Someone will want to jot down the ideas that come up so you can refine them together.

When you arrive at a handful of clear agreements, write them down and post them somewhere you all can see. It's best to keep these simple but meaningful. They may not contain all the little details that you talked about as a family, but they'll serve as reminders.

Here are some examples:

- We agree to take responsibility for our own feelings and ask for help when we need it.
- We agree to be honest with each other and maintain open channels of communication.
- We agree to pick up after ourselves and help keep our shared spaces tidy.

Agreements like these apply to everyone and should be held equally for parents and children. They also cover a lot of ground in just a few words. Depending on the specific circumstances of your family and the discussion that generated it, the agreement about honesty and clear communication could include keeping each other informed of our whereabouts, answering texts promptly or being transparent about what we're doing and who we're spending time with, for example.

When things feel like they're going astray and like connection and communication are breaking down, or when an agreement has clearly been violated, you can come back to the agreements together as a family. Instead of designing a punishment, this is an opportunity to try to figure out why the agreement was broken and how to repair the situation. (See the following Restorative Justice in the Home practice for some ideas on how to approach the violation of an agreement.)

Restorative Justice in the Home

When family agreements are broken, instead of determining blame and doling out punishments, New Paradigm Parents can use practices inspired by Restorative Justice (RJ). Mirroring the traditional wisdom and justice practices of many Indigenous cultures and non-POP communities, Restorative Justice was formally coined and developed in the 1970s by Howard Zehr[12.7] as an alternative within the criminal justice system in the United States. It has since become widely known throughout the world and has been integrated into communities, schools and households as a foundational framework for transforming our approach to discipline.

The central tenet of RJ is to restore collective wellbeing by repairing harm. In this practice, when an agreement has been broken or a boundary violated, all the people who are involved in or affected by the breach come together to hear from each other and figure out together what needs to be done to repair the damage and restore a sense of trust and wellbeing within the relationships. Instead of being shamed or ostracized for being "bad," the person who caused the damage is given the opportunity to make amends and work toward fixing what has been broken. When they hear directly from the person(s) affected by their actions, they're able to gain a greater perspective on the situation and are often motivated to make things right.

When you create a Restorative Justice circle at home, you'll move through the following phases:

- Establish the container
- Express what happened (just facts, no feelings/judgments yet)
- Share feelings and judgments
- Assess the impact
- Co-create resolutions
- Close with gratitude

Steps for your Restorative Justice circle:

1. Gather the people involved in and affected by the breach, along with at least one relatively neutral and lovingly grounded person to facilitate the communication. This person could be a parent, an adult friend of the family or even an older child if they are able to facilitate the process effectively.
2. The person facilitating will begin by creating a clear and safe container for the process. The facilitator will make sure everyone knows the steps of the process and what to expect. They will let the group know that they'll be guided through the process and that the facilitator will make sure that everyone is kind to each other and stays focused on working together towards a resolution. Before beginning, be sure to establish some very basic agreements for communication and determine how long you've set aside for the process.
3. The facilitator will then share a basic, facts-based statement of what they understand to be the breach. Refrain from including any judgments or feelings in this statement. You can refer to your family agreements as a baseline if that's helpful.
4. Then, each person is given a specific amount of time (use a timer) to share what they understand to be the breach, basically answering the question "What happened?" without including judgments and feelings at this point.
5. Then, each person is given a specific amount of time (use a timer) to share how they felt about the situation at the time and how they have been feeling about it since. This is an opportunity to express and understand the impact of the action and harm it caused.
6. Next, the facilitator will provide an opportunity to check in about who has been affected by this situation. If anyone who has been affected is not there in the circle with you, this is a chance to express and consider what they may have experienced.

7. Then, each person is given a specific amount of time (use a timer) to share what they think could be done to remedy the situation, repair the harm and restore balance and wellbeing in the relationships involved. It's a good idea for the facilitator to jot down some notes during this sharing to capture specific ideas and language around possible resolutions.
8. Once everyone has had the opportunity to share their ideas, the person facilitating can summarize the possible restorative paths that were presented. They will then check in with each of the people involved to find out if they are willing to follow through with the proposed actions and if they feel these actions would successfully restore wellbeing in their relationships.
9. Then, clarify the agreed upon path forward and get it down in writing. Be sure to be clear about who is going to do what and in what timeframe. This step is important to support accountability and integrity and to rebuild trust.
10. Before closing, be sure to express gratitude and appreciation for each other.

If there is no neutral person available to facilitate, the people involved (kids and parents) can work together to move through the steps, being mindful to prioritize connection and cooperation along the way. Remember, this is a way forward from harm and an opportunity to heal and repair harm together. Everyone involved, whether they caused the harm and/or were impacted by the harm, has a role to play in restoring wellbeing in the relationships connected to the situation.

In addition to the work of Howard Zehr and the Zehr Institute for Restorative Justice,[12.7] there are many brilliant people and communities who have contributed to the development and practice of Restorative Justice over the past several decades. I encourage you to research and explore the many resources available online and in print for a deeper understanding of Restorative Justice and for tools to support your RJ practice at home. The International Institute for Restorative Practices has collected some powerful accounts of Restorative Practices being used by tribal justice systems and Indigenous communities in North America.[12.8] One of the people who has been most inspiring to me in this work is Fania Davis. I heard her speak at the Bioneers Conference[12.9] when she was the Executive Director of Restorative Justice for Oakland Youth (RJOY).[12.10]

13

THRIVING LIFE EDUCATION

> *"...the whole process of education occurs within a social framework and is designed to perpetuate the aims of society. [...] The paradox of education is precisely this – that as one begins to become conscious, one begins to examine the society in which he is being educated. The purpose of education, finally, is to create in a person the ability to look at the world for himself, to make his own decisions."*
>
> – James Baldwin [13.1]

Both what children learn and the ways in which they learn massively influence how they come to understand themselves and the world. Over the course of their young lives, their educational experience molds and refines their paradigm. As parents raising children for Thriving Life within a Power Over Paradigm society, we must constantly navigate the paradox that James Baldwin describes in his quote above. Through attentive awareness that *"all education occurs within a social framework,"* we can support our children in learning *how to learn* in a way that allows reflection and critical analysis of *what* they're learning, *how* they're learning and the *outcomes* of their education.

This is no small feat! On top of everything else we're doing as parents, grappling with our children's education in this way can feel like an impossible task. Most parents rely on the schools available in their local community to play a significant role in caring for and occupying their children. In most households, sending the kids to school is essential for allowing both parents to work and making it possible to cover the bills. Also, in many places and situations, education for youth is mandated by the government and educational choices are limited, especially for those without access to wealth.

Additionally, since formal education is a central method for the perpetuation of societal structures, it often feels risky or taboo to bring it into question. The topic of children's education is deeply layered with personal emotions, strong opinions and a complex history of politics and power that is woven into our personal and collective lineages. As people educated into society, we each have our own blinders, assumptions and misconceptions about that society and its education systems. This makes it very difficult to analyze education clearly from within. It also limits our ability to imagine beyond the bounds of these systems into what our children's education really could be.

As New Paradigm Parents, we can turn to the Thriving Life Paradigm to guide our deep consideration of our children's education. Aligning with mutual thriving using the principles and qualities we've explored in this book can help us to imagine new possibilities for our children's education. My Thriving Life Education framework has grown from my observations and experiences supporting children's education in these pivotal times. It integrates precepts and practices that I've learned from Indigenous methodologies and modern alternative approaches to education with the massive paradigm shifting work we're being called to do in this generation.

I define Thriving Life Education as *a natural, continuum-based experience that supports the healthy social, emotional, intellectual, practical and ecological learning necessary to provide fertile roots for healthy, responsible, innovative and caring future adults who are able to contribute to mutual thriving.* It includes learning about the living world and our place as humans within it, ideally in an experiential way that strengthens our loving relationships with our more-than-human kin. It is held within a web of intergenerational, long-term relationships of mutual respect and care with other humans in community. It involves developing a clear-eyed assessment of what has happened throughout history and what is happening now regarding human dynamics and systems of power and oppression. It engages imagination and creativity as we envision a positive, healthy future and practice the skills necessary to cultivate it.

If circumstances allow, this framework can provide a rich basis for a homeschooling or unschooling experience. A complete educational experience can be crafted by carefully unpacking the elements outlined above and adapting them to your unique situation and accessible resources. These elements can also be woven into a conventional schooling experience, as you're able, by supplementing what your kids are learning at school with other skills, qualities, experiences and inquiries that support Thriving Life.

Making it Work for Your Family

There's no "right" answer or one-size-fits-all approach to Thriving Life education. The same type of education doesn't work for every family. Even within a singular family, many parents find that the same type of education may not work for each of their children or that their children's needs change over time. Some families have access to choices for their children's primary form of education while others don't. Depending on your specific situation and where you live, you may be limited by local laws, accessibility, financial constraints and other practical factors. As you partner with your children, you'll also have to balance your preferences and opinions with your children's desires and what's actually working for them at each step along the way.

When your vision of Thriving Life Education meets the constraints of the real world, it may end up looking quite different than you had initially imagined. Many parents feel overwhelmed by the challenges and limitations they face around their children's education. The frustration and disappointment of not being able to manifest their full vision causes many parents to acquiesce to conventional schooling and disconnect from their children's education to some extent. They may simply send their kids to the school that's available and leave the education part to the teachers.

However, our relationship with our children's education doesn't have to be all or nothing. Compromise, flexibility and creative adjustments are definitely part of making Thriving Life Education work for each of our unique families and circumstances in these modern times. I desperately wanted to homeschool my child, but our circumstances and her needs didn't allow for that path. So, we found our way together through the ins and outs of her educational experience, weaving different types of schooling together with other forms of education throughout the years. I have witnessed countless other parents and children navigate their educational experience in a similar way, each one discovering a different combination of resources and methods to support their journey. You and your children can also find your way through their educational experience in a way that centers Thriving Life.

As you move through this journey with your children, I encourage you to explore and learn about different methods and models of education. Follow your intuition and the leads that arise in your life to learn about methods like Montessori,[13.2] Waldorf [13.3] and the Reggio Emilia Approach[13.4] and to explore models like project-based learning,[13.5] experiential education[13.6] and self-directed learning.[13.7] Educate yourself on the different types of learning styles,[13.8] as well, so you can understand how your child learns best. Your knowledge in these areas will help you understand how their current schooling situation is working for them and how you may be able to adjust it or supplement it based on their needs.

In this exploration, seek out learning environments and methods that inspire your children and keep them engaged in learning while supporting their social and emotional development. While this is especially important in their early years, as they are learning how to work with others and navigate social dynamics in healthful ways, I also think it is essential throughout their teen years. When possible, you can supplement their primary source of education with other learning experiences that are particularly supportive to their social and emotional development and wellbeing. If you're part of a faith-based community, you can explore the options they provide. In my experience, Unitarian Universalist congregations often have very high-quality religious education programs for children that are mostly centered around social and emotional development and wellbeing.[13.9] Other programs can also provide these types of experiences. You can seek out similar opportunities in your part of the world or create them in your community.

If your children are being educated by someone else, ask them about what they're learning and talk with them about it regularly. Be curious and let them teach you their new skills and the concepts they are coming to understand. This is a great way to stay connected with your children and to empower them to deepen their learning experience by teaching what they've learned. Engage them in meaningful explorations and critical thinking about what they're being taught, especially in areas where the POP is being heavily reinforced and untruths or distorted perspectives are being passed off as fact. Instead of refuting or discounting what they are learning, ask questions that help your children think about the topics more deeply and consider them within the larger context of Thriving Life.

Make sure your children's education experience includes high-quality, place-based, experiential, ecological connection. This is essential. Children being raised to contribute to Thriving Life need to have meaningful learning experiences that inspire wonder as well as fondness for and actual intimacy with the natural living world. It is not enough to learn *about* nature. Children must learn *from and with* nature by exploring, playing, getting dirty and feeling themselves to be part of the thriving world of relations. Many forms of outdoor education are becoming more popular and accessible in communities around the world, from fully immersive Forest Schools[13.10] to garden-based curriculum[13.11] and outdoor learning adventures[13.12] within public school settings. If your children's primary source of education doesn't already include this, you can seek out extra-curricular programs for them, plan family nature time and/or volunteer to support initiatives and programs for nature immersion and outdoor learning at your children's school.

Children, like all of us, learn best when they are interested in and inspired by what they're learning. Pay attention to what lights your children up and makes them want to learn more. Then, give them more of that. Whether it's in a school setting, a homeschooling experience or through extra-curricular activities, try to provide opportunities for your children to pursue their passions and interests. If they are particularly interested in a certain topic or skill, seek out ways to support them in developing mastery in that area, especially if it involves any form of beauty-making or life-nurturing. The cultivation of magnificence and elegance feeds Thriving Life as it sculpts humans into beings of dignity and honor who can provide for the world through our delicately honed skills.

This is one of the many great reasons to engage mentors in your child's life. Helping your children establish meaningful, long-term, intergenerational learning relationships with people beyond your immediate family will help them hone their skills over time and connect with their own purpose and brilliance. In *The Healing Wisdom of Africa*, Malidoma Somé [10.2] says, *"There are certain things without which young people cannot survive and flourish, and mentoring is one of them. Westerners see adolescents as fundamentally naïve about life. By contrast, the tribal mentor sees a youth as someone who already contains all of the knowledge that he or she needs, but who must work with an older, more experienced person* to 'remember' what they know." He goes on to say, "The mentor perceives a presence knocking at a door within the pupil, and accepts the task of finding, or becoming, the key that opens the door. There develops a relationship of trust between mentor and pupil, motivated by love, and without which success would be unlikely."

In these pivotal times, Thriving Life Education must also include the thoughtful cultivation of a livable future – in our hearts, minds and hands. Envisioning and working towards a future of mutual thriving for all beings are important aspects of our children's learning experience. Critical thinking, creative problem solving and innovation are also essential, but *must* be applied in service to mutual thriving. Humans are innately innovative, which can be both beautiful and problematic, depending on the paradigm with which we're working. Many of the existing programs that encourage innovative thinking for youth are heavily focused on technological development and are geared toward human-centric survival, without a full recognition of the mutuality of thriving. As you engage your children in addressing the challenges of our times through creative problem solving (or find programs that do this), be sure to help them continually orient within the framework of mutual thriving.

As I mentioned before, these elements of Thriving Life Education can be woven into our children's educational experience whether we are homeschooling, unschooling or supporting our children as they attend school. In any of these cases, as New Paradigm Parents, it's important for us to deeply consider and reflect on *what* they are learning, *how* they are learning it, and what the *outcomes* of their education are likely to be.

Liberatory Education

What we now know as "formal education" has a complex history. In important ways, it has been used both to enforce the oppressive structures of the Power Over Paradigm *and* to liberate people from them. Because of this, there are many layers of complexity around the economic, social and racial privileges (or lack of privileges) that affect our educational choices and our feelings about these choices.

On one hand, high quality, freely accessible education is generally considered to be essential for a functional democracy and for equality within a population. At various times throughout history, and in many parts of the world, withholding education (or the poor quality of education) for certain sectors of society - such as people of color, girls and economically disenfranchised people - has been (and continues to be) used to keep them out of power. Many people across many generations have struggled to achieve the right to education for all. Increases in access to education have significantly affected the balance of power in our societies, making possible massive social movements and activating powerful changemakers throughout history. For these reasons, many parents deeply value this right and feel a profound sense of responsibility to ensure that their children receive high quality, formal education.

On the other hand, conventional, compulsory schooling has been used (and continues to be used) to separate children from their families and the ways of Thriving Life, while training them to conform to the expectations of the Power Over Paradigm. Schooling children has been (and continues to be) one of the primary tactics of colonization used throughout the "developing world" and an essential pillar of maintaining the status quo throughout established "first world" societies.

The format of conventional schooling and the content it covers are geared towards supporting industrial capitalism, keeping kids occupied while their parents are at work and conditioning them to comply with the factory standards and power hierarchy that this economy requires. During the school closures of the Corona virus pandemic, the relationship between the economy and having kids in school was highlighted as many parents struggled to do their jobs with their children suddenly at home. When school is in session, most children spend more waking hours at school than they do with their parents. What was once a privilege reserved for the elite is now mandated in many places and has turned into a means to keep the economy chugging along and maintain control over the masses.

As you consider your children's education in alignment with the Thriving Life Paradigm, I encourage you to explore beyond conventional models of schooling and seek out opportunities to engage in their education as a decolonizing, liberatory, paradigm-shifting practice. Over the past few decades, movements for unschooling, homeschooling and other alternative approaches to education have grown in popularity and in quality as they develop to meet the real needs of children with thoughtful and evidence-based practices and principles. Even if your children attend conventional school for some or all their school-age years, these alternative methods and the principles they teach can be woven into their educational experience to augment and support a deeper practice of learning and growing that can help your children move beyond the limitations of the Power Over Paradigm.

There's a common myth that alternative education is only for wealthy or racially privileged families. There are, indeed, many expensive private schools and programs that use alternative educational methods, but they're not all practicing paradigm transformation, and they aren't the only way to engage in alternative education. Many of the movements and projects I find most inspiring in alternative education are led by BIPOC (Black, Indigenous and People of Color) folks who are opening and defining these alternative educational pathways as acts of radical paradigm transformation and reclamation of freedom, autonomy and connection with Thriving Life.

Akilah S. Richards is one of these brilliant people and is at the forefront of the unschooling movement. In her book *Raising Free People*,[11.1] she shares about the messaging she received about education as a young Black girl, recently arrived in the United States from her home in Jamaica. She says, "*...our families were all in consensus that the path to excellence, this route to liberation, was tucked firmly inside a good education. Just like in Jamaica, I gathered from the messages around me that I could...and should be Black and proud – but not if that interrupted being Black and* *educated. As I started my American schooling, I began internalizing the idea that I had to tuck away my personhood (personality, preferences, opinions, too much Blackness) to excel at studenthood."*

She did excel as a student, and when she became a parent, she and her husband first approached their daughters' education with this same belief that a high-quality formal education was the key to liberation. When their daughters failed to thrive in a conventional school, they initially thought it was their responsibility, as good parents, to force and coerce them into adjusting to school and complying with the conventional model so they could succeed. However, by paying attention to what was going on with their children, and listening to their intelligent, heartfelt responses to their experience, they began to understand their children and to see schooling through an entirely different lens. In response to their children's needs and in a commitment to partner with them deeply, they took the outrageous risk of trusting their children and beginning a dynamic journey together into unschooling.

Led by Thriving Life principles and practices, they found a freedom and depth of empowerment that far surpasses what they could have experienced on a conventional path. Years into this journey, Akilah shares this about unschooling; *"Our family defines unschooling as a child-trusting, anti-oppression, liberatory, love-centered approach to parenting and caregiving. As unschoolers, the four of us operate with a core belief that children own themselves and that parents and other adults work with children to nurture their confident autonomy, not their ability to obey adults' directives."* [11.1]

As we consider education through the lens of the Thriving Life Paradigm, it's important to interrogate *how* the learning experience occurs, *what* is being taught and learned and *why* that content and those methods are being used. The educational methods and content most of us are familiar with through our experience with modern schooling are not the only way for a young person to learn. As modern colonialism has ravaged intact Indigenous communities throughout the world, these modern methods have interrupted, replaced and attempted to erase sophisticated systems of education that have been in use for countless generations. Although each community has its own unique and culturally specific methods, content and systems for educating their young people, intact Indigenous approaches to education generally share some Thriving Life principles that are distinctly different from modern schooling. They are commonly experiential, community-based, place-based, Earth centered, intergenerational and in service to the collective wellbeing of the community and of all Life.

Gregory Cajete, Ph.D. of the Tewa people of Santa Clara Pueblo (New Mexico, USA) speaks to Indigenous ways of learning and knowing in his book, *Native Science*,[13.13] by saying, *"Native science is a metaphor for a wide range of tribal processes of perceiving, thinking, acting, and 'coming to know' that have evolved through human experience with the natural world. Native science is born of a lived and storied participation with the natural landscape. To gain a sense of Native science one must participate with the natural world. To understand the foundations of Native science one must become open to the roles of sensation, perception, imagination, emotions, symbols, and spirit as well as that of concept, logic, and rational empiricism."*

Fortunately, some of these traditional practices have been preserved against all odds through courageous acts of resilience and resistance. In some communities, certain children in each generation were hidden from the missionaries and government officials who came to round them up for boarding schools (or residential schools). These children were kept with the community so they could learn and carry on the old ways. Some communities have taught their forbidden languages and passed on stories to younger generations in clandestine ways, sometimes encrypting sophisticated cultural knowledge in "fairy tales" and games for children so it could slip passed the attention of the colonizers. Many Indigenous people and communities around the world are now focused on reviving their traditional methods of education for their children as an essential practice of colonial resistance and decolonization. Languages and skills that were nearly wiped out are being revived and passed on to younger generations in projects such as the Keres

Children's Learning Center[13.14] in Cochita Pueblo (New Mexico, USA) and Te Wānanga o Aotearoa,[13.15] a Maori higher education learning center that has over eighty locations in New Zealand.

Dr. Lyla June Johnston is one of the many advocates for the revitalization of Indigenous education. In many of her talks, she shares reflections about her own educational journey, as a young Diné woman, moving through the conventional colonial schooling system in the United States and eventually learning to subvert it to serve the revitalization of Indigenous ways of learning, knowing and living. She studied Human Ecology as an undergraduate at Stanford University, got her Master's degree in Indigenous Pedagogy at the University of New Mexico and then completed her Ph.D on Indigenous Studies at the University of Alaska Fairbanks with a dissertation called *Architects of Abundance: Indigenous Regenerative Food and Land Management Systems and the Excavation of Hidden History.*[13.16]

For her Master's thesis, *Diné Bina'nitin Dóó O'hoo'aah/Education For Us, By Us: A Collective Journey in Diné Education Liberation,*[13.16] she stretched outside the box of colonial education and engaged with her community to explore what Indigenous education could be for them at this time. In her comments about her thesis, she wrote: *"It's a story of how I came to work with over 300 Diné community members to dream, plan, implement and enjoy our very own school. Thank you for peering into a world of living and learning that grows from the seeds of The People's dreams and from the soil of The People's hearts. May it help us to revalue our own epistemologies and walk free from these intellectual fetters that the colonial state has placed on us for far too long. May it give all Indigenous peoples greater courage to be just exactly who we are."*

I join my voice with hers in this prayer for *all* people and for all of us, as parents. May we all walk free from the intellectual fetters that the colonial state has placed on us, so we can raise and educate our children in service to and alignment with Thriving Life. I know, from personal experience and from working with hundreds of families over the last twenty years, that this is no easy task. I know that there are many practical factors to contend with and significant pressures on us throughout our children's school-aged years. I also realize that many of us engaged in this work are several generations away from any intact, place-based cultural knowledge in our own lineages. But we are all part of this living Earth, and we can all learn. As we seriously contemplate the possibilities for Thriving Life education, we may find a unique path forward that weaves many of these elements into our children's education and helps us guide their learning experience towards being in service to Life.

Rooting Out Lessons in Oppression

Guiding our children along their learning experience in a Thriving Life way includes helping them recognize and understand the systems of power, privilege and oppression that exist within Power Over Paradigm society. It also involves helping them understand the importance of co-liberation within the context of the Thriving Life Paradigm. It compels us to deepen our understanding that *no one can truly be free or thriving so long as anyone is oppressed.*[13.17] It calls us to live with respect for the inherent worth and dignity of all people. It requires honestly taking stock of our own privilege and making conscious choices to leverage our privilege towards collective liberation. This paradigm-shifting work is based in an understanding that freedom is the natural state of being of *all* people, and that it is only infringed upon by false authorities and illegitimate structures of power.

In our efforts to disentangle ourselves and our children from the Power Over Paradigm, it's important to beware of the common pitfall of mistaking "climbing the ladder" for actual freedom. The "powers that be" would have us believe that striving for more recognition and clout within their pyramid of oppression is the pathway to equity and justice. While gains in the recognition of rights and safety within our current system are important, they do not fundamentally change the system. It's not enough to make sure that our classrooms, city parks and TV commercials represent an equally distributed range of skin tones if everyone is playing into the model of extractive capitalism that grew in cahoots with white supremacy. Instead, we need to transform our society entirely towards radical justice and authentic connection so we can learn again how to care for each other and the Earth and live in mutual thriving with all our relatives.

This may seem like a lot to take in. Let's remember, though, that our kids are paying attention and taking it all in, all the time.

As New Paradigm Parents, supporting Thriving Life Education includes making conscious choices about the messaging our children receive from their earliest years, to prevent the same old Power Over Paradigm constructs from being perpetuated in their young minds. As our children grow and their awareness increases, we can also have open conversations with them about this. We can share our observations and understandings with them, listen to their observations and encourage them to think critically and feel compassionately. At the same time, we can help them develop their capacity to recognize and understand the systems of power and privilege that function within the POP.

We can raise our kids in a way that dismantles white supremacy (especially if we're raising white kids). This starts by educating ourselves about how white supremacy has functioned and continues to function as the basis of the Industrial Growth Society. As our kids learn about the world, we need to be honest with them about racial history and the way our economy and society are structured so they understand why white people in many countries get certain opportunities and tend to have more of a certain kind of wealth and security than people of color. We can also seek out and make sure that our children have opportunities to develop meaningful, authentic relationships with people from a range of ethnic backgrounds, including with role models, teachers and mentors of color.

We can raise our kids in a way that dismantles the patriarchy (especially if we're raising boys). From a young age, boys need to understand their true worth and the value of caring for and protecting Life all around them. They need the opportunity to feel competent, capable and honorable within a model that doesn't favor them over girls or degrade them for being boys. Toxic masculinity and all forms of misogyny are symptoms of the deep self-loathing and lack of confidence that boys and men suffer as a result of the Power Over Paradigm. This paradigm robs *everyone* of their personal power and natural self-worth, even the ones it supposedly favors. They also need to learn how to take *"no"* for an answer, accept their limitations and assess their actions through the lens of mutual wellbeing.

We can raise our kids in a way that dismantles the illusion of material luxury without consequences (especially if we're raising kids with financial wealth). This begins by being mindful of our choices and their impact on others and the planet. Even if you have a lot of money, you don't have to live the prescribed life that has been marketed to you. You don't have to have a big environmentally abusive house filled with a bunch of toys. You don't have to play into consumer culture, have a big TV and throw elaborate birthday parties. When you have financial security, you have more freedom to consider which values you want your children to imbibe as they grow and to create a life based on those values. Every choice you make will influence what your children learn and experience, the friends they'll have and the systems they'll be plugged into. Your choices will also impact the environment, the market and other people. If you choose to do something different from the status quo with your money, you can teach your children about why you've made those choices and how they can also live their lives with this level of intentionality.

New Paradigm Media and Toys

An important place to interrupt these messages is in the media our children are exposed to when they're young. Most of the media available to our kids reinforces the POP in a variety of ways. Children's books, TV shows, social media content and all other forms of media reflect the world and the worldview of their creators. So, it makes sense that we would see a lot of expressions of the POP in the media popularly produced for kids. Generation after generation, we've been telling stories that uphold, perpetuate, and fortify the dominant paradigm. To interrupt that cycle, we have to consciously consider the stories we tell our children and the lessons that are woven into them, overt or subtle.

When I was working as a nanny in other people's homes, I often found myself thumbing through collections of children's books to search for the ones that felt appropriate to read to children. Looking at these books through the lens of the Thriving Life Paradigm revealed that only a small percentage of them didn't promote and perpetuate some form of oppression. Most of the books included expressions of injustice, racism, industrialization, extractive capitalism, and the many other structural components of the POP.

One of the little boys I cared for particularly loved *Curious George.* Although the mischievous little monkey can be endearing and the more modern books and TV shows created from this character are presented as harmless, cute stories, this story and character stand on a foundation of white supremacy and colonialism. The original series, published in 1941,[13,18] is full of outdated cultural assumptions that many people may write off as "signs of the times." But they are more than just signs of the times. They are signs of the disconnection and power imbalances at the root of the Power Over Paradigm that our kids imbibe along with the entertaining story.

I also notice that zoos and circuses are commonly used as themes in children's media. Since they are so commonplace, it could be easy to think of them as fun, harmless content for kids' stories. But upon examination, they reveal how easy it is to be seduced by the worldview of the POP into thinking that something is normal. The circus is a perfect example. Picture a nicely illustrated children's book depicting the circus with colorful cartoon-like figures. The audience is all lined up in the bleachers with exaggerated expressions of delight and wonder on their faces as they watch the animals and clowns in the ring do their tricks. There are smiles on the faces of the animals, too, and they almost look more like cartoon *people* than actual animals. They appear to be willing, joyful participants and collaborators in the show. There's absolutely no evidence of the kidnapping and enslavement at the core of this form of entertainment. It's a perfect display of the way the amnesia and ignorance of Business As Usual plays out to support privilege and injustice in our real lives. Normalizing this framework from a young age and reinforcing it year after year helps create the mindset that allows people to carry on with the show of "first world" Industrial Growth Society, despite all its consequences.

Another common theme for children's media is exploring and extolling the working parts of industrial society. With books like Richard Scarry's *Busy, Busy Town* and *What Do People Do All Day?* [13.19] kids are trained to pay attention to and learn all the roles that make up an industrialized city. Our toddlers learn about the policeman, the mailman, the foreman, etc. and all the structures and rules of conventional urban life. Other popular books focus on industrial construction, turning big gas guzzling, earth moving machinery into lovable characters with cute cartoon faces.

Much of the media marketed to our young people also perpetuates a false sense of luxury and a desire for material wealth based on the "first world" dream. The characters in many of the TV shows made for our kids and teens live in huge houses and have an exaggerated access to wealth. There's a dreamlike absence of the environmental and social consequences of their extravagant lifestyles that can confuse our children about how things are in the real world.

Another, often overlooked, way our children are conditioned into the POP mindset of materialism and consumerism is through the toys marketed to them. The trend toys of earlier decades, like Barbies, Cabbage Patch dolls and GI Joes hooked children of those eras into wanting to own and collect these coveted treasures. But in recent years, the tactics and results of trend toys have gotten more and more intense, with new collectible product lines like LOL toys and Hatchimals. Toy trends like these can manipulate kids into a greedy frenzy, stimulating adrenal responses of suspense, acquisition, frustration and comparison. In my experience as a nanny, I had far too many opportunities to witness this rollercoaster firsthand. These toys are well marketed but poorly constructed. They are generally made of chintzy, overly complicated plastic pieces that break easily and are frustrating for little hands. As soon as the toy has been opened, kids usually just want the next one in the collection, which fulfills the collectible marketing strategies of the companies and encourages overconsumption and excess.

These expressions of the Power Over Paradigm in our children's media, toys, education and environment are pervasive. It can feel overwhelming to take it all on and to resist the tsunami of marketing and the strong current of the mainstream. But these are the ways in which the POP sneaks into our children's worldview, little by little, in every direction, convincing them that this is the way the world works. As paradigm shifting parents, this is an area where we can make conscious choices, lead by example and provide a counterbalance to the onslaught of influences to which our children will be exposed.

PRACTICES FOR THRIVING LIFE EDUCATION

Regardless of the path or combination of paths your children's educational journey traverses, you can weave Thriving Life Education into their learning experience. By supporting their social, emotional, intellectual, practical and ecological learning, you'll help them grow into adults who are deeply rooted in mutual thriving and able to contribute to it throughout their lives. The practices below are here to help you explore how the concepts shared in this chapter can be integrated into your household in playful and empowering ways. Please experiment with them and adapt them, as needed, to meet your family's needs.

Thriving Life Education: Open Sentences for Co-Parents and Kids

Please refer to the instructions for Open Sentences in the practice section of Chapter 5: Grounding in Gratitude.

Open Sentences to use with your co-parents:

1. Some ways that we could enhance our children's education to support a deeper alignment with a Thriving Life worldview are…
2. What I love (or don't love) about our children's current educational path is…
3. In my vision of the most radically Thriving Life education, our children would learn and experience…
4. Some ways that we can root out lessons of oppression by how we raise and educate our children are…
5. Some of the POP messages I notice coming through our kids' media and toys are…

Open Sentences to use with your kids:

1. My educational situation is working (or not working) for me because...
2. When I'm at school (or engaged in homeschooling) I feel...
3. The biggest challenge or struggle I have with school (or homeschooling) is...
4. My favorite types of learning experiences are...
5. One of the subjects or skills I want to learn a lot about is...

Thriving Life Education Reflection

This practice is an opportunity to reflect on your children's educational experience in the context of Thriving Life. If you work with closely with a partner or co-parent, it may be a good idea to do this together. For each of the children in your care, go through each of the elements of Thriving Life Education listed below, one at a time, and ask yourself these two questions:

1. How is their current educational situation fulfilling these aspects of Thriving Life Education?
2. How could we weave more of these elements into their experience, either by making a different educational choice or by augmenting their current education path?

If you are doing this practice with another parent, make sure to give plenty of time for each parent to fully explore and express themself on each aspect. Taking notes or journaling the responses is helpful for capturing key insights that could be applied later.

Elements of Thriving Life Education:

- Practical – experiential, skills-based education that enhances a child's competency and confidence over time
- Relational – rooted in social and emotional development and wellbeing, ideally in an intergenerational and community-based context
- Intellectual – teaches a child *how* to learn, emphasizing critical thinking and problem-solving, while stimulating curiosity and a hunger for lifelong learning
- Ecological – place-based, Earth-centered experiential education that deepens a child's understanding of the living world and our place within it as humans
- Liberatory – addresses societal cause and effect and supports a clear-eyed assessment of what has happened throughout history and what is happening now in terms of power, privilege and oppression
- Visionary – engages imagination and creativity as we envision a positive, healthy future and practice the skills necessary to cultivate it
- Purposeful – always in service to collective wellbeing of the community and of all Life

After your reflection practice, look over your notes and identify a few manageable action steps for bringing your children's educational experience more fully into alignment with Thriving Life. You can come back to these notes or repeat the practice again from time to time to identify additional action steps as you further align your children's education with Thriving Life.

Privilege Assessment

In a society based on the Power Over Paradigm, each of us experiences an array of privileges and disadvantages based on our lived experience and the aspects of our identity that make up our social location.[13.20] As we seek to disengage with this oppression-based framework, it's essential for us to understand our unique position within it so we can be mindful and responsible about how we move through the world, what we teach our children and how their positionality will influence their experience.

This practice is an opportunity to reflect on the unique combination of privileges and disadvantages you and your family experience. Again, if you work closely with a partner or a co-parent, it may be a good idea to do this together.

Power Over Paradigm societies are designed to privilege certain types of people, catering to their needs and desires while disenfranchising other types of people. Privilege is often hidden from the awareness of the privileged, well-cloaked under the guise of society's norms. Those who are disenfranchised are often acutely aware of the oppression they're experiencing because of the stress, danger and extra labor it requires for them to navigate a society that is explicitly *not* designed for them.

Although there are differences from country to country and within different communities, the modern POP society is generally designed for and privileges upper middle class, cis-gendered, straight, able-bodied, neurotypical, white, male, English speaking, Christian-rooted, consumers from North America between the ages of 25 and 60.

As you reflect on the aspects of your identity below, I invite you to consider them in terms of your lived experience, both within our shared global society and in the context of your local community. In your home country, you may experience nuanced privileges and disenfranchisements regarding race and ethnicity, religious affiliation, economic class or other aspects. Consider who has the power in your local community, who is safe and who is not, who has to struggle to get by and who is comfortable.

Look over the list of identity aspects below and ask yourself:

1. Which aspects of your identity are privileged by society? Often, these are the ones you aren't forced to think about or consider in your daily life.
2. Which aspects of your identity are disenfranchised by society? Often these are the ones that cause extra effort, stress, fear and/or danger in your daily life.

Aspects of Identity:

- Race/Ethnicity
- Economic Status/Class
- Gender Identity
- Sexual Orientation
- Religious Affiliation
- Physical and Mental Ability
- Citizenship/Nationality
- Age

"Where we are born into privilege, we are charged with dismantling any myth of supremacy. Where we are born into struggle, we are charged with claiming our dignity, joy and liberation."

– adrienne maree brown [13.21]

Once you've completed your personal identity assessment, consider this quote from adrienne maree brown. Then, with your partner, reflect on and/or talk about what you can do as parents to dismantle myths of supremacy in the areas within which you experience privilege and to claim your dignity, joy and liberation in the areas within which you experience oppression. We may not be able to make immediate, sweeping changes to society. However, by raising our children with a deep dedication to co-liberation and mutual thriving we can play a significant role in shifting the tides of society.

Media and Toy Inventory

Now it's time to dig around in your bookshelves, video collections, streaming apps, social media platforms and toy boxes to consider what messages your children are imbibing through their media and toys. Put on your Thriving Life goggles to see the messages in terms of which paradigm they affirm. Do they reinforce elements of the Power Over Paradigm? Do they support a Thriving Life worldview?

Once you get a sense of which messages are being conveyed through your children's media and toys, see if you can subtly and gently phase out the most POP items in your family collection without raising alarm. Then start infusing your collection with more Thriving Life material, as you're able.

Quest for New Media

Our lives and our children's lives are awash in media. The stories, imagery, videos and news we're exposed to daily shape our concepts of the world and our place in it. Part of your New Paradigm Parenting practice can be a quest for media that tells the story of Thriving Life. It may take some special sleuthing to reach beyond the easily accessible mainstream media and find alternatives, but it will be well worth the effort.

If your kids are very young, you may choose to curate what they are exposed to. You can intentionally surround them with stories, movies, and songs that tell the tale of mutual thriving and the natural way of the world. If your children are older, you may try to connect their interests with some form of alternative media that shows them there is more to the world than the mainstream narratives. Bringing Thriving Life Paradigm media into your household is beneficial for children and adults of all ages. As it helps to connect you with the living world beyond the status quo, you can all enjoy the ways that it nourishes your lifeforce and your inherent worth as a vital member of the Web of Life.

You can begin your quest by visiting my website www.Radiant-Balance.com to access the Thriving Life Media Resource List and following the leads there.

Musical Interlude: Maiden the Flower

"In every child lives an innocence
Unbound before this world
So, let them live inside the magic
Of imagination's swirl

And don't you ever take advantage
Of those open eyes on you
Teach by example
To respect all life
And speak only love true

In every mother-father-adult
At the peak of sacred life
We see a mountain goat of will
To build the temple up on high

So, let the mothers-fathers-adults
Find the sacred in their work
To soon bear fruit and let it fall
Fall to bless us all."

From the song *Maiden the Flower*
on the album *Teach, Inspire, Be Real* by my dear friend and folk
singer extraordinaire, Diane Patterson

14

PHASES AND STAGES

"Parenting has seasons. Seasons where we are in full mama bear mode, instinctively pulled to overprotect and lead the way. And there are seasons when we are just here to love and support while they find their own way. The art of motherhood is knowing when the season is changing and having the courage to change with it."

– Brooke Hampton [11.4]

Constant Change

The only constant about childhood is change. Change is essentially what's going on in every moment of every day, year after year. Change. Growth. Transition. Learning. It's constant and unrelenting. Your children will go through many different phases and stages as they learn about their world and experiment with how to be in it. Some of these phases will last a few hours or a day. Some will last months or years.

Our job, as loving parents, is to be the steady shore against which their tides can move and shift. To be present and steadfast as they ebb and flow. To let them explore, experiment, challenge, question, grow and learn along their own paths without ever feeling that we've abandoned them. In our best expression, we would do this while exemplifying the core values we most want them to embody in their lives. We would show them the way into adulthood by being personally centered in honesty, respect and love all the way through their wild oscillations.

Understanding the unique qualities and needs of each stage of childhood within the context of New Paradigm Parenting helps us anticipate the changes we can expect and learn how to navigate them with grace.

When a two-year-old I cared for began experimenting with defiance he learned how to express his frustration in a very dramatic (and also extremely cute) way. He would slam his fists down on his lap and make a really grumpy face. Then, he started coupling this expression of frustration with a refusal to do things we asked of him (like sit down to eat lunch). My job, as one of the loving adults in his life, was to allow him to express his feelings while also holding the steady, loving reality that lunch is what is happening. I knew he needed to fill his belly before naptime. I knew that his body needed that food and that he'd sleep better if he had a good lunch. I also know that he'd enjoy eating it if he could come around to it.

To be the steady adult in that situation, it was important to recognize that this was a temporary phase, to see that he was just testing something out, and not to react to his behavior and feed into it or to get concerned that he was becoming a "naughty" kid. In order to respect his feelings in this situation, it was essential that I did not dismiss or ignore his expression and that I didn't laugh at how cute he was being (even though that was really hard.)

In situations like these, it's important to verbally validate what a child is expressing while at the same time, lovingly holding the line of what needs to happen. *"I see that you're frustrated"* and *"I understand that you don't want to eat lunch right now. But it is lunchtime so we're going to sit here and eat before naptime."* It's often helpful to create a little space for children to emote so they can arrive at the ability to shift gears into acceptance on their own. My approach was to put him in his booster seat with his plate of food nearby. Then I would sit next to him and start looking at books and eating, pleasantly enjoying my lunchtime moment. He could fuss and pout without having a head-on conflict with me. Gradually, his energy would start to align with mine because, truly, it felt better than being grumpy. When he was ready to read a book with me, I'd read a page or two and then slip a forkful of food into his mouth. As soon he tasted the food, he would forget his struggle and his hungry little body would get right into eating lunch.

This is an example of how we can hold that steady, loving groundedness during a shorter, simpler phase. The same principles apply as our kids grow up and their phases and stages get longer and more complex. We might not always understand the changes that are happening, and at times they might challenge us or push our buttons. Through it all, our task is to stand strong, steady and loving to the best of our ability.

As your children get older, they might try out different ways of behaving, dressing, identifying themselves or relating to their world. Let them experiment and don't give them a hard time about it. Refrain from belittling their experiences by telling them that they're just going through a phase. It might be helpful for *you* to realize that every little change they experience isn't permanent, but it's not helpful for them to hear that from you. Their experience is their own. It's real, valid and extremely important to them. Some of the changes may endure. Some may be fleeting.

If they're doing something or experimenting with something that you feel may be unsafe or that you don't understand, then you can *and certainly should* talk with them about it. But be mindful to engage with them respectfully, without judgment or panic. Ask them what's going on and why they're choosing to do what they're doing. And listen! *Really listen.* Show them that you are there. Breathe through any of your own fears, judgments and projections that arise and just show up for them, fully, as one of the people who loves them most in the world. If you've been cultivating a high-quality partnership with them based on respect and trust throughout their childhood, these conversations during their tween and teen years will be *much* easier.

As our children move through their phases and stages we can be the steady shore against which their tides shift. We can toe the line. Stand strong. Love deeply. Respect their process. Let go, let go, let go, lovingly, without indifference or apathy. Vibrant, openhanded, unconditional, fierce, courageous loving is what they need.

We can get good at sensing the shifting seasons of our children's growth, stay alert to the constantly unfolding changes and learn to respond to them with flexibility. We can enjoy the process of getting to know our children again and again and again as they reinvent themselves and develop new aspects of their personalities and identities. If you've been making peanut butter and jelly sandwiches for your child for years and they loved them every time, don't be alarmed when they suddenly tell you, *"I don't like peanut butter!"* Things change. All the time. Don't make a big deal about it. Just roll with it and ask them to keep you posted.

As your children enter their tween and teen years, one of the best gifts you can give them is your willingness to see them with fresh eyes and learn who they are becoming, day by day. Release them from the limitations of who they were as little ones. Resist the urge to cling to their babyhood or to reinforce aspects of their reality that they are working hard to outgrow. Each stage has its own indescribably valuable treasures. As you learn to be flexible and open to each new phase, you'll get to experience those treasures in full presence with your growing children.

> *"What is rooted is easy to nourish.*
> *What is recent is easy to correct.*
> *What is brittle is easy to break.*
> *What is small is easy to scatter.*
> *Prevent trouble before it arises.*
> *Put things in order before they exist.*
> *The giant pine tree*
> *grows from a tiny sprout.*
> *The journey of a thousand miles*
> *starts from beneath your feet."*
>
> – Lao-Tzu [14.1]

Laying the Groundwork for Babies (Birth to Walking)

Babies, toddlers and little kids are delightfully honest. They are fully and authentically human. Each one is exquisitely unique and full of life-force energy. They have a natural curiosity and sense of humor. Their commonalities and vulnerabilities show us how tender and precious we are as a species and how much we truly need each other. I've always felt most at ease around very young ones. As the situation on the planet worsens and people raise doubts about the value of the human race, I see the light in each new baby as a reassurance of our worth and our place in this world. Having the privilege of caring for and getting to know a baby is an invaluable opportunity to reorient ourselves and align more deeply with the pure, brilliant, authentic humanness they carry into this world.

Although every single one of us began our lives as babies, we generally can't remember the experience. This lack of memory often causes us to dismiss or underestimate the richness and importance of this time in our children's lives. If we pay close attention to babies and observe their responses to their environment, it becomes crystal clear that they experience, feel and understand *way* more than most people think they can. They can't tell us about their experience in words and they process very differently from adults, but the experience they're having is complex, important and completely valid. Learning to respect babies requires tuning into their unique experience, even though we may not fully understand it. It means keeping our minds and hearts open with loving curiosity, knowing that they are doing the unfathomably difficult work of becoming oriented to the experience of being a human on planet Earth. When we engage in this type of relationship, babies can teach us a lot.

From a purely adult perspective, it can seem like not very much is going on. Sleeping, pooping, drinking milk, gurgling, on endless repeat. Many new parents, in their enthusiasm and pride, treat their baby as a prize, an accessory or an extension of themselves. They celebrate "having" a baby instead of honoring the experiences their baby is having. Many parents don't even put a lot of thought into conscious parenting until their children are a bit older and more interactive, assuming that there's not much to do in this early stage but change diapers and feed. But these are precious moments that lay the groundwork for the rest of their lives.

This early stage has an enormous impact on your children's lifelong wellbeing: physically, emotionally, psychologically and spiritually. During this precious, foundational time, you have the opportunity to make conscious choices about their environment, experience and exposure in a way that you won't have for most of their lives. Most of your parenting experience will be about letting go and most of their lives will be outside of your choice and control. However, what you provide for them at this early stage will create the inner compass that will guide them as they grow. It will become the fertile ground of mind, body, spirit and emotions that they'll grow from and return to throughout their lives.

As I mentioned earlier, the wisdom conveyed by Jean Liedloff in *Continuum Concept*,[9.3] significantly influenced how I cared for my daughter in infancy and my understanding of what babies need. The teachings of Joseph Chilton Pearce, especially those from his book *Magical Child*,[9.5] also influenced my approach to caring for infants and babies. Both sources emphasize the importance of loving connection, physical touch and bonding for healthy development.

In the first three years of a child's life, their brain grows to almost adult size and creates the neural patterns that will define how they function for the rest of their life. The most important things that a baby needs for this brain development to go well are to feel safe and loved. Babies need to be held in our warm, loving arms or carried in a wrap close to our bodies. They need to feel the rhythm of our movements and to hear the beating of our hearts. They need to gaze into loving eyes and receive a loving response to the expression of their needs. When this early brain development is supported by loving safety, it increases the capacity they'll have for presence, centeredness, empathy and love as older children and adults.

In the first weeks and months of a baby's life, they spend a lot of dreamy time drifting between asleep and awake. They are liminal beings hovering around the threshold of birth. I get the strong impression that they are swimming with memory and connection to the realms they inhabited before arriving here. I get the sense that they are surrounded by helpers. In quiet, tender moments, you may notice your baby staring off at "nothing" or smiling, laughing and babbling at "nobody." I cherish these moments and often feel a presence that I like to imagine comes from the "more than human" realms of spirit helpers. If you are open to it, these moments are a great opportunity to do what you can to make your baby's helpers feel safe and welcomed and to receive any guidance they care to share with you. As you hold your sweet baby, you can cultivate sacred space, tune in, meditate, listen and just enjoy the blessing of this new precious life.

The first months and years of your children's life are a gradual progression of countless, tiny, little learning moments and growth thresholds as they learn how to use their physical bodies and understand the world around them. Building the strength and motor skills necessary to fulfill their curiosity and get around is a big focus for the first year or more. This process is rich and involved. Every little step is a huge accomplishment. Wrapping fingers and thumbs around that rattle. Wahoo! Lifting that head up off the mat when they're on the tummy. Yeehaw! Scooting, rolling, kneeling, crawling. It all takes such incredible strength, perseverance, courage and patience. As I observe babies, I'm always struck by how intense it must be to grow, learn and transform so rapidly. Let's give our babies credit for the hard work they're doing and encourage them along the way.

As you witness these incredible feats of strength and perseverance, see if you can settle your adult mind enough to really witness and appreciate their experience. Imagine what it must be like. Feel a sense of appreciation and respect for this brave little being who is determined to learn and struggle through all these thresholds. A book that I've found helpful for staying oriented in this appreciation (and for knowing what to expect next) is *Wonder Weeks: A Stress-Free Guide to Your Baby's Behavior*.[14.2] This book explains what's going on for our children as they're moving through certain thresholds and working towards certain milestones. It explains what struggles and challenges our babies experience at each new step and how these might affect their moods and behavior.

I've found that this understanding can increase our compassion for a baby's experience and help us understand how to help them successfully move through these important growth thresholds. It can keep us from reacting to their fussiness, frustration, moments of clinginess and temporary regressions. Using this book has helped me understand that all these behaviors are signs that a new threshold is approaching. At each new stage of growth, you can go to the book to see which threshold the baby is passing through and get some helpful tips on how to support them. In my experience, this helps with maintaining the steady groundedness they need from us and makes the transition periods much smoother and shorter.

Although I've found this book to be uncanny in its accuracy, it's important to note that every baby is different, and they all pass through their developmental thresholds at different times and in their own ways. I've noticed that a lot of emphasis is placed on milestones in parenting and childcare circles these days. This emphasis can create an obsession with "accomplishments" along a linear timeline and disconnect us from being truly present with our babies and respecting their processes. Please don't compare your baby with other babies or be anxious or disappointed if another baby did something before yours did. It is not a competition. It is a naturally unfolding miracle and organic learning process that happens differently for each child.

When your babies are little, sing a lot! Little brand-new humans thrive on melody and rhythm. Music has a powerful impact on brain development and is an important tool for learning. It's also a wonderfully effective way to shift a baby's energy and to make the baby feel included in the world. I love to sing throughout the day when I'm caring for little ones, to keep the energy light and help us dance through our learning journey together.

If you've never thought you could sing or someone told you that you have a bad voice, this is your chance to let that go! This little being loves you beyond compare, and they need to hear *your* voice. All the time. In loving, playful melodies. Play with this and explore. Find songs that you love to sing. Find songs that are meaningful to you. Find songs that are prayers for the life you want this little one to experience and then sing them as prayers, from your heart to the Universe on behalf of this precious being.

Just before I got pregnant, I met a dear friend who loved to sing. She played the guitar and wrote songs and would sing for hours around the fire at night. Although I had always loved to sing along to my favorite songs in the car or the shower, I had been under the impression that I had a pretty bad voice, so I never really sang in public. But this dear friend wouldn't take no for an answer when she wanted me to sing with her. She coaxed my voice out of me and made singing an important part of my daily life.

She and I both got pregnant around the same time and spent a lot of time together throughout our pregnancies. We sang to our babies the whole time they were growing in our bellies and every day after they were born. I am so grateful to her for the way this singing practice has changed my life and what an important, positive role it has played in my daughter's life and in the lives of all the kiddos I've cared for. My daughter's life has been woven with song and prayers that she continues to call on to this day in her moments of joy and challenge.

As a nanny in Portland, I've also had the great pleasure of bringing babies and toddlers to their Music Together classes.[14.3] These are a series of parent/child music classes that immerse little ones in a cornucopia of musical influence and play. They are tons of fun and incredibly effective. One little boy I cared for learned an astonishing amount from this depth of musical exposure in his early years. And he loved it! I highly encourage finding or creating some sort of musical experience like this for your little ones if you can.

Babies are physical, naturally embodied, sensory beings. When caring for them, you're not just dealing with a personality. You're dealing with a real, embodied *being*. Tune into your baby with all your senses and engage them with all their senses. In addition to using music to change the energy for your baby, you can use sensory cues. When a baby continues to fuss even after their immediate needs have been met, sometimes the simplest solution is to step outside. The change in air and temperature and environment often releases them from their fuss. A little bit of cold water or warm water can help too, on their hands, face or feet. Movement, touch, tickling and gently blowing on their face and body are other ways to engage their senses to help soothe them or shift their focus.

Framing the World for Toddlers (Walking to Age Three)

As your children begin to walk, climb and explore their world, they become toddlers. This is a great time to let them teach you about being human. Look at the ways they use their bodies. Look at their resilience and fortitude. Their ingenuity. Their curiosity. Their openness and emotional fluidity. Their love and tenderness. Their sense of humor. Notice what they find interesting. Notice their presence. Through their innocent expression of their own true nature, they show us what is possible for human beings. They show us human nature, free from the perversion and distortion of societal indoctrination.

I'm not saying that toddlers have it all figured out and we should all act like toddlers. But I encourage you to use this time with your toddler to study and reflect on all the genius and brilliance of humanity that shines through them in their innocent expression. This is your chance to learn from them and reclaim some of the parts of yourself that were educated out of you.

Toddlers are driven by passionate desire and curiosity. Desperately wanting to grab (and taste) the toy that's just out of reach is what motivates little ones to learn how to crawl and walk and climb. Their enthusiasm and alertness to the details and pleasures of life can help us remember to enjoy the little things and savor our experiences.

Toddlers can also show us how our bodies are meant to move and how to reside deeply within our bodies. They show us how to feel strong emotions and let them move through us like weather, letting them go when they're done and moving on to the next interest or emotion with equal enthusiasm. Toddlers show us how to focus our full attention on something we care about, and they show us how to play and be silly. The way toddlers learn through play, movement, experience and connection teaches us quite a lot about how we are meant to learn. Play is an essential element that your toddler can bring back into your life if you're open to it.

Toddlers are outrageously intelligent. Little geniuses, perhaps! Through the books, media, songs and direct experiences they're exposed to in the first few years of their lives, they form the basis of what they will unconsciously hold true about the world. During these years, they are intricately cataloging their world with every new word, concept and skill they discover. By the age of two, most of them have already learned about everything from the animals of the rainforest to dinosaurs, from excavation equipment to rocket ships. Whatever they've been exposed to, they've picked up, committed to memory and cataloged in their little growing brains. They learn through repetition, play and story. Every single moment is a learning moment.

During these early years, while they are cataloging their world, you have a great opportunity to be intentional about what you expose them to, what you teach them, how you want them to understand their world and what you want them to notice and see. This process can re-awaken our own senses and help us relearn the world right alongside our little ones. It invites us to shift our focus away from the things the Power Over Paradigm wants us to focus on and tune into some of the bigger, more enduring truths of Life.

For example, as I bopped around to the playgrounds and parks of Portland with a toddler, we could easily have only noticed the play structures we visited and failed to notice the vibrant community of Life surrounding them. Instead, I always made it a point to try to take it *all* in. We'd stop and say hello to the trees and greet them with love and respect. We'd put our little hands on their trunks and look up to notice how tall and beautiful they were. We'd talk to the crows and watch them flock and fly. We were constantly on the lookout for mushrooms, moss, worms, flowers, bees, birds and all our other living relatives. And when we saw them, we'd greet them with love and respect.

As their brains develop rapidly, toddlers are building neural pathways and experiencing synaptic pruning (the elimination of functional synapses that are not used and therefore, not needed).[14.4] Basically, their brains are being designed and sculpted by their experience and exposure. The more they do and experience a certain way of thinking and seeing, the more that will be incorporated into the design. The parts of their brains and the connections that they don't use will be pruned away and ultimately, not incorporated into the design. This is an important time to orient them to what is real, important, special, precious and worthy of our respect and attention.

For example, if we want to teach children how to love and respect animals as their relatives, we may choose to limit the way animals are objectified, belittled, commodified or personified and distorted in their toys, clothes and books. Instead, we can consciously provide opportunities to learn about, explore and enjoy getting to know animals as they exist in the real world. If you can tend animals at home, you can teach children about our reciprocal relationship with animals and develop a deep sense of mutual respect through direct experience. We can also show them nature shows like BBC's *Planet Earth* [14.5] and provide resources like the *Smithsonian Visual Encyclopedias of Animals*.[14.6]

I nannied for twin four-year-old boys and their two-year-old sister for several months. They loved this book and would pour over it for hours. The real-life pictures provided a great basis for exploration and storytelling about real animals and real experiences. They loved to open to the section on bears and ask me to tell them all my stories about real life encounters with bears from my time living in the Rocky Mountains of Colorado. They would ask me what I knew about each of the animals, and I would tell them. The ones I didn't know, we would make guesses about and then look them up to see what was true.

During this phase of rapid mental cataloging and the shaping of neural pathways, they can learn an incredible amount about the living world, our place in it and the relationships that make it all work. If you walk with them in curiosity and exploration of the living world, they could learn all about the plants and trees and other lifeforms that grow around them in their home ecosystems, instead of just cataloging the elements of the commercial industrial world. You'll be amazed at how much they are capable of learning (and how much you'll learn in the process) and how this orientation of attention creates a framework of learning based in Life.

One of the things I love most about toddlers is that they generally have a great sense of humor. Now that they know so much about the way things are, and how they're supposed to work, they love to joke and laugh about things that are not the way they are supposed to be (i.e. putting pants on your head or books that invite them to point out what's right/wrong in a picture, like *Wacky Wednesday* [14.7]) They want to know how things are supposed to be and they want to show you that they know. This can be a lot of fun.

Toddlers have *way* longer attention spans than we typically give them credit for. I find that it's usually adults who get bored and want to move on or complicate an activity when a baby or toddler just wants to *"do it again!"* I invite you to challenge yourself to follow their lead to see if you can stay present and enjoy the slow exploration of whatever activity or thing is fascinating your child. If it's peek-a-boo 1,700 times, see if you can enjoy it as long as they do. If it's a slow toddler walk, checking out every bug and rock along the way, see if you can slow yourself down enough to explore in wonder with your child, even if you only make it 25 feet from your front door. If they want to stand and watch the trucks for 20 minutes or run the blender with soapy water in it over and over again for a half hour, see if you can drop into the learning opportunity and the joy of that activity without trying to complicate it or rush them out of it.

Making space for the development of this level of focus and attention is critical to their development. As we notice older children struggling with "attention issues" I think it's essential that we reflect upon and take responsibility for the ways that we stunt our children's ability to develop attention and focus by the ways we "distract" them when they're little. We train them to expect rapid shifts in focus with the media, activities, toys and experiences that they are typically exposed to while they're babies and toddlers.

I recently spent over an hour playing with *oobleck* [14.8] with a not-quite-two-year-old. My adult attention span felt done after about 20 or 30 minutes, but I noticed he was still *really* interested. So, I challenged myself to just hang with him and follow his lead. We dropped into this lovely trance-like exploration of the sensations. It was nice, simple and exactly what he needed.

Keep in mind, of course, that you can't control this or count on them having a long attention span for what *you* think they should want to do. They have to be into it, and it has to meet them at the right moment and stage of their development. Our job as parents is to pay attention to what they're interested in and provide meaningful opportunities for exploration and learning. Whether or not the child really dives into an opportunity has to do with their age, temperament, mood and stage of development. Sometimes you hit the sweet spot. In those moments, I hope you can drop into that presence with the child and allow them to stick with the activity as long as they want to. And sometimes you don't hit a sweet spot. They might just not be that interested, or they might have gotten everything they needed from the activity in five minutes. In moments like this, I hope you'll be able to let it flow and move onto the next thing.

Depending on the child's age and disposition, they may need you to stay with them and match their level of attention in order to sustain their focus. If I had walked away, or even just stopped playing with the *oobleck,* this toddler would have lost his attention much sooner. He needed me to be there paying attention to it, too. But sometimes, even with a young one, you can step away and let them dive into whatever they're exploring on their own. These moments are extremely rich and valuable for development. Look for these opportunities to recede into the background, not so you can "go get stuff done" but so the child can experience sovereignty and the joy of their own unique presence.

This solo play and exploration allow them to develop the intrinsic motivation, independence, personal intuition and sense of self that are all essential qualities they'll need as they grow into thriving life. As these qualities develop more and more in your child, you will also be able to "get stuff done" in the background, but that's just a happy side effect of the real magic taking place. And, of course, every child is unique. Some tend more easily towards being on their own, while others require more companionship. And everyone needs a bit of both.

When your children are toddlers, be sure to manage your time as well as you can, so you'll be able to be deeply present with your kids during some parts of the day and week, without feeling pressured, distracted or drained. If you possibly can, be sure to get some time to yourself. If you're a mom and you've been nursing, make sure you have some time *every day* when no one else is touching you so you can reconnect with your own body. If you're in a partnership, make sure you and your partner get some adult time together *every week*. If you get good at this type of time management and at meeting your own needs, you'll be more able to be fully present and available for your kids when you're with them.

As we explored earlier in the book, adults are the ones who set the tone. As the adult, you can create a smooth experience for your toddlers by making certain choices, learning how to anticipate needs, manage expectations and tend to your own energy and attention. Doing this well will not only benefit your toddler and their development in significant ways but will also make your life *way* easier. The foundation of this practice is modeling and carrying a certain steadiness and presence to help them learn how to be centered as they navigate their world. Be aware of the impact your mental or emotional state has on these tender little beings. They are like sponges in many ways. We have to do our own work so we can provide good energy for them to absorb.

Another key is creating healthy rhythms that are responsive to your toddler's needs and then maintaining those rhythms with loving boundaries and consistency. For example, if you, as the adult, know that it's time for nap, it's your responsibility to hold that knowledge and create the conditions necessary for a smooth and non-traumatic transition from whatever is going on into naptime. Non-traumatic doesn't mean the child won't fuss. It doesn't mean the child will be docile and cheery the whole time. It means that their experience will be respected to the extent that they can adjust and come to terms with naptime, moving through whatever layers of shifting gears and relaxing and soothing are necessary for them.

On the day that the eighteen-month-old boy I cared for had his first ice cream cone (and, with it, more sugar than he had ever had in his life), his mom and sister were spending the day with us, so our normal rhythms were interrupted to some extent. We had had a fun sunny day out at the park. His big sister was playing out front with the neighbor kids and everyone was having a lot of fun. But it was time for his afternoon nap. I knew that if he didn't head in for a nap by a certain time, he wouldn't make it to bedtime without a meltdown. So, I started moving him in that direction. I asked his mom to come into the house with us, so he didn't feel like he was being taken away from *all* the fun. (That worked well.) Once we were inside his mom started getting together supplies for making slime to bring out to the big kids. The toddler recognized what was going on and started freaking out. (That didn't work well.) I then took him downstairs to change the laundry and get his mind off all that and give his mom a chance to get out of the house again. (That worked well.)

Once we were back in his room, he freaked out about getting his clothes changed because he didn't *want* a nap. I took a moment to rinse his face and hands with cold water and let him play in the water for a short moment to shift his energy. (That worked well). We enjoyed some little jokes while I changed his diaper, keeping him focused and moving forward towards nap. (That worked well). I talked calmly to him the whole time, staying steady, not wavering, not letting myself get distracted, swayed or defeated by his fuss, and not dragging anything out too long or indulging him, but using humor, play and physical shifts to help him transition. I used all the regular rhythms of our naptime ritual as anchors for the experience. Crossing those thresholds one by one brought him closer and closer to sleep. By the time we got to the singing part he was ready and oh-so-tired from his big day. He conked right out.

As toddlers are learning and testing boundaries with you, refrain from laughing at or indulging misbehavior, even if it's adorable or entertaining. (This can be hard.) There are a lot of other ways and times to enjoy your child's cuteness and have fun with them. You can play chasing games when it's play time, not when it's time to put on shoes or get ready for bed. You can also be playful as you get things done, so long as they are cooperating and working with you. These are important moments to guide the experience with a steady hand and hold your boundaries firmly by giving your toddler clear feedback about which behaviors work and which don't. Make sure the boundary is respected and the needs of the moment are met *before* you lose your patience and snap harshly at them.

Talk to your toddlers with the level of kindness and respect you want them to use when they talk to you and their friends. Pause and listen to yourself often to check in. You are the adult in the situation and, even if they're acting wild and ornery, you can draw the line and hold it firmly with love and kindness. The way you speak to your children when they're young will become their inner voice that will be with them throughout their lives. Practice speaking to them in empowering, uplifting, loving ways so they don't have to battle with and recover from your voice when they're grownups.

As early as 12 months old (possibility earlier), babies can learn to wait when necessary and to ask nicely for what they want. You'll need to stay tuned into your toddler's growing abilities to keep your expectations reasonable. But, for example, if you are reading a book, you can teach them to wait until the right moment to turn the page. Be kind and clear and firm in your expression. With little ones, a physical gesture along with words is helpful. Gently remove their little hand from the page and say, *"Please wait until we're ready."* When it's the appropriate time, say, *"Okay. Now you can turn the page."* They will quickly learn to wait and feel excited when they get to turn the page instead of just tearing through a book and not getting the full experience of being read to.

If your toddler starts to whine, squeal or stomp around demanding something they want, you can clearly, kindly and firmly remind them to ask nicely, say please or show you what they want in a calm and respectful way. Simple sign language [14.9] is really helpful for this. If they know how to sign *"please," "food," "up," "down," "water,"* etc. that will help them a lot. But even if they don't know the sign for what they want, they can still calm down and show you in a kind way. Resist the urge to just give them what they want to make them be quiet. This is directly teaching them that the best way to get their needs met quickly is to be obnoxious. If you take a moment to connect with them and give them a chance to ask nicely and then, when they do, directly fulfill their request, you are teaching them how to get their needs met in a functional and empowered way.

You can also teach toddlers to ask for help as soon as they can talk (or sign). Let them know that they can always ask for help and that they can ask for it nicely instead of demanding it or throwing a fit. Toddlers often get frustrated. The world is so big and there are so many things they don't know how to do yet. When frustrations arise, let them know that they can ask for help. Guide them in calming down and asking nicely. When they ask nicely, be sure to provide the help quickly and in a satisfying way. Just enough to get them to be able to do it themselves. Be mindful not to take things out of their hands or steamroll them. Just assist, with respect, and empower them to learn how to do what they're trying to do. The simple skill of learning how to ask for help nicely and how to receive it gracefully will go a long way for them throughout childhood and well into adulthood. This is one of the things that can start in very early childhood.

As you teach them to speak to you with respect, be sure that you are also speaking to them with the same level of loving respect. Remember, even though they are still tiny, this is where your partnership with them begins. This is when they begin to learn how to work together with you. If it's going well, some of the phrases you might often hear yourself saying are: *"Thanks for listening," "Thanks for asking," "Thanks for helping,"* and *"Thanks for cooperating."* These early years create the basis for your children's whole understanding of the world and their place in it. Be sure to orient them into a world of reciprocity, love and connection as you teach cooperation and mutual respect.

Empowering and Uplifting Big Kids (Ages Four to Ten)

This is when kids really start to come into their own. They begin to understand themselves as distinct from their parents and start to develop their own agency and capacities. Respecting a big kid means giving them space to try new things and letting them fail and try again. Letting them work hard at what they're interested in and practice their growing capacities. Letting them feel age-appropriate responsibility. Letting them make their own choices, whenever possible. It also means letting them be silly and have fun and be interested in weird kid stuff.

Our work as New Paradigm Parents in this phase is to support their developing sovereignty and let them become their own people. This includes being mindful about the projections we may be inclined to hurl at them based on our own conditioning, fears, hopes, plans and preferences. In *Raising Free People*,[11.1] Akilah Richards encourages us to question everything we do with our kids against whether it supports their authentic wellness as free people. She talks about the "adult gaze" and how our own judgments or fear of judgment from other adults can cause us to force certain behaviors and activities onto our children, even if they're not in service to their wellness. Children know they are being observed by adults. They naturally look to their parents and the adults around them to get a reading on their level of acceptance and belonging (essential components of their wellbeing as social creatures). If we're not aware of our own conditioning and fears, we may be unconsciously projecting certain judgments onto our children and pushing them into performing a specific type of conditioned acceptability, instead of living authentically.

Here are some questions we can ask ourselves during this phase of our children's growth:

- Am I worried about what other adults will think of my children's behavior and performance?
- Am I worried about what other adults will think of my parenting?
- Am I training my kids to prioritize my opinions and other people's opinions over their own needs?
- How much of my choices (or the choices I push onto my kids) are about trying to make other people comfortable or trying to conform to a standard that is not connected to my kids' authentic wellness?

This part of your children's life is critical to their lifelong wellness and their ability to make it through their teen and young adult years safely. The field of Positive Youth Development[14.10] identifies an array of Protective Factors that children can develop during their big kid years. It makes a clear case that these Protective Factors play a significant role in protecting children from experiencing risky behaviors and negative outcomes as teens (such as drug use, unplanned teen pregnancies, self-harm and suicide, etc.) Gaining skills and growing in confidence during this big kid time, along with having a strong sense of belonging and of being needed by your family and community are some of the protective factors that will help them successfully navigate through their teen years.

As guides for our children during this stage, we can help them develop their capacities and feel a genuine sense of worth by providing meaningful work for them to do at every age. This helps them feel included and valued within their family unit and gives them a sense that their help makes a difference. The activities and interests that they discover during this part of their life will begin to shape their identity and, when nurtured well, can become the foundation of their confidence and sense of self as they venture into their teen years. Paying attention to their unique interests and helping them build their skills in the directions in which they are drawn is an important way to support this confidence.

In our modern parenting culture, there is a lot of emphasis on academic performance and extracurricular activities. At times, there can be a lot of external pressure around what our children should be involved in and how they should be performing. It can be easy to get wrapped up in the frenzy of filling the schedule and the competitive aspect of giving your children a "leg up" in the world by building strong, well-rounded transcripts starting in kindergarten. But the "leg up" they truly need is based in quality of connection and competence, not quantity of activities and accomplishments.

In the midst of it all, keep your sacred partnership with your children in focus. Stay tuned in to what *they* need, what's working for them, what excites them and allow the spacious energies of play and discovery to be central to their experience. They have to love what they're doing and be doing it because they *want* to. At times, we may have to push them a bit to stay focused or follow through with something, but we have to be careful not to make it about us or some external target or to keep them unnecessarily bound to responsibilities that take the playfulness and joy out of what they're doing.

During these pre-adolescent years, be sure to listen to what your children have to say. Beyond listening to their preferences for extracurricular activities, listen to their ideas, thoughts and stories. Typically, kids in this age range have *a lot* to say. If you don't listen to them now, they won't talk to you when they're teens. Find ways of being interested in what they're interested in (to the extent you can, honestly). Listen to their music and learn about their games, even if they go through weird phases and silly trends. Let them show you their world and share it with you.

When my kid was in this zone, I got into all sorts of pop music that I *never* would have listened to without her. I enjoyed listening to it with her and all her friends and let them feel valid in their interests. One of my biggest parenting challenges, however, was trying to listen while my child talked at length about movies and TV shows she watched. She would describe the whole show to me in great detail. It was a stretch for me. I would stretch as much as I could (or felt was reasonable) and then I would let her know when I'd reached my limit. Because I respect her, I didn't just blow her off or ignore or belittle her. I'd respectfully let her know when I started to get overwhelmed and couldn't follow anymore.

Just as we can validate our children's interests and ideas by listening to them, we can validate their feelings by listening too. If they want to talk with you about their challenges and struggles, listen to them with full respect. Even if what they're telling you seems small or simple from your adult perspective, remember that their struggles are very real to them and are in proportion to their lives. Try to pause your adult mind for a moment and really pay attention to what is going on for them.

Your children may or may not want to talk or be able to talk about their feelings. And yet, they may still have them. Many children in these times are expressing and experiencing anxiety beginning in this age range. In the context of everything we've already covered in this book, I feel it's very important not to react to this anxiety as though it is a problem or something that is wrong with them that needs to be fixed. It's very common and natural for our children to feel anxious in a world with so many converging crises, whether they are cognizant of them or not. Instead of treating their anxiety like a personal pathology, you can take this opportunity to help them accept anxiety as a messenger about what we need to change in our world and you can help them breathe through the discomfort and listen to what their feelings are telling them.

Modern parents have the challenge of providing children with the resources they need for healthy growth (including education, community, meaningful skills and initiations) within a society that is largely deficient in these resources. This requires a combination of creative problem solving and a gentle yielding to our personal and collective circumstances. We may not be able to give them everything we know they need, but we can creatively stretch beyond Business As Usual to meet their needs in the best way possible, like we explored in the Thriving Life Education section in Chapter 13.

In addition to high quality education, rites of passage (or meaningful initiations) are another resource that's essential to human wellness and childhood development but severely lacking in modern society. Meaningful initiations are integral to all intact human cultures and have been throughout human history. Although the specific details of rites of passage initiations are unique to the people, land, history and cosmology of the culture from which they emerge, the experience of being initiated into an intact culture through a series of rites is, historically, a universal human experience. In the context of the evolutionary expectations[9.3] introduced in Chapter 9, that likely means that our children expect this initiation on some evolutionary level and feel its absence when it doesn't exist.

In his book *Long Life Honey in the Heart*, Martín Prechtel gives us a glimpse into the depths of these rituals as he describes a specific Tz'utujil Mayan youth initiation in poetic detail.[14.11] Through his sharing of this experience, he shows us how these rituals traditionally involve an entire intergenerational community and the long lineage of intact cultural wisdom that grows from the intimate relationship between human beings and their place on the Earth. He shows us that these initiations are typically not about giving something *to* the children. They are about children *learning how to give,* so Life can keep on living. As the community comes together to feed Life, the children play a vital role, and through that experience, they learn how needed they are in their next stage of maturity and service.

Those of us who aren't connected with an intact cultural lineage may not be able to provide this depth of initiation for our children. But we can do what we're able to do to let our children know that they are needed and valued as they move through certain thresholds of growth. An appropriate time for this type of experience may be at age seven or age nine, depending on the child. Another threshold moment may present itself around first menstruation or maturation into young adulthood.

If you're fortunate enough to live among people whom you and your children trust, you can build these traditions into your community. You can gather the people who form the "community" that your child is part of (parents, aunties, uncles, mentors, teachers, grandparents, older siblings and cousins) and create an experience that challenges that child and gives them an opportunity to serve. If there are multiple children in this community passing through the threshold at the same time, they could all be held in this initiation together.

Although our "invented" initiations won't be able to replace a true rite of passage that grew out of countless generations of intact human culture in dynamic living relation with the unseen world and the Holies that nourish Life, we can allow these initiations to be guided by the real and current needs of the living world. Tune in, listen to the Earth and follow your intuition and the guidance you receive to find your way in marking these major growth thresholds for your children in meaningful ways that help them feel the sacred duty of caring for their community and the Web of Life. In this time of unraveling and collapse, we often just need to do our best and leave the rest to Grace.

Partnering with Passion for Teens (Ages 11 to 19)

Yes, the teenage years begin as early as eleven-years-old. Actually, for many kids there could be a noticeable shift as early as nine. If children are exposed to a lot of media (even cartoons) you might notice "typical teenage" attitudes and tones of voice coming out even sooner. Mainstream media tends to glorify teenage characteristics and little kids will cling to them and emulate them if they're exposed to it.

In my experience and observation, I've found the middle school years (11 to 13) to be more of a tumultuous teenage experience than the high school years (14 to 18). During the middle school stage, children often struggle with their identity and self-worth as they straddle the threshold between childhood and adulthood. They are venturing into the unknown as they deal with changes in their bodies and changes in their social circles and external expectations. This transition happens in different ways and in different timing for each child, so within a friend group or a class, it's common for some of the kids to still look and behave very much like children while others are developing quickly and losing interest in childish play. In this phase of development, it's normal for kids to be obsessively interested in the approval of their peers and to desperately want to be older than they are. All of this can make them act erratic and awkward at times.

If you can ride through this time with them and maintain partnership, respect and presence using the tools we've explored throughout this book, then the later teen years can be a really rich and fruitful time of deepening maturity, refining partnership and practicing increased autonomy. It can all be very manageable, and actually even fun!

As your teenagers get older and you build on the years of respectful partnership you've been cultivating with them through childhood, you can work with them to discover their path into adulthood. You can support them in creating a path that ignites their passion and gives them an opportunity to be of service in a meaningful way by weaving together their unique interests and skills with the needs of your community and the world.

These years at the end of childhood are precious. Be sure to savor them and enjoy them as much as possible, not by coddling or clinging, but by being as present as you can. Cherish these moments by consciously getting to know the developing young adult in your house. By being curious and interested in this new person. By being available to chat or connect in those (possibly rare) moments when *they* want to. By helping them reflect and recover when they've faltered. And by holding that steady light in their sometimes-stormy seas.

Respecting a teenager means letting them change. Let them reinvent themselves as often as they need to. It also means realizing that it is insanely stressful to be a teen. It always has been. But the experience of the teenagers in this generation is exponentially more intense than ours was. They know what's going on in the world. They hear it all. From cataclysmic climate change to school shootings and deadly pandemics. They're freaking out inside. They're being pressured to plan their future, while being told that they might not even have a future. On top of all that, this socially dominated phase of life has become unfathomably harder to navigate with social media, cyberbullying and online sexual predation. So, give them a lot of credit for hanging in there and making it through.

Even though they don't need you in the ways they used to, parenting doesn't end when kids start dressing and feeding themselves and driving themselves around. Teenagers and young adults need us to stay present with them all the way through. Don't think that there's nothing to do or nothing you *can* do just because things have changed so much. There's still plenty of active parenting that needs to be done. It's just different.

As you venture into the teenage zone with your kids, all the aspects of your parenting will become more complex, more subtle and more sophisticated. The issues they face and the lessons they need to learn will require a more thoughtful approach and may be quite challenging. They tend to need you less often but more deeply. Now, instead of guiding their growth by spotting them while they climb on the playground, you will have to spot them while they learn how to drive, get a job, navigate love and heartbreak, suffer through loss and grapple with big life decisions. All these moments are still opportunities to help your children build strength and competence and to support them in earning their way through their stages of growth. Every little (and big) moment is a learning moment that helps them develop into the young adult who will be ready to move into the world with confidence.

For this part of the parenting job, you really have to listen, observe respectfully and carry a strong abiding presence, as always, but now with a lot more space. As your teenagers do weird things and make questionable decisions, you may be stretched to the limits of your ability to respect them. They will likely do things that trigger memories, experiences and self-judgments from your own teenage years. Be mindful not to judge them for being in this underdeveloped moment of their lives. Don't judge or compare them against yourself or by the standards and values that you've developed over decades of trial and error. They are where they are. Brand new to adult life, like you were at their age, but with more fear, anxiety, information, pressure and conflicting feelings than you could ever imagine.

The sage advice I've heard Martín Prechtel offer in regard to what we may do for teenagers has to do with bearing witness to how they see and experience the world. Instead of sitting across from them and telling them what you know, what they should do or whether you approve, you can sit down beside them and behold the world from their view. You can honor them for being who they are in this moment in time. You can hold them in presence, respect and love. And when they talk, you can listen. *Really listen.*

No matter how stellar your partnership skills have been throughout their childhood, you and your teenager will have ups and downs. There will be rough moments and times when they push you away to some degree. They will have a lot of opinions about their world and about you. Don't get discouraged when they give you negative feedback. Listen to them. Take them seriously and consider what they're saying. There may be a lot of insight and wisdom in there. Reflect on what they say, and make changes if you determine that's appropriate. Or just stay the course and allow them space to vent if that's all that seems necessary. Sometimes, they just need to let off steam with the person they feel most comfortable with.

Managing behavior during the teen years should really be centered around transparent communication and high-quality agreements, made with mutual respect and clarity. Ideally, your agreements will be made during "peacetime." If you make any deals or agreements while in conflict, be sure to revisit them soon, in a moment when you're both calm and centered.

Your agreements should be made in a way that allows for teens to have agency within the widest margin that you determine is safe and reasonable. As the adult in the situation, you have the opportunity and responsibility to be very clear about the needs, expectations and parameters of whatever situation for which you're making agreements. Reflect deeply with respect for your teen's growing sovereignty and offer clear, reasonable boundaries with straight forward, understandable explanations. Ask for their input and feedback. Make sure you both understand. Give them the opportunity to ask questions, seek clarity and propose adjustments without having to be defensive.

When the agreement is made, be sure that it is crystal clear. Be explicit about the timeframe and what will occur if the agreement is not upheld. Make sure you can follow through with the consequences you agree on. Don't set yourself up for something you'll feel bad about enforcing or something that you can't realistically enforce. Realize that all agreements are two-way streets, and you have a responsibility in this practice. It's not all about getting your kid to do something. It's about working together to create healthy conditions for your mutual wellbeing.

In a partnership like this, individuation can happen without harm. Your teenager *has* to individuate from you. It's a necessary and important part of growing up. Knowing this, you can see it coming and choose not to take it personally when it does. You can make space to allow for it graciously, so it can happen without emotional damage and scarring and without creating a painful rift between parent and child. It will happen in many different little and big ways throughout their teen and young adult years. Be prepared so you can roll with it to the best of your ability.

What if it feels too late?

It's never too late to orient our relationship with our children towards high quality presence and authentic respect. In fact, if you feel you haven't quite hit the nail on the head with that throughout their childhood, the teenage years are a perfect time to press the reset button. Everything is changing. Teenagers want, more than anything, to be seen and respected. To do this well, you have to do your own work to stay grounded, be honest, communicate clearly and all the other things we've covered in this book.

Even adult children will appreciate your efforts to connect with them authentically and respectfully. We're all in this together. We need each other. When we take our own responsibility and honor our children's sovereignty without projecting our fears and judgments on them, we open up worlds of possibility for wellness and connection.

15

FORGET THE PERFECT OFFERING

"Ring the bells that still can ring. Forget your perfect offering. There is a crack in everything. That's how the light gets in."

– Leonard Cohen [15.1]

New Paradigm Parenting invites us to let go of our attachment to normalcy as defined by the Power Over Paradigm. It urges us to release our illusions of perfection and our fantasies about how the world "should" be so we can face the realities of our world-in-crisis, honestly and courageously. This is the world and the planet-time into which we were born and into which our children were born. Despite all its hardships and challenges, all the suffering and the unraveling, it is *our* time. It is *our* world. We were made for this moment. And so were our children.

Our children need us to meet this moment of the Great Unraveling and Great Turning with them, fully and deeply. New Paradigm Parenting encourages us to embrace the messiness of this time and to learn how to dance in the cracks[15.2] of our changing world. It implores us to say *"yes"* anyway, wholeheartedly. Yes to being here with *and for* our kids. Yes to being with the mystery and moving through the obstacles we encounter with as much flexibility and grace as we can muster. Yes to persevering with resilience on behalf of our children, the ones yet to be and the Earth. Yes to feeding that which feeds us.[15.3] Yes to serving Thriving Life.

Obstacles Abound

This parenting path is deeply rewarding, and in many ways, it ultimately creates much more ease, joy and wellbeing than following along with the status quo. But it's not *easy*, especially at first. As we commit ourselves to Thriving Life and practicing New Paradigm Parenting, we'll have to face and overcome many obstacles. Being aware of how these obstacles may present themselves and being prepared to meet them can help us move through them more skillfully.

Obstacle #1: The POP Sets Us Up to Fail

The Power Over Paradigm society does not release its subjects readily. It is designed for our perpetual servitude to the pyramid of power in which we're always striving for the top. It is designed for our failure in that pursuit. It relies on it. It feeds on the struggle and the disempowerment of individuals. For it to function, each of us is meant to strive and strain throughout our lives, kept busy and stretched thin, motivated by the promise of more success and more ease, if we can just make it a little further up the pyramid. It feeds on our kids too. It tries to hook them while they're young, attempting to disconnect them from themselves, from their families, from the Earth and from their innate relationship with all Life.

As the Power Over Paradigm approaches the end of its viability, it can seem like it's becoming stronger in some ways. With its dying breaths, it clings to its false power. The surge in authoritarianism and nationalism around the world today is a symptom of this. The feverishly desperate attempts from big oil companies to claim and defile every last corner of the Earth for their dead-end fuel source is another symptom. World leaders doubling down on preserving their own power instead of responding to the climate crisis with the urgency it deserves is another symptom. As the POP struggles to maintain its dominance, the increase in these symptoms can make us feel like the path forward is hopeless.

However, these are in fact signs of positive disintegration.[3.10] They announce the imminent end of "the way it has been done" and herald an opportunity for us to find a new path forward. If we can remember this, it will help us shake loose from the grip of the POP. Instead of letting it have power over us and take us down with it, we can see it for what it is and let it go compassionately. We can imagine that we sit bedside through its unraveling, hospicing modernity[15.4] tenderly, as we weave connections with Life beyond modernity.

Obstacle #2: Fear and Overwhelm

Even if we recognize the symptoms of the positive disintegration of the Power Over Paradigm for what they are, they are still manifesting with real consequences. Recent increases in violence, social injustice, economic instability, climate chaos, food insecurity, political tyranny and personal desperation impact people and communities in tangible ways every day. The intensity of suffering caused by these symptoms can be overwhelming and terrifying as we struggle with these impacts, consider how much worse it may get and worry about what the future may hold for our children.

The fear itself can be paralyzing. It can keep us from being present and taking positive action. It can keep us from being available for our kids to help them navigate their feelings and find their own ways forward with creative resilience. In the paralysis of the fear and overwhelm, we can become fixated on trying to protect our kids and control their outcomes. In this state, parents tend to cling to their kids and project their anxieties onto them. This often pushes them away and leaves them even more vulnerable to the challenges of the world.

To maintain authentic closeness and truly partner with our children through these tumultuous times, we need to do our own adult work to metabolize our fear and other big feelings. Using the guidance and practices in this book and following the Spiral of the Work That Reconnects[15.5] (especially in group practices with other parents) helps us let the lid off these feelings and move beyond them into deeper presence. Allowing ourselves to safely and fully feel our feelings – to grieve our losses and express our rage – moves our congested energy through us so we can feel on a visceral level and understand on a soul level that we are intricately woven into the fabric of Life.

This awareness of our interconnection with all Life makes it possible for us to surrender and experience a sense of trust. Trust in Life. Trust in the perfect imperfection of our lives and our children's lives. In this process, we may see that our children came into this life to do something and be someone in direct relationship with this living, changing world. We may feel a sense that we and our children *are* this world, moving together through these changes with all our relations in this vast and complex Interbeing.[2.2] Moving through our fears and releasing the paralysis of overwhelm frees us up to dance with the Great Mystery and the unanswerable questions of life so we can be truly present and meet each moment with courage and resilience.

Obstacle #3: Getting Distracted and Giving Up

Parenting in this way requires a significant amount of intention, consistency and discipline. It can be hard to keep it up – day after day, year after year – especially when the world around you pulls so strongly in the direction of the Power Over Paradigm. Mainstream media, politics, the economy, conventional education and all our major social institutions are designed to reinforce POP principles and practices. Your extended family, friends and even your partner may not understand why you want to question your POP conditioning and raise your children in this unconventional way. They may want to just go along with the status quo. All this can make it incredibly hard to stay persistent and focused on cultivating a Thriving Life household.

A dear friend of mine who has a four-year-old and a nine-year-old told me that she and her husband have come to understand parenting as a major "counter cultural" operation. As they have been raising their children, they notice that, in order to take good care of their children and center their children's wellbeing, they have to constantly intervene and interrupt the influences of mainstream culture. She noted that vigilance and attention are required at every step along the way. I completely agree.

This vigilance is well worth it and will return to you as blessings many times over throughout the years. If you consistently show up for your children with loving, respectful presence during their childhoods, you'll build a strong foundation of trust with them that will make all your interactions more meaningful and easeful. The significant shift around how we work with power and support mutual empowerment in New Paradigm Parenting diffuses power struggles and makes decisions, boundaries and accountability infinitely easier to navigate. The depth of love, safety and belonging fostered by New Paradigm Parenting provides our children with high quality protective factors [14.10] that support their mental health and strengthen their resilience for facing life's challenges. As we embrace and practice New Paradigm Parenting, we also heal and grow along with our children, deepening our own connection with Life and contributing to the Great Turning in meaningful ways.

The best way to ensure your perseverance on this path is to surround yourself with support. If possible, share this learning journey with your partner(s) and/or co-parent(s) so you can collaborate in service to Thriving Life. Find other parents who are concerned about the world, struggling with the POP mainstream and may be interested in caring for their children and Life in this way. I would encourage you to form a book group to read through this book together and have conversations about what it brings up for you. You might also choose to move through the Spiral of the Work That Reconnects[15.5] together, supporting each other with simple ways to practice facing the challenges and joys of these times with honesty, resilience and creativity.

Another great way to generate support is to put yourself and your children in learning environments and community experiences that support Thriving Life practices and principles so you can experience the joy of connection and comradery around caring for Life with others.

Weaving New Paradigm Parenting into Your Life

Unlike other parenting philosophies and methods, New Paradigm Parenting is not a prescribed collection of practices and steps. It is an orientation to parenting as a powerful form of postactivism.[4.13] It is a call to do everything you can to care for your children and to care for Life in these uniquely challenging times. It invites you to embrace parenting as a learning adventure and healing opportunity that supports mutual wellbeing – for you, your children and all beings.

The practices and principles we've explored in this book are here to support and inspire you along your learning journey as you orient towards Thriving Life. Some of the practices shared here may have already emerged in your parenting, either through your intuitive response to the needs of your children or through one of the many parenting approaches that overlap with New Paradigm Parenting. Some practices may have been completely new to you. Take your time with them and notice what brings you and your family into greater connection with each other and with Life.

Weaving new ideas and practices into your parenting can be awkward and challenging, especially if they are imposed without consideration for the actual needs of your family members and adapted accordingly. New Paradigm Parenting encourages you to pay attention with presence and to learn directly from the needs of each of your family members in relation to each other and the needs of our world.

This means it's going to manifest differently from household to household. As you engage in this learning journey, it will unfold in its own way for you and your family. Completing this book is not the end of the learning. It is just the beginning. As you move through your years of dynamic living relationship with your children and our world, I encourage you to let the concepts from this book swim around in your mind and heart. Pay attention to the adult/child relationships you come across – whether in your personal life, your community or even as represented in the media – and contemplate them in the context of New Paradigm Parenting. Then turn your attention, again and again, to your own relationships, spiraling back to this book for support as often as needed while your children grow, and your journey deepens. Adapt your learnings to the unique needs of your family and weave them into your daily life, to the best of your ability, always in service to mutual thriving.

As I continue my learning journey, leading and growing alongside the evolving community of New Paradigm Parents around the world, I want to hear about your experiences. I want to hear about your successes and your challenges and what you're learning along the way. I also want you to have support and connection through your New Paradigm Parenting journey. I invite you to connect with me on social media and through my website: www.RadiantBalance.com to share your stories and questions, to learn from the other parents who are following this path, to stay connected with our ever-deepening collection of New Paradigm Parenting resources and to join me for the Work That Reconnects experiences that I design and facilitate specifically for parents.

"We live in a kind of dark age, craftily lit with synthetic light, so that no one can tell how dark it has really gotten. But our exiled spirits can tell. Deep in our bones resides an ancient, singing couple who just won't give up making their beautiful, wild noise.

The world won't end if we can find them."

– Martín Prechtel [4.10]

Leaving it All on the Field, for the Love of Life

Life is calling to us. It is urging us to bend our ears to hear the singing of those Holy Life-Giving Beings that keep spinning around each other in ecstatic dance within our bones and all around us. It is coaxing us to listen past the incessant newscasts of doom and gloom, and to hear beyond the clarion calls to "save the world" so the sweet sound of the still-thriving living world can guide us back into purposeful relationship with Life.

As we orient deeply into the Thriving Life Paradigm, we understand the world as a complex Interbeing within whom we are dynamically entwined, instead of some sort of separate "thing" that we could destroy or save. Within this orientation we're no longer compelled to scramble to protect ourselves and our children by preserving some little scraps of "safety" or comfort for ourselves against the hardships of the world. We are compelled, instead, to respond to the needs of the world with loving mutuality and courageous reverence.

Although life has been teaching this to me slowly in little ways for many decades, I am most deeply indebted to Martín Prechtel for helping me truly understand that life is *not about getting what we want or protecting ourselves*. It's not about human success and survival, at all. It's about serving the thriving whole with as much beauty as we can muster so there is a possibility that the beauty and the large sacred Mystery of Life can continue beyond our own time.

During the years that I was blessed to study with Martín at Bolad's Kitchen,[15.6] I felt a radical shift in my entire orientation to Life. What I learned from him deepened and widened my sense of what is happening in the world at this time and my understanding of our role as humans within it. New Paradigm Parenting grew, in part, from the rich soil of these understandings. In his own words, Martín teaches, *"life is not about function or getting there, it's only the beauty of how you go that really matters."*[15.7]

I've experienced this to be a great relief! It's not a relief as in "getting off the hook." It's a relief to be *on* the hook. To be hooked onto all of Life and capable of responding to *and with* Life. In this way, we can focus deeply on the beauty of what we do, the quality of the relationships within our care and the depth of connection and reverence for Life that we cultivate. And we can take extra care in leaving steppingstones of wellness for our children and the ones yet to be so they have the possibility to thrive in a future that we will never see and probably can't even imagine.

When we release our attachment to human success and accept that, as Martín puts it, *"humans are here to give the juice of their unique beauty and grief to cause the Holy in Nature to succeed,"*[15.8] we no longer feel the need to hold back and guard ourselves against hardship. Instead, we meet the present moment with courage and curiosity, as open-hearted and generous servants to the sacred Mystery of Life, inspired to pour all our love and creativity into this service, leaving it all on the field, for the love of Life.

There is no guarantee that our New Paradigm Parenting efforts will succeed in seeding a Thriving Life future for the coming generations. There is no know way to know if we will be able to heal and learn our way out of all this damage we've caused and are still causing. There's no guarantee that human beings will be able to continue to thrive on the Earth. There is also no way to completely safeguard ourselves or our children against suffering in our lifetimes. Life offers no such guarantees and safeguards. Only possibilities.

Even without a guarantee that our efforts will work, is there any other choice but to do *everything* we possibly can to pour our love into these precious young people in our lives?

If there is breath in our lungs and children to care for, if the Earth still spins and flowers still bloom, if the Sun shines and there is any chance that any of this could work, we have no other choice. Our love demands our best effort. Even if we may fail, may we fail beautifully while loving deeply.

As we give ourselves fully to parenting in the best way possible, for the sake of Thriving Life, we move beyond perfect and into *Beautiful*. In this way our lives and our children's lives become gifts that nourish the wellbeing of the world.

About the Author

Jo delAmor is a mother, personal coach and Work That Reconnects facilitator who has dedicated over twenty years to the care of children and their families. She has led dozens of parents from around the world through her signature group program: *Parenting in Tumultuous Times* – a practical, fun and supportive course for parents looking to do right by their kids in these times of converging global crises. The frameworks and activities outlined in this book have been tested and refined by these parents.

Jo has worked as a personal coach for over fifteen years. Upon graduating from the Institute for Integrative Nutrition in 2007, she launched her private practice as a Holistic Health Coach, working mostly with moms. As she supported her clients in improving their physical and mental health, it became clear to her that their main struggles were embedded within the illnesses of the larger society. She began to identify as a personal transformation coach and dedicated her practice to *supporting personal and cultural transformation as a catalyst for planetary healing*. Her coaching work is deeply holistic, incorporating reconnection to self, all our relations, the Earth and the Divine across Deep Time in service of the ones yet to be.

Since 2013, Jo has been facilitating the Work That Reconnects with a focus on dismantling oppression, transforming our cultural paradigm and supporting parents through these unprecedented and challenging times. She has also been one of the core staff members of the Work That Reconnects Network since 2019.

About the Author

Jo delAmor is a mom and a stepmom to two young adults who graduated high school in 2020, in the middle of Covid lockdowns and school closures. For over twenty years, she has also cared for and worked with hundreds of other people's children of all ages in a wide variety of contexts. She was blessed to live in and care for children within a long-term co-parenting community throughout her child's upbringing. She has also designed and facilitated after school programs in low-income public schools, been a lead teacher for Unitarian Universalist Sunday school, mentored high school students, chaperoned many field trips and school social events, been a wilderness camp counselor, taught in preschools and daycare facilities, and worked as an in-home nanny. In all her work with children, she has paid close attention to what this new generation needs at this pivotal time on planet Earth, charting what works, what doesn't and what is being called forth from us as parents.

Jo is on a lifelong journey of remembrance and reconnection that is guided by being a mother, a caregiver, a grower of food, a spinner of wool, a maker of beauty and a disciple of Life.

Learn more about Jo and her work at www.RadiantBalance.com

Acknowledgments

As all things in this living, breathing, Interbeing of Life are, this book is a manifestation of countless relationships, generations of experience and profound rivers of wisdom that flow through to our current troubled times from the Deep Past and the Deep Future. In these final moments of the epic project of compiling this book, I must first bow down with gratitude and acknowledgement to the Holy Beings that make Life thrive and to the teachers – both human and more than human – who have planted the seeds and cultivated the growth of New Paradigm Parenting in my life.

I am eternally grateful to my child, Luna Blue delAmor, who has been my greatest teacher and my greatest joy since he/they first graced my life. I'm also so grateful for the ways he/they has supported the writing of this book, talking with me about the concepts and reviewing all the personal stories. I'm particularly grateful for the rich conversations and collaboration that we got to experience as we worked closely together on preparing the gender identity section. Thank you for teaching me and trusting me. I love you to the moon and back.

My heart is overwhelmed with gratitude for my amazing husband, Mountain Ross, who has provided unwavering support and encouragement to me throughout this whole book writing process. Thank you for picking up the slack for all those hours when I was stuck on the computer and for being my faithful companion and fearless partner in life and parenting.

Deepest gratitude to my sister, Allison Wonderland, for her sincere commitment to the quality of this work, for giving me loving, honest feedback and helping me fine-tune the contents of this book in its early stages. I am also profoundly grateful to her for introducing me to the Work That Reconnects and for always forging the path ahead as my "big" sister and teaching me all along the way, in literally all the most important areas of life, from growing food to living our lives as a gift to Spirit to being a mom in the deepest way. The fierce love and dedication with which she raised her son and continues her parental partnership with him in his adulthood planted the first seeds of New Paradigm Parenting in my heart when I was just twelve years old and has been my most enduring example of the potential we have as parents in this time.

I also extend my heartfelt gratitude to all the parents who have participated in my *Parenting in Tumultuous Times* programs and private coaching sessions over the past few years. I feel deeply honored by their trust and vulnerability and their willingness to explore and embrace New Paradigm Parenting. Their insightful feedback and the experiences we've had together in WTR practice have contributed immensely to the content of this book and the development of New Paradigm Parenting. I feel so blessed to know each of them and share in this learning journey together in our growing global community of New Paradigm Parents, with active members from Mexico, New Zealand, Australia, Switzerland, Sweden, Germany, the United Kingdom, Canada, across the United States, and in many places in between.

I am deeply grateful to Simone Hanchet for her brilliant copyediting and heart centered support through the grueling process of coaxing this book across the finish line. I couldn't have dreamed up a more perfect person to comb through this manuscript and bring it to its full potential. Her humor, honesty, integrity, steadfastness and undaunted cheerleading have been a profound blessing and have been instrumental in making this book a reality. There is no way this book would have made it into the world without her meticulous, thoughtful and poignant editing. As a fellow Work That Reconnects facilitator, coach and participant in my *Parenting in Tumultuous Times* program, her belief in the value of this work has meant the world to me.

Thank you to my dear friend and mentor, Catherine Gregory at Modern Wisdom Press who midwifed the first draft of this book into being with her brilliantly designed *Birth Your Book* program for new authors. Great thanks to Alissa MacGowan of Red Pen for Rent and the insightful feedback that saved this book and made it possible to publish. Much gratitude to Eileen Kelly-Aguirre for her proofreading work and her enthusiasm for this project.

Endnotes

This endnotes section is meant to be a resource for you to seek out further information about the many concepts introduced in this book to help you dive deeper into your learning and experience. Please follow these threads and enjoy!

The endnotes below are grouped and numbered by chapter. In the cases where a reference is repeated in the book, the endnote will point back to the chapter in which it was first mentioned.

Many of the notes below include references to websites as they existed in 2023. Due to the dynamic nature of the internet, please note that any links shared below may have changed since publication or may no longer be valid. If the direct links provided don't work, you can use them as leads for further exploration to find the most current resources in that area.

Introduction

0.1 L.R. Knost, award-winning author, feminist, social justice activist, founder and director of the children's rights advocacy and family consulting group, Little Hearts/Gentle Parenting Resources, and Editor-in-Chief of Holistic Parenting Magazine. www.littleheartsbooks.com

0.2 Joanna Macy, PhD is the beloved root teacher of the Work That Reconnects. She is a mother and grandmother, a lifelong activist, a scholar of Buddhism, General Systems Theory, and Deep Ecology, and a translator of the poetry of Rainer Maria Rilke. Her ability to articulate the connection between our personal anguish and our pain for the world in this time of collapse and transformation has been widely appreciated by people around the world. Through her decades of facilitation, and the development and sharing of the Work That Reconnects, she has fostered profoundly transformative group experiences in which participants are invited to access their own deep knowing and empower their creativity and resilience for contributing to the Great Turning. The wide range of emotion that Joanna holds in her heart – from the courageously honest lens with which she witnesses collapse to her playfulness and adventurous love of life – has been a tremendous inspiration to me and my work. Thank you, Joanna!

Learn more about Joanna at: https://workthatreconnects.org/joanna-macy-root-teacher/ and https://www.joannamacy.net/

0.3 Martín Prechtel is the most intelligent, knowledgeable and deeply loving person I've ever been blessed to know. Carrying both Native American and European lineages, he was raised within a Pueblo Indian community in Northern New Mexico. As a young adult, he left New Mexico to live in the village of Santiago Atitlán, Guatemala, eventually becoming a full member of the Tzutujil Mayan community there. His unique life experience and the calling given to him to "keep the seeds alive for a time of hope beyond our own" have made him an incredible gift to the world in this time of great transformation. There are truly no words worthy of expressing my sincere gratitude for and admiration of his commitment to Life and the miraculously mysterious way that he resuscitates the Indigenous Souls of the shimmering amnesiacs (like me) that have had the rare opportunity to study with him at his hands-on village-style school of forgotten things and endangered excellent knowledges, Bolad's Kitchen. In addition to being a brilliant teacher, he is a devoted father, a loving partner, a caregiver and friend to fine old-time horses, an artist, a musician, a signer of sacred songs, a tender of ancient seeds and the author of numerous books, each one a masterpiece of layered wisdom about how sacred and spectacular this blessing of Life truly is. Thank you, Martín!

Learn more about Martín at: https://www.floweringmountain.com/

0.4 Woman Stands Shining (Pat McCabe) is one of my dearest teachers, elders and comrades in this walk of life and learning. She is of the Diné Nation (often known incorrectly as Navajo) and was also adopted into the Lakota Spiritual Way of Life, receiving the name Weyakpa Najin Win (Woman Stands Shining). She is a mother, grandmother, activist, artist, writer, ceremonial leader, and international speaker. Her teachings about the Law of Nature, personal will, sovereignty and the importance for humans to understand paradigm as a matter of choice have been central to the development of my work and the content of this book. Having a deep understanding of and access to both dominant Power Over Paradigm society and Indigenous Thriving Life Paradigm community, she carries essential wisdom about the calling that we are receiving at this critical moment in time to uphold the honor of being human. She encourages us "holy earth surface walkers, five-fingered beings" to remember our place in the Sacred Hoop of Life and become Omnibenificient beings, like the rest of our relatives. Her open-hearted commitment to joy and beauty, her courageous commitment to healing through the trauma of her lineage and her humble, loving, generosity as a friend and ally on this path of unlearning and learning have been a deep nourishment and inspiration to me. Thank you, Pat!

Learn more about Woman Stands Shining (Pat McCabe) here: https://www.patmccabe.net/

Chapter 1

1.1 from *Let This Darkness Be a Bell Tower*, a poem by Rainer Maria Rilke as printed in *A Year with Rilke: Daily Readings from the Best of Rainer Maria Rilke*, translated and edited by Joanna Macy and Anita

Barrows, HarperOne (2009). This poem was originally from Rilke's book, *Sonnets to Orpheus*.

1.2 The Work That Reconnects (WTR) is a philosophy and body of work that has been developed by Joanna Macy and her colleagues over more than forty years. This form of group work grew out of the anti-nuclear movement and engaged Buddhism in the late 1970s. It has evolved over these decades to meet the changing circumstances of our world and provide a framework and practices for *"how to face this mess we're in without going crazy."*

The book *Coming Back to Life*, co-authored by Joanna Macy and Molly Brown, is a complete manual that details the concepts and practices that form "the Work" and make this work accessible to anyone that wishes to practice it. It is an outrageously generous and profoundly useful resource for our time. In addition to the books written by Joanna Macy and co-authors, the Work That Reconnects Network has created a living platform for connection and extensive WTR resources at www.WorkThatReconnects.org

I have been blessed to study, participate in and facilitate the Work That Reconnects since 2013 and completed the yearlong Spiral Journey WTR facilitator development training in 2018. This work has deeply affirmed and informed the development of my work, my concept of the world and the direction of my goals since it has come into my life. I had the great pleasure of working on the administrative team for the Spiral Journey WTR facilitator development program from 2018-2022. I have also been on the staff and Weavers Team for the Work That Reconnects Network since 2019. These positions have given me the opportunity to directly engage with incredible, passionate people from all around the world who are dedicated to serving the Great Turning. For that I am deeply grateful and continually inspired.

1.3 Business As Usual, the Great Unraveling and the Great Turning are terms used in the Work That Reconnects to describe the Three Stories of our Time. These stories are playing out simultaneously and each one reveals a profoundly different lens through which we can understand our world.

Business As Usual (BAU) is the story of the Industrial Growth Society, and the European-based colonial empires from which it emerged that functions to maintain the status quo and the power and privilege of the wealthy.

The Great Unraveling refers to the ongoing and worldwide unraveling of biological, ecological, economic, and social systems. It is the story told by scientists, journalists, and activists who have not been bought off or intimidated by the forces of the Industrial Growth Society.

The Great Turning is the story of the transition from the Industrial Growth Society to a Life Sustaining Society. This term originally appeared in the 1980s and was used in the title of the book *The Great Turning: Personal Peace, Global Victory Paperback* by Craig Schindler and Gary Lapid, Bear & Co (1989)

Definitions borrowed from the WTR Network website: https://workthatreconnects.org/glossary-of-wtr-terms/

Chapter 2

2.1 Quote attributed to Maya Angelou by her dear friend Oprah Winfrey in 1995 and throughout the years. This video shares the lesson she learned from this simple statement: www.oprah.com/oprahs-lifeclass/the-powerful-lesson-maya-angelou-taught-oprah-video

2.2 The term Interbeing was proposed by Thich Nhat Hanh and explored in his book, *Interbeing: Fourteen Guidelines for Engaged Buddhism* by Thich Nhat Hanh, Parallax Press (1998). He explains that "to be means to InterBe" and that there is no separate existence. Each aspect of Creation is co-existent with all other aspects of Creation.

This understanding of radical and dynamic interconnectedness is also expressed by many other people from a variety of cultural contexts. It is a universal aspect of animist cultures worldwide that recognize the interweaving and interdependence of all of Creation, sometimes depicted as the Web of Life of ancient Earth-based cultures or the Sacred Hoop (Cangleska Wakan) of the Lakota people. In his writing and teachings, Martín Prechtel shares the traditional Tz'utujil Mayan understanding of K'as Limaal, which he translates as mutual indebtedness or mutual ensparkedness. Another version of this understanding of mutuality is expressed in the Bantu term, Ubuntu, from central and southern Africa. Loosely translated as "I am because we are," it is a philosophy or understanding that supports collectivism over individualism.

Chapter 3

3.1 Bayo Akomolafe is a brilliant, revolutionary, mind-bending public intellectual and deep-rooted human being, partner and father with an incredibly loving heart. His generosity of spirit and his ability to articulate beyond the dominant paradigm are unparalleled and extremely helpful in the process of aligning with the Thriving Life Paradigm. This quote is from the foreword on the homepage of his website: www.bayoakomolafe.net

3.2 When using the words "we" and "us" it's always important to be clear about who that "we" really is. The "we" in this book refers to parents who are engaged in, complicit to, dependent on and/or imposed upon by the Industrial Growth Society in relation our income, housing, food, civic services, education, entertainment, etc. There is *a lot* of diversity within that "we." The use of the word "we" isn't meant to imply that we all see things the same way or have the same experiences. It is not meant to overshadow the important differences that exist within our cultural lineages and positionality within the Industrial Growth Society. It is meant to indicate that "we" are all affected by the Industrial Growth Society and the Power Over Paradigm on some level and therefore have a shared interest in and need to understand it and respond to it consciously.

3.3 Many Indigenous peoples from around the world carry traditional stories describing a time or times in the past when the old world collapsed, and they were born into a new world. In consideration of this mutually corroborated oral history, I recognize that humans may have faced this level of existential crisis before. However, these events would have occurred a very long time ago and this knowledge is not included in the annals of conventional "modern human history." I am very interested in learning more about how native peoples survived catastrophic collapse and rebirth and what they learned from it. It lifts my heart to consider that such a devastating crisis could have given birth to some of the most intelligent and sophisticated cultures on the planet. It makes me think that there might even be hope for us yet, if we're willing to learn.

3.4 Climate Change 2023 Synthesis Report Summary for Policymakers, a report of the International Panel on Climate Change (IPCC): www.ipcc.ch

"Climate change is a threat to human well-being and planetary health (very high confidence). There is a rapidly closing window of opportunity to secure a liveable and sustainable future for all (very high confidence)."

3.5 Woman Stands Shining (Pat McCabe) speaks about the Power Over Paradigm in many of her talks and interviews. One example is the first episode of This Mythic Life podcast by Dr. Sharon Blackie: Interview with Pat McCabe (Feb 16, 2018): https://soundcloud.com/thismythiclife/pat-mccabe For the full website for this podcast visit: https://sharonblackie.net/podcast/

3.6 *The Chalice & the Blade* by Riane Eisler, HarperOne (1988). Dr. Eisler is a social systems scientist, cultural historian, futurist and author of several other books, including *Nurturing Our Humanity: How Domination and Partnership Shape Our Brains, Lives, and Future* Oxford University Press (2019) and *The Partnership Way: New Tools for Living and Learning, Healing Our Families, and Our World*, Harper San Francisco; First Edition (1990). Learn more about Riane's work at: www.rianeeisler.com

3.7 *World as Lover, World as Self* by Joanna Macy, Parallax Press (1991); anniversary edition (2021)

3.8 *Coming Back to Life* by Joanna Macy and Molly Brown, New Society Publishers; Revised edition (2014), page 39

3.9 Living Systems are discussed in *Coming Back to Life* by Joanna Macy and Molly Brown, New Society Publishers (2014) on pages 37-41. For further explorations, see the paper *Living Systems Theory* by G.A. Swanson, Tennessee Technological University, Cookeville, USA and James Grier Miller, University of California, Los Angeles, USA here: www.eolss.net/sample-chapters/c02/e6-46-01-03.pdf

3.10 In *Coming Back to Life*, on page 52, Joanna Macy and Molly Brown credit psychiatrist Kazimierz Dąbrowski for the term "positive disintegration."

3.11 *Coming Back to Life* by Joanna Macy and Molly Brown, New Society Publishers (2014), page 53

3.12 With much gratitude in my heart, I give credit to Woman Stands Shining (Pat McCabe) for the sharing the phrase "Thriving Life Paradigm" and I give deep thanks for her teachings on the Law of Life, free will, sovereignty and mutual thriving. She speaks about these topics in many of her talks and interviews. She shares beautifully on these topics in episode #17 on the Sounds of SAND podcast – January 12,

2023 (www.youtube.com/watch?v=3iob2inGAyQ) and in the Work That Reconnects Network webinar, Paradigm as Choice in the Great Turning – March 25, 2023 (https://vimeo.com/812227409)

3.13 *War Talk* by Arundhati Roy, South End Press (2003)

Chapter 4

4.1 University of Portland commencement speech by Paul Hawken, May 3, 2009

4.2 Industrial Growth Society and Life Sustaining Society are terms used in the Work That Reconnects.

Industrial Growth Society refers to the economic and social systems developed by colonial-based empires and is based on the exploitation of human and natural resources. In Work That Reconnects framing, the Industrial Growth Society is often referred to as Business as Usual.

Life Sustaining Societies refer to cultures in which the interlocking economic and social systems function to maintain the health of the natural world and the vibrancy of human communities.

Definitions borrowed from the WTR Network website: https://workthatreconnects.org/glossary-of-wtr-terms/

4.3 As quoted in *Beyond Civilization: Humanity's Next Great Adventure* by Daniel Quinn (1999), p. 137

4.4 Joanna Macy speaks to this in her speech *The Hidden Promise of Our Dark Age* for the Bioneers Conference in 2018 www.youtube.com/watch?v=vzmjF1jE2K0

4.5 *Sacred Instructions* by Sherri Mitchell, North Atlantic Books (2018), page 20

4.6 *Braiding Sweetgrass* by Robin Wall Kimmerer, Milkweed Editions (2015). I don't know if there is a more perfect book. The exquisite brilliance with which Robin braids together her love for the living world with her deeply rooted Indigenous Thriving Life worldview and her extensive knowledge of botany in well-crafted stories that break the reader's heart open to the wonder of the world is beyond compare. It is a paradigm shifting work of creative genius.

4.7 *Hope in the Dark* by Rebecca Solnit, Haymarket Books (2016). The teachings from this book have been a great help to me in moving through certain levels of emotional paralysis and despair about the state of the world.

4.8 *Refuge: An Unnatural History of Family and Place* by Terry Tempest Williams, Vintage; Reprint edition (1992)

4.9 *Coming Back to Life* by Joanna Macy and Molly Brown, New Society Publishers; Revised edition (2014), page 169

4.10 *The Secrets of the Talking Jaguar* by Martín Prechtel, TarcherPerigee (1999), page 283. These are actually the last words of this incredibly moving, life-changing book. I encourage you to read it from the beginning and all the way through.

4.11 *Saving the Indigenous Soul: an Interview with Martín Prechtel* by Derrick Jensen, April 2001, www.thesunmagazine.org/issues/304/saving-the-indigenous-soul

4.12 Founder of Meaningful Ideas: Conscious Parenting with Vivek Patel, www.meaningfulideas.com

4.13 *What I Mean By Postactivism* by Bayo Akomolafe, https://www.bayoakomolafe.net/post/what-i-mean-by-postactivism

4.14 *This is Why I Speak of "Postactivism"* by Bayo Akomolafe, https://radicaldiscipleship.net/2019/03/03/this-is-why-i-speak-of-postactivism/

Chapter 5

5.1 *In My Grandmother's House: Black Women, Faith, and the Stories We Inherit* by Rev. Yolanda Pierce, Broadleaf Books (2023)

5.2 *Body of Truth: How Science, History, and Culture Drive Our Obsession with Weight--and What We Can Do about It* by Harriet Brown, Da Capo Lifelong Books (2015)

5.3 *Upstream*, selected essays by Mary Oliver, Penguin Press (2016)

5.4 *Peace Is Every Step: The Path of Mindfulness in Everyday Life* by Thich Nhat Hanh, Random House Publishing Group (1992)

5.5 This phrase "coming back to life" is the title of the foundational book of the Work That Reconnects by Joanna Macy and Molly Brown. I love how clear and simple it is as a practice. It reminds us to return, again and again, to the basic structures and systems of Life. It also inspires us to "jump up and live again," as my dear teacher Martín Prechtel always says. This is a call to wake up and revive our vitality and our connection with the living world we are inextricably woven within.

Chapter 6

6.1 Andrew Harvey, https://www.andrewharvey.net/

6.2 *World as Lover, World as Self* by Joanna Macy, Parallax Press (2021) Joanna also speaks to the importance of Honoring Our Pain for the World in many of her recorded talks and other books, including *Coming Back to Life* and *Active Hope*.

6.3 Martín Prechtel teaches about the importance of metabolizing grief in his school Bolad's Kitchen (https://floweringmountain.com/bolads-kitchen-general-information/) and in many of his recorded interviews. He also covers this topic quite thoroughly in his book, *The Smell of Rain on Dust: Grief and Praise,* North Atlantic Books (2015) and in the recorded lecture of great renown from 1997 *Grief and Praise: an evening with Martín Prechtel.* https://floweringmountain.com/product/grief-and-praise-lecture-on-cd/

6.4 *The Unbroken,* a poem from the book *Beyond Brokenness* by Rashani Réa, Xlibris, Corp. (2009) https://www.rashani.com/

6.5 *The Darkside of the Light Chasers* by Debbie Ford, Riverhead Books (2010). I have found this book to be an essential resource for personal growth work, learning to recognize the dysfunctional patterns and cycles that often hide in the shadows of our awareness and interrupting them before passing them down, unchecked, to our children.

6.6 Extinction Rebellion is a decentralised, international and politically non-partisan movement using non-violent direct action and civil disobedience to persuade governments to act justly on the Climate and Ecological Emergency. https://rebellion.global/

6.7 *Coming Back to Life* by Joanna Macy and Molly Brown (2014), page 121. Joanna shares this beautiful teaching of the companion emotion that accompanies each of the painful emotions we experience as part of facilitating the Truth Mandala practice.

Chapter 7

7.1 *Whispers Through Time* by L.R. Knost, Little Hearts Books, LLC (2013)

7.2 *A Sense of Wonder* by Rachel Carson, Harper Perennial; Reprint edition (2017)

7.3 Joshua Gorman is the founder of Generation Waking Up, a non-profit organization igniting a generation of young people to bring forth a thriving, just, and sustainable world. http://www.generationwakingup.org/

7.4 Excerpt from Severn Cullis-Suzuki's speech at the 1992 UN's Earth Summit in Rio de Janeiro. Listen to the full speech on YouTube under "Severn Cullis-Suzuki - The Speech that Silenced the World for 5 Minutes": https://www.youtube.com/watch?v=lhesdVrawgc

Learn about her current life and work on her website: https://severncullissuzuki.com/

7.5 Autumn Peltier, 13-year-old water advocate, addresses UN, 2018: https://www.youtube.com/watch?v=zg60sr38oic

7.6 Xiuhtezcatl Martinez Speaking at National Event at six years old in 2006 https://www.youtube.com/watch?v=6sus-1rZG8c. Xiuhtezcatl spoke and performed extensively as a climate activist throughout his youth and served as the Youth Director of Earth Guardians until 2019.

7.7 In 2015, 21 young Americans filed their constitutional climate lawsuit, *Juliana v. United States*, against the U.S. government. Their complaint asserts that, through the government's affirmative actions that cause climate change, it has violated the youngest generation's constitutional rights to life, liberty, and property, as well as failed to protect essential public trust resources. Learn more at https://www.ourchildrenstrust.org/juliana-v-us

7.8 Greta Thunberg addressed world leaders at UN Climate Action Summit in 2019: https://www.youtube.com/watch?v=KAJsdgTPJpU

Her school strikes for climate awareness inspired the global movement Fridays for Future: https://fridaysforfuture.org/

7.9 The Bioneers Conference is a vibrant, engaging annual conference of visionary thinkers, activists, ecologically aligned scientists and changemakers that has been occurring every year since 1990. Their slogan (which I love) is, "It's all alive. It's all connected. It's all intelligent. It's all relatives." On their website they describe the conference as "a real-time co-creation story of social transformation and movement building. It's a social coral reef of nourishment, fertility, innovation and mutual aid." Learn more about the conference here: https://conference.bioneers.org/

One of the aspects I love most about the conference is their commitment to youth leadership. Every year there are many powerful presentations and performances by young people and there is a rich Youth Leadership Program that provides an interactive, empowering space for young people at the conference and a rich program of offerings designed by and for youth. If you ever have the opportunity to bring a group of young people to the conference, I highly recommend it. Learn more about the Youth Leadership and Education Program here: https://bioneers.org/youth-leadership-and-education-program/

Over the past few decades, Bioneers has grown into a learning community that provides a wide range of educational resources throughout the year, beyond the conference. Visit their full website to learn about their projects, listen to their podcast, read articles, explore their online courses and more. You can type "youth" into their search bar to find keynote speeches, performances and articles by and for youth that you can explore with your kids to inspire and empower them. https://bioneers.org/

7.10 I credit the term "heartstorm" to my dear friend and co-mama, Cristina Cabeza-Kinney. It's like brainstorming but it reminds us to let our hearts lead the way, as we dig deeper and listen more lovingly while sharing ideas with each other. Just like in brainstorming, all ideas are welcomed and included without judgment.

7.11 Lyla June Johnston speaks about these practices and the importance of making sure you're offering the type of support that is actually desired by the Indigenous communities in your area. I first learned about the concept of voluntary land tax from her. This is one way in which people living on occupied land can contribute to the wellbeing of the Indigenous communities in their area and support rematriation and landback projects. One of the examples of the voluntary land tax that Lyla speaks about comes from the Sogorea Te' Land Trust, an urban Indigenous women-led land trust that facilitates the return of Indigenous land to Indigenous people in the San Francisco Bay Area (Turtle Island/California, USA). They call this contribution the Shuumi Land Tax because Shuumi means gift in the Ohlone language, Chochenyo. They have a great website with information about their projects and about the voluntary land tax, including a calculator to help people decide how much to contribute on a monthly or annual basis. Wherever you live, you could use this information and the calculator to help inspire and guide your choices about the amount to contribute to the Indigenous communities in your local area. Here's the page with that information: https://sogoreate-landtrust.org/shuumi-land-tax/

7.12 This passage is from a Facebook post written by ALisa Starkweather for Mother's Day 2019.

ALisa Starkweather began her visionary work four decades ago and her contributions include the Red Tent Movement, Women in Power, Priestess Path and Daughters of the Earth Gatherings. She offers deep healing immersions with individuals in the mythic realms of our psyche to shift old stories, shadows and patterns. You can connect with her at alisastarkweather@me.com and www.facebook.com/alisa.starkweather

Chapter 8

8.1 *The Prophet* by Kahlil Gibran, Knopf (1923)

8.2 *The Disappearance of Childhood* by Neil Postman, Vintage/Random House (1994)

8.3 Sadhguru (born Jagadish Vasudev) is the founder and head of the Isha Foundation, based in Coimbatore, India. https://isha.sadhguru.org/us/en

8.4 See Chapter 4: Parenting as Activism for reference on Bayo Akomolafe's concept of "touching the box" as part of the practice of postactivism.

8.5 This passage is from *These Wilds Beyond Our Fences: Letters to my Daughter on Humanity's Search for Home* by Bayo Akomolafe and was written by Ijeoma Precious Clement-Akomolafe, Bayo's wife and the mother of his children.

8.6 *Letters to a Young Poet* by Rainer Maria Rilke, translated by M.D. Herter Norton, W. W. Norton & Company; Revised edition (1993)

Chapter 9

9.1 *The Parent's Tao Te Ching: Ancient Advice for Modern Parents* by William Martin, Da Capo Lifelong Books (1999)

9.2 Pennie Brownlee (1947-2023) was a passionate advocate for the well-being of babies, children, and parents. http://www.penniebrownlee.com/

9.3 *The Continuum Concept* by Jean Liedloff, Da Capo Press; reprint edition (1986), original (1975) This website provides a dynamic resource for readers of the book, including helpful articles and a community listserv https://continuumconcept.org/

9.4 Charles Raison, M.D., Professor of Human Ecology at University of Wisconsin-Madison

9.5 *Magical Child* by Joseph Chilton Pierce, Plume; Reissue edition (1992)

9.6 For more of Pam Leo's teachings on Connection Parenting visit her website at https://connectionparenting.com/

9.7 From *Wild Geese*, a poem by Mary Oliver; included in *Wild Geese: Selected Poems,* Bloodaxe Books Ltd (2004)

9.8 This is a reference to *The Continuum Concept* by Jean Liedloff (see endnote 9.3) Here is a simple summary of the concept of evolutionary expectations from the Continuum Concept website: "According to Jean Liedloff, the continuum concept is the idea that in order to achieve optimal physical, mental and emotional development, human beings — especially babies — require the kind of experience to which our species adapted during the long process of our evolution."

9.9 The term elimination communication was coined by Ingrid Bauer in her book, *Diaper Free! The Gentle Wisdom of Natural Infant Hygiene*, Plume (2006)

Chapter 10

10.1 In 2016, the USA's National Public Radio (NPR) researched the origins of this proverb but was unable to pinpoint them, although academics said the proverb embodies the spirit of several African cultures. https://www.npr.org/sections/goatsandsoda/2016/07/30/487925796/it-takes-a-village-to-determine-the-origins-of-an-african-proverb

10.2 *The Healing Wisdom of Africa* by Malidoma Somé, TarcherPerigee; Reprint edition (1999)

Chapter 11

11.1 *Raising Free People: Unschooling as Liberation and Healing Work* by Akilah S. Richards, PM Press (November 1, 2020)

11.2 This concept is explored in Chapter 5 of *The Healing Wisdom of Africa* by Malidoma Somé, TarcherPerigee; Reprint edition (1999)

11.3 Martín Prechtel shares extensively about the birth and death rituals and beliefs of the Tz´utujil Mayan people in his books, *The Unlikely Peace at Cuchumaquic: The Parallel Lives of People and Plants: Keeping the Seeds Alive,* North Atlantic Books (2012) and *Long Life, Honey in the Heart: A Story of Initiation and Eloquence from the Shores on a Mayan Lake,* North Atlantic Books (2004)

11.4 Brooke Hampton is a writer, business owner, mother and Huffington Post contributor. This quote was taken from a blog post written by Brooke that was no longer available online at the time of the publication of this book.

11.5 From the article *Gender is Over* on the Raising My Rainbow blog: https://raisingmyrainbow.com/

11.6 *Beyond the Gender Binary* by Alok Vaid-Menon, Penguin Workshop (2020)

11.7 From the interview Dr Gabor Maté on Childhood Trauma, The Real Cause of Anxiety and Our 'Insane' Culture posted on humanwindow.com (2020) https://humanwindow.com/dr-gabor-mate-interview-childhood-trauma-anxiety-culture/

11.8 Deep Time is a term used by Joanna Macy in the Work That Reconnects. It frames the present moment in the context of the great river of time in which we all live, presencing both our ancestors and the ones yet to be. You can explore more about Deep Time in Chapter

9 of *Coming Back to Life* by Joanna Macy and Molly Brown or by visiting the Work That Reconnects Network website at www.workthatreconnects.org

11.09 Woman Stands Shining (Pat McCabe) speaks to her experience of working with intergenerational trauma in many podcasts and interviews. One example is this panel interview with Gabor Maté for Science and Nonduality's series on The Wisdom of Trauma: *Examining the Root Cause of Addiction from an Indigenous Lens* https://scienceandnonduality.com/videos/examining-the-root-cause-of-addiction-from-an-indigenous-lens/

11.10 There are many interviews and articles in which Lyla June Johnston speaks to her own intergenerational healing experience and the ways in which we can collectively work to heal intergenerational and inter-cultural trauma. Visit her website at www.lylajune.com to explore her offerings. This article, *Reclaiming Our Indigenous European Root*, published online in The Moon Magazine is one example of these teachings (http://moonmagazine.org/lyla-june-reclaiming-our-indigenous-european-roots-2018-12-02/). The interview in episode 208 of the Last Born in the Wilderness Podcast, *All Nations Rise: Undoing Intergenerational Trauma & Healing Through Solidarity* with Lyla June is another example: https://www.lastborninthewilderness.com/episodes/lyla-june

Chapter 12

12.1 Brooke Hampton is a writer, business owner, mother and Huffington Post contributor. This quote was taken from a blog post written by Brooke that was no longer available online at the time of the publication of this book.

12.2 Ashleigh Warner, Holistic Family Psychologist: https://holisticfamilypsychologist.com/

12.3 Restorative Justice for Oakland Youth (RJOY) defines Restorative Justice as "a set of principles, a philosophy, focused on mending broken relationships to create a better future. It is a fundamental shift in the way that we think about and do justice, in the way that we do community." They ask the questions: "What happens when we stop thinking about justice as 'an eye for an eye'? What happens when we think about harm in ways that don't involve retaliation or vengeance, but healing and transformation?" https://rjoyoakland.org/what-is-rj/

12.4 There are many resources online for learning more about Restorative Practices. The article *Bringing the Lessons of Restorative Justice Home* (October 4, 2018) on the Parent Today website provides a good foundational understanding of Restorative Justice as it relates to parenting practices: https://www.parenttoday.org/bringing-the-lessons-of-restorative-justice-home/ and the Designing for Equity Toolkit from Next Generation Learning includes a great description of Restorative Practices: https://www.nextgenlearning.org/equity-toolkit/school-culture

12.5 from Joseph Chilton Pearce's introduction to the book *Teaching Children to Love: 80 Games & Fun Activities for Raising Balanced Children in Unbalanced Times* by Doc Lew Childre, Heartmath, LLC (1996)

12.6 *Redirecting Children's Behavior* by Kathryn J. Kvols, Parenting Press; 3rd Revised edition (1998)

12.7 Zehr Institute for Restorative Justice: https://zehr-institute.org/staff/howard-zehr/

12.8 The International Institute for Restorative Practices: https://www.iirp.edu/ published *Restorative Justice Practices of Native American, First Nation and Other Indigenous People of North America: Part One* (April 27, 2004) by Laura Mirsky: https://www.iirp.edu/images/pdf/natjust1.pdf and *Restorative Justice Practices of Native American, First*

Nation and Other Indigenous People of North America: Part One (May 26, 2004) by Laura Mirsky: https://www.iirp.edu/images/pdf/natjust2.pdf

12.9 Fania Davis - Restorative Justice's Promise – 2015 Bioneers Conference https://www.youtube.com/watch?v=g63g1GwAneQ

12.10 Restorative Justice for Oakland Youth (RJOY) https://rjoyoakland.org/

Chapter 13

13.1 *A Talk to Teachers* by James Baldwin, delivered October 16, 1963: https://www.zinnedproject.org/materials/baldwin-talk-to-teachers

13.2 Montessori education is child-focused approach to education developed by the Italian physician, Dr. Maria Montessori. Learn more on the website for the American Montessori Society: https://amshq.org/About-Montessori/What-Is-Montessori

13.3 Waldorf education is based on the insights, teachings and principles of education outlined by the world-renowned artist, and scientist, Rudolf Steiner. Learn more on the official website for the Association of Waldorf Schools of North America (AWSNA) https://www.waldorfeducation.org/

13.4 "The Reggio Emilia Approach® is an educational philosophy based on the image of a child with strong development potential and subject to rights, who learns through the hundred languages belonging to all human beings and who grows in relationships with others." Learn more on the Reggio Emilia Approach website: https://www.reggiochildren.it/reggio-emilia-approach/

13.5 "Project Based Learning (PBL) is a teaching method in which students learn by actively engaging in real-world and personally meaningful projects." Learn more on the Buck Institute for Education's PBLWorks website: https://www.pblworks.org/

13.6 "Experiential education is a teaching philosophy that informs many methodologies in which educators purposefully engage with learners in direct experience and focused reflection in order to increase knowledge, develop skills, clarify values, and develop people's capacity to contribute to their communities." Learn more on the Association for Experiential Education website: https://www.aee.org/

13.7 Self-Directed Learning is "education that derives from the self-chosen activities and life experiences of the learner." Learn more on the website for The Alliance for Self-Directed Education: https://www.self-directed.org/

13.8 The VARK model of Student Learning developed by educational theorist Neil Fleming identifies four distinct learning styles: Visual, Auditory, Reading/Writing Preference, and Kinesthetic (VARK). Learn more on the Teach.com with edX website at: https://teach.com/what/teachers-know/learning-styles/

13.9 I was raised as a Unitarian Universalist and attended the full religious education program offered by my childhood congregation (First Parish Brewster, in Brewster, MA) from kindergarten through high school, including the Our Whole Lives (OWL) program and youth group. When living back in my home community for a few years while my child was young, they also attended the same programs and when living in Oregon when my child was in high school, I was a Sunday School teacher for second graders at First Unitarian Portland. To learn more about Unitarian Universalism and explore congregations and offerings in your area visit the website for the Unitarian Universalist Association: https://www.uua.org/

13.10 "Forest Schools are nature-based communities where trained practitioners nurture learner-led exploration and discovery, nurturing meaningful experiences for positive lifelong impacts." Learn more on the Forest Schools website at: https://www.forestschools.com/

13.11 The School Garden Network of Sonoma County, CA, USA has some great curriculum resources and examples of what garden-based learning can look like in school settings: https://www.schoolgardens.org/

13.12 These websites include some great examples of resources for outdoor learning adventures: National Center for Outdoor and Adventure Education: https://ncoae.org/ and Outward Bound: https://www.outwardbound.org/

13.13 *Native Science: Natural Laws of Interdependence* by Gregory Cajete, Clear Light Publishers (2016)

13.14 "The Keres Children's Learning Center (KCLC) is a not-for-profit educational organization that supports Cochiti Pueblo children and families in maintaining, strengthening, and revitalizing their heritage language of Keres." Learn more at their website: https://kclcmontessori.org/

13.15 "Established in 1984, Te Wānanga o Aotearoa provides holistic education opportunities of the highest quality for Māori, peoples of Aotearoa and the world." Learn more at their website: https://www.twoa.ac.nz/

13.16 You can access and read Dr. Lyla June Johnston's academic research papers on her website: https://www.lylajune.com/academic-papers

13.17 This understanding of the mutuality of freedom has been expressed by many great teachers and thinkers, including Dr. Martin Luther King, Jr. and Audre Lorde. In his *Letter from Birmingham Jail* (August 1963) Dr. King wrote, "Injustice anywhere is a threat to justice everywhere. We are caught in an inescapable network of mutuality, tied in a single garment of destiny. Whatever affects one directly affects all indirectly." In Audre Lorde's keynote presentation at the National Women's Studies Association Conference (June 1981) she said, "I am not free while any woman is unfree, even when her shackles are very different from my own. And I am not free as long as one person of Color remains chained. Nor is any one of you."

13.18 *Curious George* written and illustrated by Margret Rey and H. A. Rey, Houghton Mifflin (1941)

13.19 *Busy, Busy Town* by Richard Scarry, Golden Books (2000) and *What Do People Do All Day?* by Richard Scarry, Golden Books (2015)

13.20 Social location "refers to an individual's place or location in their society and includes race, class, gender, sexuality, religion, age, education, marital status, and political view." This definition was taken from *Creating Caring and Supportive Educational Environments for Meaningful Learning* by Kisha Daniels and Katrina Billingsley (2018)

13.21 Excerpt from *Sublevel: Report* by adrienne maree brown (March 12, 2018) https://adriennemareebrown.net/2018/03/12/excerpt-from-sublevel-report/

Chapter 14

14.1 *Tao Te Ching* by Lao-tzu, translated to English by Stephen Mitchell, Harper & Row (1988)

14.2 *The Wonder Weeks: A Stress-Free Guide to Your Baby's Behavior* by Hetty van de Rijt PhD, Frans X. Plooij PhD and Xaviera Plooij, Countryman Press; 6th edition (2019)

14.3 Music Together is offered at more than 3,000 locations and 40 countries. Their early childhood music classes give families with children from birth through age 8 the chance to get in touch with their inner musician and connect with other families. Learn more at: https://www.musictogether.com/

14.4 *How Synaptic Pruning Shapes Neural Wiring During Development and, possibly, in Disease* by Jill Sakai (2020), from The Proceedings of the National Academy of Sciences (PNAS), a peer reviewed journal of the National Academy of Sciences (NAS): https://www.pnas.org/doi/10.1073/pnas.2010281117

14.5 *Planet Earth* is a television series produced by the BBC Natural History Unit and first aired in 2006.

14.6 *Animals: A Visual Encyclopedia* by DK, DK Children (2012)

14.7 *Wacky Wednesday* by Dr. Suess, Random House Books for Young Readers (1974)

14.8 Oobleck is a fascinating substance to create, explore and play with. Children of all ages and adults become easily enthralled with this non-newtonian fluid made from water and cornstarch. For more information about it and the recipe to make it, visit this post on the PBS Kids website: https://www.pbs.org/parents/crafts-and-experiments/how-to-make-oobleck

14.9 *Baby Sign Language Made Easy: 101 Signs to Start Communicating with Your Child Now* by Lane Rebelo, Rockridge Press (2018)

14.10 Positive Youth Development (PYD) is a proactive approach to supporting young people and promoting positive outcomes for them. It focuses on their strengths and capabilities, while encouraging community connections and providing opportunities that help youth overcome adversity and develop resiliency. It is used widely across social spectrums and within many youth support programs. To learn more and access PYD resources, visit: https://youth.gov/youth-topics/positive-youth-development

14.11 *Long Life Honey in the Heart: A Story of Initiation and Eloquence from the Shores on a Mayan Lake* by Martín Prechtel, North Atlantic Books (2004)

Chapter 15

15.1 From the song *Anthem* on the album "The Future" by Leonard Cohen (1992)

15.2 Credit to Bayo Akomolafe for this phrase he often uses and the ways he encourages us to "dance in the cracks," responding to collapse, breakdown and failure with curiosity, presence, playfulness and creativity.

15.3 Credit to Martín Prechtel for this phrase and his teachings about the importance of "feeding that which feeds us." In his school Bolad's Kitchen, his students learn (among many other things) to recognize, remember and nourish the holy life-giving forces that make life live.

15.4 This phrase "hospicing modernity" is borrowed from the title of a book by Vanessa Machado de Oliveira, *Hospicing Modernity: Facing Humanity's Wrongs and the Implications for Social Activism*, North Atlantic Books (2021)

15.5 Visit my website (www.RadiantBalance.com) or email me at jodelamor@gmail.com to inquire about facilitated WTR experiences designed specifically for parents. You can also refer to the book *Coming Back to Life* by Joanna Macy and Molly Brown or visit the Work That Reconnects Network website (www.WorkThatReconnects.org) for information about the WTR spiral and for guidance on facilitating

WTR experiences. The Resource Library of the WTR Network website includes all the original WTR practices, new and adapted practices and other related resources. See the Event Calendar on the WTR Network website for upcoming WTR experiences (both online and in person), facilitated by experienced WTR facilitators from all around the world.

15.6 Bolad's Kitchen is Martín Prechtel's school of forgotten histories and delicious endangered knowledges. In this one-of-a-kind learning experience, Martín teaches ways of being and understanding that give "humans a real usefulness within the whole, instead of a fearful rationalist synthetic flight away from life into depression and extinction." Learn more here: https://floweringmountain.com/bolads-kitchen-general-information/

15.7 *The Wild Rose: Stories of My Horses: volume II* by Martín Prechtel, North Star Press of St. Cloud (2022)

15.8 From the course description on the webpage for Bolad's Kitchen: https://floweringmountain.com/bolads-kitchen-general-information/